I0649779

A Colorni-Hirschman International Institute 6

Art, Aesthetics, Politics

Eugenio Colorni

Art, Aesthetics, Politics

Edited by Luca Meldolesi and Mario Quaranta
Translated by Michael Gilmartin

Bordighera Press

Library of Congress Control Number: 2021953526

Printed in the United States.

Published by
BORDIGHERA PRESS
John D. Calandra Italian American Institute
25 W. 43rd Street, 17th Floor
New York, NY 10036

A Colorni-Hirschman International Institute 6
ISBN 978-1-59954-191-4

TABLE OF CONTENTS

I: YOUNG EUGENIO

II: YOUNG EUGENIO

III: Adult Eugenio

IV: Adult Eugenio

"My weakness and shyness were what pushed me into philosophy. I was perfectly aware of this and said it even then. In aesthetics I felt a sense of satisfaction for the first time. I immediately felt stronger, more secure in my judgments, more independent. I no longer depended on the approval of Mother and my friends — I depended on philosophy. I wanted to continue. More and more I became aware of philosophy's typical method — this taking a word and putting it in quotation marks: 'thought,' 'concept,' 'art,' etc. And I discovered I had a certain skill in 'untangling things,' clearing up misunderstandings, and getting to the bottom of word games. This is where I got the habit that gets on Silvia's nerves so much of asking, whenever we get into a discussion — of thought, for example: 'what do you mean by thought?' And it is also what made me aware of the vanity, the arbitrariness of this word — a facade, as you say, that hides what lies behind it."

— Eugenio Colorni, Letter to Ursula Hirschmann,
Ventotene, 21 February 1939[1]

"I don't care about being cited or publicly remembered. The only thing dear to me is the thought that I will continue for a while to be a part of my friends' conversations — those conversations which were perhaps the purest joy of my life."

— Eugenio Colorni, "Last Wishes," Melfi, 2 May 1943[2]

---

[1]Colorni, *Lettere* 3 (1939): 63–67. Cf. below, sec. 1 (and "The Philosophical Illness" 1939; now 2020a: esp. p. 124–33). Silvia Colorni Schwarz was Eugenio's sister.

[2]Now in Colorni 2019, p. 150. This is the ending of Colorni's last will and testament, where he also says: "I leave my manuscripts and scientific typescripts to Ludovico Geymonat. If he has the will and patience to use my puerile and incomplete notes to trace the main line of my research, and either make use of it as his own or transmit it to others, one of my most vivid desires will have been fulfilled. The same goes for my philosophical and literary manuscripts, which I entrust to Guido Morpurgo Tagliabue."

INTRODUCTION[1]

In memory of Eva Hirschmann Monteforte and Mario Quaranta.

"Sorry I'm late, Eugenio!" — I felt like exclaiming in reference to this second epigraph, thinking with a pinch of self-irony about my own conversation with Colorni (almost like the famous Naples football championship that before Maradona, never arrived!). Because it has taken a good bit of effort — two or three generations (more than seventy years after his death), along with some intense "reinterpretation" — to be able to revisit (from my point of view, of course, and . . . mutatis mutandis) our author's desire for conversation. Of course we will have to see whether Nicoletta Stame and our collaborators and I will be able to truly renew "the friendship with Eugenio Colorni" — as Albert Hirschman wrote to us in the spring of 2004.[2] And we shall also have to see whether, from up there, Eugenio will want to welcome us among his friends. . . . But be that as it may, I want to give you an idea of what I intend to put together this time around. It is inevitable that a thousand questions come to mind concerning Colorni. And each of them brings others with it, in clusters. The problem is not so much what I (or we) would like to know as it is how to approach the objective of posing such questions to Eugenio. We need to build on what we already know and then find a gateway (perhaps previously unheard of, perhaps off to one

---

[1]It might seem at first sight that the present *excursus* represents a step backward with respect to my introduction to Colorni 2020a. It is true, in fact, that at that time I argued the need (which I then felt) to postpone the analysis of Eugenio's early writings to another occasion, in order to focus instead on the "break in continuity" of thought and action that occurs in his work in the late thirties of the last century — also as a starting point for a careful examination of his mature theoretical and political development. And yet it requires but a moment of reflection to realize that in Colorni's work, this sprinter's burst from the blocks coexists with a measured progression in his intellectual interests. So that to explore these interests it is also necessary to briefly review their progression. This is what I shall try to do (in part) in the pages that follow, at the same time introducing a new style of communication (made possible by the results achieved) — a posthumous dialogue with Eugenio. This is essentially another way of talking about (and with) Colorni, whom — let us not forget — Albert Hirschman thought of as always present.

[2]Personal communication; now in Colorni 2019, back cover. In this spirit I shall once again question, alone and/or in the company of others, what I/we have managed so far to obtain, to give and to do.

side).[3] *We need to verify the "thread" (or perhaps, more modestly, one of the possible threads) that we thought we could see in Colorni's work. And finally, as an hors d'oeuvre, we should say something about what readers (if they so desire) may find below.*

In other words, following the editing of a very considerable part of the original theoretical-political work of our author, I reflected once more on the road he had traveled, and in particular — recalling the brief words of Eugenio's selected above as an epigraph — I went back in my mind to the incredible intellectual tension Colorni had endured at Ventotene: within himself, in the condition in which he found himself and within his "circle." The challenge he had set himself was (and is) "astronomical," "sidereal" — a break with a western culture complicit in and/or guilty of the tragedy of the war, and at the same time a useful reinterpretation of some of the key saplings growing in its various fields (natural and social sciences, philosophy, literature, etc.) as a way of unlocking his own thought and action.

Yet in spite of so much anxiety and adversity, . . . Eugenio did manage to move forward — mysteriously, victoriously!

For this reason, his discussions with his friends (and the famous Ventotene dialogues linked to them) are an important part of the happiest times of his life. At the time, Colorni's thinking returned continually to scientific knowledge, and particularly to theoretical physics and mathematics as more evolved disciplines than the other natural, social and humanistic sciences. It was a focusing of intellectual interests that

---

[3]If nothing else, to avoid the spontaneous tendency of thoughts sometimes to slip off . . . in the usual humdrum direction. This is therefore an unpremeditated work arising from a stratagem that Hirschman taught me — that when dealing with a complex theme it is preferable to find an indirect, collateral angle of view. As soon as I posed this problem, two ways forward immediately came to mind (regarding Colorni's political and intellectual journey): his youthful studies (mainly) in aesthetics and his research on the work of Leibniz. I therefore decided to tackle the first one with the invaluable assistance of my friend Mario Quaranta (and his fortunate retrieval of two large and illuminating unpublished works by the young Colorni). And yet in retrospect I had to ask — is this really a collateral angle? Well, I replied, it depends on the position of the observer. Because I believe it has indeed been essential (and legitimate) to focus attention on the core of Colorni's political and theoretical work, as I have tried to do in previous volumes. But it is also true that the youthful texts of Eugenio's presented below play an important part from a genetic point of view — such that they can help us better decipher the above mentioned works and the overall process, by following moreover a typical mental process (leading from the specific — within certain limits — to the *more* general). The conclusion is therefore Solomonic, and the overall enrichment of the work does not seem to me at all in doubt. . . .

was perhaps indispensable in giving him a way forward. But it left a key question unanswered — what about the other disciplines?

Apart from philosophy, they had only figured in a few particular digressions, while Eugenio's point of reference seems to have remained physics.[4] *At times Colorni seemed to expect developments in other sciences to move in the same direction, at others he expected them not to.*

At this great distance in time it is necessary to understand, above all, Colorni's enormous effort of thought (not least aimed at getting specific results, actual and potential — possibly with the help of specialists in the different fields).[5] *At the same time, however, it is essential to note the existence of a multiplicity of possible solutions that is by no means transient — as seen in his "Recantation" regarding Economics.*[6] *It is useful to have a grounding in different disciplines and to make use of the comparative method (within reasonable limits). Then there is "trespassing" from one science into another (the ability, making necessary allowances, to graft onto one field what has been learned in another). And it is also useful — as Albert Hirschman later suggested — to carefully observe different intellectual zones, the cracks that separate disciplines, and the wide uncharted territories that still exist.*

The important thing is that, while respective methodologies are preserved, knowledge is (mutually) kept open and in continuous growth.[7]

Looking at things in this way I will say at once, to get back to Colorni, that along with his writings on the work of Leibniz (which will enliven another volume), there still exists, without doubt, a central area to explore — after we have spoken of politics, philosophy, physics, mathematics, psychology, psychoanalysis, autobiography . . . and that is aesthetics[8]

---

[4]In all of this he gave the impression that he was announcing a sort of second, great phase in the history of philosophical thought — following the one in which the discoveries of Galileo, Copernicus, Kepler, and Newton had led philosophy to construct a series of all-encompassing mechanistic systems. A reconsideration of the germinal intuitions of Kant in the light of the progress of modern physics instead led Colorni to abandon all-encompassing systemic logic, and to offer a healed and reformed philosophy a possible role as a stimulus *urbi et orbi* — that would lead to a further harvest of discoveries in many different directions, those of the natural sciences first and foremost.

[5]A bit like what Mario Quaranta (philosophy) tried to do with his son (physics).

[6]Now in Colorni and Spinelli 2020, p. 172–73.

[7]Here, as is well known, Hirschman enters the field. It is his research, in fact, that seeks the intellectually possible across an astonishing number of themes, social sciences, and "pathways."

[8]Both for the importance of the position it held in the overall panorama of Colorni's work,

(together with literary criticism, and literature).

I

1. It is well known that Ursula Hirschmann and Eugenio Colorni met in Berlin shortly before the rise of Hitler. When they met again in Trieste, Ursula recalled,[9] Eugenio "immediately mounted a full-scale attack on my Marxist way of looking at things. The conversations I had with him were for me a liberation from the lightweight cultural world of 'basic' socialism and dialectical materialism which had until then satisfied my need for culture and political action. Like all liberations it came when I felt a need for it — that is, when I felt an emptiness in the answers that had until then seemed satisfactory, and I was open to breaking out of the patterns I was still moving in. During these discussions I continued to play the advocate for Marxist sophistry, but I felt happy every time with the defeat I suffered at the hands of a freer and higher logic. Nevertheless, in spite of this willingness of mine, the 'enlightenment' was violent and definitive."[10] The first question I would seek an answer for is precisely this. How did Colorni acquire that security, that ability to liberate himself and his interlocutors that comes up continually in the mem-

---

and for the consequences it brought with it (regarding historicism and Italian culture in general). On the other hand, concentrating attention on that aspect can also lead to an inversion in the reasoning. Basically, Eugenio was a student of humanistic studies who had developed a passion for philosophy. Agreed, but what would happen, I had to ask myself, if one took the opposite path — starting out from philosophy to focus rather on the Colorni of the fine arts?

[9] Hirschmann, U. (1974) p. 158.

[10] "I fell in love," the passage continues (ibid., p. 159), "with his cheerful and irreverent way of attacking every tabu and bringing to politics all the freedom of his learning. In this way his political commitment did not fade — indeed, it became stronger, losing dogmatic security but gaining enormously in vitality and the imagination of what was possible. Above all much of the space occupied in my mind by the 'inexorable course of history' that had always oppressed more than encouraged me was restored to the human will, because basically, being of little faith, I had never been able truly to believe it. From falling in love with his ideas to falling for him was a short, almost necessary step. I could no longer imagine living far from this constant source of fresh and original ideas that were above all always in motion. With time I also got used to living and moving naturally in this free space, access to which I owed to Eugenio. In this area our interaction continued actively throughout our difficult years of living together and even after our separation."

ory of those who had the good fortune to know him?[11] Evidently, behind the scenes, the author imposed on himself a continuous effort involving doubt, exploration, repositioning and surmounting, perhaps triggered initially by the need to combat the timidity and uncertainty that tormented him. In any case, it is a question that can be dealt with in successive phases — backwards, from Eugenio's early maturity (which I have dealt with in the introductions to previous volumes), to his youthful experiences — and/or vice versa.[12] One of the aims of the present work is precisely this — to turn the argument on its head in order to show how the whole exercise was set in motion by Eugenio's interest in aesthetics (and literary criticism).

I begin with the illuminating letter of 21 February 1939 written to his wife Ursula (which I was able to consult thanks to the courtesy of the latter's sister, Eva Hirschmann Monteforte[13]), in which Colorni clarified in a few words "how to do philosophy and abandon it," how to "absorb shocks" [and react to them], and how to "move from philosophy to psychology," where he had (finally) ended up.

It was, he writes, "a liberation from a burden that had oppressed me for years, from the weight of my entire weak and uncertain boy-

---

[11]It is a question that (obviously) involves moving beyond the presumed break in continuity between Eugenio's philosophical and political thought pointed out by the critics (Bobbio 1975, p. xxxix; and below, sec. 2). Cf. the testimony of Spinelli, Piovene, Solari, Villani etc. (now in Colorni 2021a, p. 61–69). It is certainly true that Eugenio's ability to discuss, critique, investigate, and stimulate is remembered (even by Albert Hirschman in a letter to Ursula in the early 1970s — now in Colorni 2019, back cover), more than his actual original contribution. This obviously calls for a rebalancing (long overdue) in the overall assessment in favor of the latter. But it also suggests the need for an open recognition of Eugenio's "capacity for impact," the "bite" that gave rise — as the second epigraph above reveals — to "the purest joy" of his life. . . .

[12]I am aware that even in the case of this procedure the accent is on the instructive and liberating aspect of the dialogue with Colorni. But the difference (with respect to discussions with his contemporaries) lies in the cognitive purpose that prompts it. In my view, in fact, Eugenio's interlocutors did not give sufficient attention to the importance of a thorough understanding of what he was trying to say and do. As far as I can see, it was an implicit problem that concerned "the strength and vitality of love" (Colorni 2019, Appendix; or giving in order to receive, as in the "affective method," Meldolesi 2020, Chap. 9). In actual practice, "the exchange," so to speak, turns out to be more than . . . unbalanced (for reasons of age, training, skills, etc.). Furthermore, in this specific case, we need to add Colorni's concern not to dominate his interlocutor, and also his tendency to obsessively repeat (rather than exhaustively explain) his point of view. Consequently, it has not been (and is not) easy to even partially "decode" (without actual interpretive work) what our author was actually up to. . . .

[13]And invoked above as an epigraph: Colorni 1939, vol. 3, p. 63–67.

hood." "When I was a boy, I decided to study philosophy [. . .] because I was not able to live alone, because I needed a moral guide — Mother, my older cousins. I needed 'discriminating criteria,' rails to travel on" — which he found, as we know, in aesthetics. He later added that he still felt "tied to philosophy by a debt of gratitude and by the fear of being left without a guide. I believe that this is why for years I settled for the Leibniz compromise. With Leibniz I could untangle the knots, I could search for what lies beneath the words without abandoning philosophy, dear old solid soothing philosophy. And I had become more confident, calmer, a good counselor, a valuable friend, a clarifier of problems, a supporter of the uncertain — a good teacher. When you came to me this was what you found [. . .]. But while you were leaning on me I was drawing the strength from you to live without the rails, and to be free of my posthumous gratitude to philosophy" — which of course did not stop him, a short time later, from "breaking through" intellectually . . . precisely in philosophy.[14]

This letter was written while Eugenio was waiting for Ursula Hirschmann's first visit to Ventotene, when he was about to begin "The Philosophical Illness"[15] — his autobiographical masterpiece. To my mind, it is of considerable importance, especially for those who, like the writer, seek to verify the meaning of Colorni's adult theorizing by questioning its roots. Following the tracks of the two clear indications it contains ("aesthetics" and the "Leibniz compromise"), I got to thinking. Perhaps it is possible to "take by surprise" (retrospectively) at least some of the factors that eventually made Colorni so comprehensively incisive and decisive "in word and deed" — in the development of knowledge in the human, natural and social sciences, as well as in bold and deliberate political action for a better world.

---

[14]Colorni 2021b; Colorni and Spinelli 2018.

[15]Cf. the letters to Ursula of 4, 6, 8, 24 and 26 April (now in Colorni 2019a, p. 115–17). Cf. also "Beginning of an Autobiography" and "Justification," the two pieces from 1936 and 1937 that precede "The Philosophical Illness," and the latter as well (now in Colorni 2021a, p. 75–78, 79–80, 91–116).

II

2. But before dealing with this issue, I think it is essential to briefly "disentangle" an aspect of the question that is somewhat muddled.

Norberto Bobbio has written of Eugenio Colorni's work[16] that
"even disregarding the real difficulties faced under a censorious regime by anyone who wanted to write about politics with the same
freedom with which they expressed their ideas in literary or philosophical criticism, [. . .] the dualism between science and life, or the
gap or even lack of communication between theoretical reason and
practical reason can serve, at least in the case of Colorni, to explain
not so much the small number of political writings as the fact that
between these and the philosophical writings it is difficult to find
a connecting bridge, much less a common trait. The few political
writings bear no trace of the philosophical travails their author was
struggling with, and more importantly, the philosophical writings
never touch the field of political discussion, even when they seem
to brush up against it."

It is my opinion that this judgment has long weighed (dispro-
portionately) on the exegesis and interpretation of Colorni's theoretical and practical contribution. This in the sense that it has involun-
tarily (but significantly) promoted a spontaneous tendency, typical
of intellectual specializations, to proceed "by field of expertise" —
such that philosophers have dealt with Colorni's philosophy, histori-
ans with his socialist and federalist engagement, and so on.

On the contrary, I believe that my profound disagreement with
the implications (including those of Bobbio's judgment) expressed
thus far has been transformed over time into a sort of driving force
for my interpretative work. It may be true that Eugenio's exasperat-
ing "dualism" left traces in many of his writings (published by Bobbio and published later, in his letters and his unpublished works —
including those that follow), but this certainly does not allow critics
to overlook the fact that this was the painstaking (and overwhelm-
ing) work of a person who thought, wrote and acted day by day,
always mindful of what he was able to understand (whether much

---

[16]Bobbio 1975, p. xxxix.

or little). It is therefore the precise duty of the critics (philosophical, historical, political, etc.) to try and understand the true meaning of what Colorni was little by little devising — aided in this by his astonishing theoretical-practical inventiveness and by the unexpected (not designed!) ex-post coherence of his own teaching. . . .

Not only that — it also seemed to me right to actually read Bobbio's reasoning in reverse.[17] Because apart from conspiratorial and professional necessities (which clearly carried weight), the absence of explicit points of connection between many of Eugenio's political and philosophical writings is undoubtedly also a result of the methodology used in his research (which, as noted, is alternative to the traditional type which is systemic or comes from a *Weltanschauung*). In fact, it requires proceeding according to intellectual interests and successive areas of thought, in each case carefully "trimmed" and delimited, which only later may show that they are connected.[18] (Not to mention, finally, that the absence of clearly expressed "bridges" may conceal many others that are more or less unexpressed and even psychological, beneath the surface — as Eugenio Colorni and later Albert Hirschman implied on numerous occasions.)[19]

It was for this reason that, in launching the publication of Colorni's works (at Soveria Mannelli and then in New York) I have preferred to focus on Eugenio's political writings (which are actually neither few nor secondary) and on the intellectual judgments contained in his correspondence (through an ad hoc choice agreed upon with Eva Hirschmann) — both because of their importance

---

[17]Undoubtedly due to training, expository convenience and intellectual propensity (in addition to antifascist prudence), Colorni was used to keeping his philosophical and political writings clearly separate from one another. But it is also true (as I have also tried to show in the several introductions written for this small series of his writings) that his work becomes comprehensible, valid, and even (more) topical when Eugenio's sources of cultural, philosophical, political and literary inspiration are gradually "called to account" and pushed to engage in dialogue with each other.

[18]Hirschman 1981, p. V.

[19]"Eugenio," Albert Hirschman once told me, "had too many ideas," presumably considering the brief span of his life and the consequent difficulty of setting them out properly. The testimony of his friends and collaborators tells us that he loved to talk about the widest variety of topics, even jumping from one to the other, and perhaps applying to one theme something he had learned in another. This was, in essence, the beginning of the art of "trespassing" later theorized by Hirschman — that is, of his repeated temptation to examine the possibility of adapting to a new theme an intellectual result achieved in another context.

and as an essential way of enriching the understanding of the theoretical and practical work of a decisive protagonist of the best of the
humanistic-scientific culture of our time.

3. On the other hand, although "art and politics" has generally been neglected by critics as a specific theme,[20] the question discussed above reappeared implicitly in my mind (like a carbon copy!)
when, with the invaluable help of the late Mario Quaranta, I started
my sixth "excavation campaign." This in fact also became easier with
a boost from the politics, rather than Eugenio's aesthetics (or literary
criticism). And in the end it helped me make some small decisions.

The first of these was to highlight the main political-philosophical essay of the young Eugenio "Utility and Morality in the Political
Philosophy of Tommaso Campanella," published in the *Rivista di
Filosofia* in 1931. I think, in fact, that in his obvious interest in Campanella as "a firm proponent of the existence of a moral conscience
and of its absolute validity in all fields"[21] we have in a nutshell Eugenio's key federalist-universalist ethical choice — and therefore his
democratic, libertarian, socialist, anti-nationalist, anti-imperialist
and (more specifically, socially) anti-verticalist spirit, *urbi et orbi.*

I will therefore take the opportunity to begin the discussion
from this angle. And to appropriately frame the theme I take my cue
from a famous little book[22] by Antonio Serra (economist, friend,
and possibly companion in arms of his compatriot Campanella).[23]
I am referring, of course, to the *Breve trattato delle cause che possono far abbondare I Regni d'oro e d'argento dove non sono miniere*

---

[20]So much so that Alberto Cavaglioni wrote that (2011, p. 96) "[Colorni's] literary vein
deserves specific study."

[21]Even though in his ongoing development Campanella did not perceive this morality: Colorni 1931, p 242 and below 68–69. (With this clarification, Eugenio evidently launched a
philosophical-political interpretation of Campanella's work which was very different from
what we find, for example, in Höffeding 1926, pp. 117–25.)

[22]Long present in the history of Italian economic thought, mentioned in Joseph Schumpet-
er's *History of Economic Analysis* (1954) and appearing in the *New Palgrave Dictionary*
(Peter Groenewegen 1987), his *Short Treatise* was translated into English in 2011 (Sophus
A. Renhert, ed.).

[23]Coming from different parts of Calabria (Serra was born at Dipignano, near Cosenza, while
Campanella was from Stilo, near Reggio), the two intellectuals probably met at Cosenza —
the most culturally progressive city in the region.

con applicazione al Regno di Napoli [*Brief treatise on the causes that can make gold and silver abundant in kingdoms where there are no mines, with application to the Kingdom of Naples*] (10 July 1613).

Written in Naples's Vicaria prison (perhaps because Serra was in debt or due to his sympathies with the Campanella's anti-Spanish conspiracy), the *Brief Treatise* is dedicated to "Your Excellency Don Pietro Fernandez de Castro, viceroy of the Kingdom of Naples" — since the author seems to have intended that the book would reveal to this high dignitary how the Kingdom could become rich and powerful (perhaps in the hope of receiving his freedom in exchange, and possibly a position at court).

It is a text that, by comparison with similar works of the time, has the peculiarity of containing an effective analytical core regarding the balance of trade and the balance of payments. In fact, in opposition to the proposals concerning the prohibition of the export of precious metals and the reduction of the exchange rate made at the time by Marc'Antonio De Santis, Serra concentrated his interest on real aspects of the economy (the quality and quantity of the production of goods and services, productive capacity, freight and trade, the role of administration, investments) and argued that a prolonged surplus in the balance of trade, obtained by encouraging exports, would lead to an abundant flow of gold and silver into the Kingdom of Naples — both as a solution to this imbalance and because of the supporting effect that this process could have on the movement of capital in the Kingdom's favor.[24]

---

[24]For this reason, the *Brief Treatise* is placed at the dawn of modern economic thought. But in my view this does not mean (as some have written) that it rivals the works of William Petty or Adam Smith in the actual foundation of modern political economy. Economics proper is the offspring, if I am not mistaken, of the formation of the internal market in Great Britain (and also, through the physiocrats, in France) and therefore has a "horizontalist" inspiration (both in the classical and neo-classical eras), while the *Brief Treatise* has a "verticalist" genesis. In this sense it has sometimes been associated with mercantilist thinking. If anything, in my opinion, it actually has a point of contact with the Hirschman of *National Power* and the writings on Latin America and with the best "dependencia" authors, such as Cardoso and Sunkel. This in the sense that it falls in with all those studies that, albeit only in part, have tried to clarify the existence (the evolution, but also the persistence) of pyramidal structures of economies and human societies. This is a need that should be gradually extended among the different countries and within each of them, and that actually embraces "n" aspects of human life.

Naturally, the viceroy and his successor (Don Pedro Telléz Giròn) did not begin to understand (much less put into practice) the advice of this particular inmate, at a time when, following the sixteenth-century loss of their political weight (relative to France and Spain), the Renaissance economic supremacy of the Italian states (understood globally) was about to "sink" definitively, to the advantage above all of the European countries to the northwest (England and Holland).

As is well known, this was a momentous process of rearrangement of the European (and world) pyramid, which is of interest here as background to the event I intend to mention — because it was precisely in this period, and not by chance, that the political preaching of the Dominican Tommaso Campanella developed.[25] Not only a tireless militant, leader of a Calabrian anti-Spanish revolt, possessed of extraordinary energy, and the political-religious herald of a more equitable society, he was also a sage — counsellor of Popes and Kings — and expert in occultism as well as philosophy and religion. Campanella was persecuted, imprisoned, tried, and tortured repeatedly by both the political and ecclesiastical authorities[26] to the point of having to feign insanity to escape death.

Campanella wrote about a hundred works, often intended as high-sounding political-religious proclamations and manifestos. Some have gone missing, while others were taken away under wraps in an attempt to prove their author's guilt, and were perhaps rewritten by Campanella from scratch during his long years of imprisonment,

---

[25]Tommaso Campanella was born in Stilo on September 5, 1568. "The warm and lively atmosphere of Calabria," wrote Aldo Testa (1951, p. 1), "permeates the spirit of Campanella in all his most characteristic impulses, as when he eagerly soaks up and seeks to revive the traditions of Magna Graecia, or when he sets as the natural background of his political dream the land of Calabria, whose climate seems made on purpose to open the soul to that broad sweep of humanity which is the ethical substance of the collective pathway he dreamed of. And above all, Calabria is in the passionate warmth of his life of action and thought, a life that has something volcanic about it. As a manifestation of a genius that is more like the expression of intense and obscure natural forces emerging in the light of thought." Höffeding (1926, p. 72) wrote that with Bernardino Telesio, Giordano Bruno and Tommaso Campanella, "we tread the soil of the southern Italy that produced such a great number of thinkers in ancient times and which in the Renaissance regained its ancient fame. [. . .] These three thinkers form a unique series; the orientation of their ideas is the same, however many different characteristics they may present."
[26]Including the ordeal known as "the vigil," lasting 36 hours.

which thus turned out in the end to be intellectually fruitful. . . .

It is easy to see how such a particular philosophical and political figure could attract the interest of the young Colorni, given
that Campanella embodied, one might say, the struggle against civil
and moral decline from the vantage point of an ill-favored area (as
Calabria already was), and fought at the same time for an ideal,
however imaginary, in his *City of the Sun*.[27] And it is easy to understand — as readers will see for themselves — how Eugenio, even
while writing in the pompous style of the *Rivista di Philosophia*,
could have pursued the idea of promoting Tommaso Campanella's
philosophical work on utility and morality — both in its own right
and as an instrument for reinterpreting the thought of Niccolò Machiavelli in such a way that the means correspond to the ends.[28] He
did so not least because, as founder of modern political science,
Machiavelli — for authors from Antonio Gramsci to Paolo Treves
— was already playing an important role in the incipient thinking
of the anti-fascist movement.[29] So this is the economic and political

---

[27]Campanella 1953. This is probably the source of some points of contact, which seem to me
quite revealing. Because, with his essay on the work of Tommaso Campanella, the young Colorni displayed a lively interest in a theoretical-practical matter that lay at the base of the Italian
economic-political pyramid. Because (as a consequence) one does not find in Eugenio that
"northern" attitude of self-referential superiority that since Carlo Cattaneo has undoubtedly
damaged the internal federalist prospects of our country. And finally because a glance at the
characteristics this "City of the Sun" was meant to have is enough to convey in a flash why Eugenio had "his own idea of socialism," as Giuliano Vassalli put it. That is to say, he demurred
before those who wished to clarify meanings, he went so far as to claim that good intuition is
enough to indicate which way to move, and he considered it a waste of time to predict in detail
the future nature of socialism, seeing this as a distraction from current commitments — in
both word and deed. In other words, according to Colorni, the socialist passions and interests
of the people ought to inspire daily action in each individual, but this action must be based on
a concrete analysis of situations and policies (of possibilism — which Hirschman would later
link to proposals and exit routes) adapted in each case to the desired end.

[28]It will be recalled that in speaking with friends and acquaintances who were critical of
fascism, but actually temporizers, the adult Colorni repeatedly engaged in dialogues of the
type: "Are you anti-fascist? Are you really? And what do you do against fascism? Nothing?
Then you are not anti-fascist." . . .

[29]This is a problem that was posed repeatedly in the postwar period, given the humanistic
background (often political-journalistic) of many of the actors on the Italian public stage.
To all of them my standard response, as always, is that they should read this essay by the
young Colorni. "If we accept with Campanella the ethical purpose of politics," I wrote,
for example, to *Il Sole-24 Ore's* Barbara Fiammeri in December 1996, "then Machiavelli's
much-criticized formula of the ends justifying the means takes on a meaning opposite to the
current one — that is to say, the means must be tailored to the ends. Otherwise the ends are

culture in which the young Colorni began to take the first steps along his philosophical itinerary, beginning as we know with aesthetics and literary criticism, yet without losing sight of the political side of the matter.

III

4. At (classical) high school, Eugenio was introduced to Benedetto Croce's *Breviario d'Estetica* [*The Essence of Aesthetics*], an "almost obligatory encounter," according to Norberto Bobbio, "for a young person going into philosophical studies in those years and coming, as all of us did, from humanist and literary studies, a field that offered no opportunity for reflection and research that was not on things concerning poetry and art."[30] As a brief overview for the reader, it will suffice to recall that these were some of the "after-effects" of an impressive cultural process that had been set in motion in the eighteenth century by the French and, above all, German Enlightenment — when in the three hundred small "Frenchified" courts of the Holy Roman Empire an extraordinary cultural flowering of poetry, drama, literature, music and philosophy began. In philosophy there then developed an additional specific interest in the arts that took the name of aesthetics and, at some point, claimed its own autonomy within the discipline (Baumgarten).[31] Then, squeezed as it was in its own progress between the enrichment of a few big businessmen and bankers, the conservatism of the German nobles and the extraordinary political processes that had their epicenter in neighboring France, Teutonic culture (not least

---

not really pursued [. . .]. Possibilism (which monopolizes the titles of my books) originates here — from the effort of identifying and tenaciously pursuing the means that I think are best tailored to the ends. This way [for example] if we really want to attack the key question of public policy in the Italian south so as to liberate social and productive energies, we need to track down the right means. Our proposals must come from a specific knowledge of the facts, they have to be effective and efficient, they must attract the attention of those whose intentions are serious, they have to be feasible, etc. And they must also dispel prejudices and capture the imagination.

[30]Bobbio 1975, p. v–vi.

[31]Croce 1990, p. 267 and ff.; Merker 1974, p. 100. Cf below, n. 42.

through Romanticism, irrationalism, the sciences of the psyche, etc.) sought to become a noble substitute for politics by creating a kind of myth (i.e. a seduction, an obsession) around itself[32] — which of course included philosophy — through idealism. As an alternative to late positivism, idealism also took hold in Italy at the beginning of the twentieth century — even in secondary education and often through Croce's *Essence of Aesthetics*. At the same time, from a subjective point of view, Colorni had, as mentioned, an additional specific reason for his interest in Crocean aesthetics — his condition of adolescent shyness, put to the test by his mother's severity and the overbearing exuberance of his Sereni cousins.[33]

"On the subject of art, for example," Colorni wrote,[34] "Pierino [i.e., Eugenio] has a certain taste for poetry and painting, and a great passion for music. But how difficult it is for him to justify his judgments and feelings! His cousins' opinions are on the contrary invulnerable, secure in a fortress of coherence that protects them on every side. [. . .] Pierino wavers, feeling unsettled. He is looking for a guiding thread, a touchstone, a key."

He finds it when he reads Croce's The *Essence of Aesthetics*.

"From that day he becomes the best in the class in composition. Writing a theme, once a nightmare, is now pleasure. All he has to do is think about it a little, 'place' the topic within the system of modules or categories, and develop the analysis in the appropriate direction. Pierino enjoys works of art much more now, and he has the elements he needs to offer sensible judgments and support them. All at once the world has revealed to him his invisible armor."[35] The evident self-irony in this passage does not in any case

---

[32]Cf. Elias 1996, Lepenies 2006.

[33]Cf. on the subject the auto-ironic and illuminating pages of "The Philosophical Illness" (Colorni 2021a, p. 93–102). In my opinion, Clara Sereni's *Il gioco dei regni* [*The Game of Kingdoms*] (1993) allows us (at times) to discern some parallels with Colorni's account, but from the standpoint of the Sereni cousins. Putting the two viewpoints together in this way, I became convinced that indeed the overbearing and effervescent competition of the three Sereni boys and the annoying consequences of this rivalry on the surrounding environment during the long summers at Forte dei Marmi had a leading role (even if sometimes in an indirect and unconscious way) in forcing Colorni "out of his shell" for the first time (or in making him react, finally, to the numerous "shocks" his cousins had over time subjected him to). . . .

[34]Colorni 2021a, p. 102.

[35]Thus, during his days as a high school student, Croce's *Essence* became a sort of provi-

hide the personal and historical evidence for such an encounter. Croce's *The Essence of Aesthetics* was the first "Trojan horse" by which Eugenio as a boy penetrated one of the main citadels of Italian idealism (with a passion for the Universal!).[36]

At the same time, in his presentation of *The Essence of Aesthetics* (commissioned for the inauguration in October 1912 of the Rice Institute, the large new University of Houston, Texas) Benedetto Croce had written that the four lessons that comprised it — 'What is Art?', 'Prejudices Relating to Art', 'The Place of Art in the Mind and in Human Society', and 'Criticism and the History of Art' "could be useful to young people who turn to the study of poetry and of art in general, and perhaps even be of service to them in secondary schools, as a reading aid to literary and philosophical teachings. Because," he added, "it seems to me that Aesthetics, when skillfully taught, is perhaps a better introduction to learning philosophy than any other philosophical discipline, since there is no subject that awakens the interest and reflection of young people so early as art and poetry."[37]

Originally from a prosperous family in Abruzzo, Benedetto Croce lost his parents in an earthquake at the age of seventeen, was brought up in Rome (in the home of aunts and uncles) and later resided in Naples at Palazzo Filomarino. As an intellectual, he started out as a historian (without getting his degree). Interested in the Hegelian school that flourished in Naples before Italian unification,

---

dential passport, at least for the time being. Nevertheless, the young man was too intelligent (and honest with himself) not to become aware later — as we shall see — of this contrived logical implant. . . .

[36]"The decision is made," he continues, "— he will study philosophy. He has only read a few books, but his determination is unwavering" (Ibid., p. 103). The few philosophy books that Colorni had already perused (or perhaps begun to read) before he enrolled at university likely included Benedetto Croce's *Aesthetics* (1st ed. 1902) — a full-blown treatise that was part of a comprehensive project on *Philosophy as a Science of the Mind* in four volumes: *Aesthetics, Logic, Practical Philosophy,* and *Theory and History of Philosophy.*

[37]Croce 1913; now in Croce 1988, p. 5–6. "The problems of art," he continued further on, "lead more easily and spontaneously not only to the acquisition of the habit of contemplation, but also to giving preference to logic, ethics and metaphysics; because, to say the least, to understand the relationship between content and form in art is to begin to understand the a priori synthesis; to understand the relationship between intuition and expression is to succeed in overcoming materialism and mental dualism at the same time; to understand the empirical nature of the classifications of literary genres and the arts is to acquire a glimmer of the difference between naturalistic and philosophical procedures; and so on and so forth."

and impatient with the positivist objectivism of the late nineteenth century, he began moving in the direction of idealism. Reasoning with the binary logic that goes back (at least) to the Italian academies of the Renaissance, he went with the humanistic rather than scientific disciplines, and initially marshaled his historical research on the side of art.[38] A prolific writer who undertook numerous editorial initiatives, he published a series of works at the turn of the century that later merged into a treatise on *Aesthetics,* and later wrote the *Essence*[39] "with no other intent from the start than to fulfill the commitment made [to the Rice Institute in Houston], and then, once the work was finished," he explained, "not without some mental satisfaction on my part, for it seemed to me that in it I had not only condensed the most important concepts of my previous volumes on the same subject, but also set them out with better coherence and greater insight."[40] It was to this exercise in the "dialectics of distinct forms" (of Herbartian and Hegelian derivation) that the adolescent Colorni initially subscribed.[41]

But it was clearly inevitable that he would start poking around behind the scenes, even plunging straight into the treatise *Aesthetics as Science of Expression and General Linguistics. Theory and History* by Benedetto Croce, which had reached its fifth edition in 1921 and exceeded six hundred pages.[42] Given his philosophical propen-

---

[38]To the extent that he called his first philosophical paper (presented at the Accademia Pontaniana in Naples on 5 March 1893) "History Brought Under the General Concept of Art." ("From the first essay of 1893 on," Colorni explains [1932 p. 10 and below p. 144], "there is an effort [on Croce's part] to make a place for history in the life of the mind. Reduced at first under the general concept of art, then identified, in the *Logica,* with philosophy, and restored afterwards to an unclear position involving both elements, history in any case is at this stage [a period of around thirty years] a particular aspect of the mind identified with one of the terms of the dialectic of distinct forms, and is not yet, as it would later appear [. . .], almost a generic substratum of every form of apprehension of reality, a participant — as the union of universal and particular — in art as well as in philosophy.")

[39]After a closer engagement with Hegelian dialectics and the publication of the well-known essay "What is alive and what is dead in Hegel's philosophy" (1907).

[40]Cit. in Bonetti 1989, p. 5.

[41]In this way, he wrote in "The Philosophical Illness" (now in Colorni 2020, p. 124) Eugenio now "feels like an initiate. Speaking with 'lay people' he has the impression of moving easily in a region filled with arrows and indicators visible only to him. With those who have 'done the reading' he feels part of a privileged caste of people who need few words to understand each other." And so on.

[42]It is therefore my hypothesis that the display of Crocean erudition we find in Colorni's "The

sities, I would imagine that Colorni was mainly interested in the first part, the theoretical part, which takes up about a third of the treatise. But then curiosity probably led him to plunge into reading the second, historical part, which he found highly interesting. The latter in fact is an unprecedented history of philosophical thought on aesthetics, and largely focuses on the modern era (the 17th to 19th centuries) — including of course the thought of Gianbattista Vico[43] and Francesco De Sanctis.[44]

Aesthetics of Benedetto Croce. A Critical Study" (1932) has deep roots. In addition, Croce's treatise *Aesthetics* contains two parts. The first of these, dedicated to theory, is subdivided into 18 chapters: "Intuition and Expression," "Intuition and Art," "Art and Philosophy," "Historicism and Intellectualism in Aesthetics," "Analogous Errors in History and Logic," "Theoretic and Practical Activity," "Analogy between the Theoretic and the Practical," "Exclusion of Other Mental Forms," "Indivisibility of Expression into Modes or Grades and Critique of Rhetoric," "Aesthetic Feelings and the Distinction between the Ugly and the Beautiful," "Critique of Aesthetic Hedonism," "The Aesthetic of the Sympathetic and Pseudo-Aesthetic Concepts," "The So-called Physically Beautiful in Nature and Art," "Mistakes Arising from the Confusion between Physics and Aesthetics," "The Activity of Externalization, Technique and the Theory of the Arts," "Taste and the Reproduction of Art," "The History of Literature and Art," "Conclusion: Identity of Linguistics and Aesthetics." The second part, dedicated to the history of philosophy regarding aesthetics is divided into 19 chapters: "Aesthetic Ideas in Graeco-Roman Antiquity," "Aesthetic Ideas in the Middle Ages and Renaissance," "Ferments of Thought in the Seventeenth Century," "Aesthetic Ideas of the Cartesian and Leibnitian Schools, and the 'Aesthetic' of Baumgarten," "Giambattista Vico," "Minor Aesthetic Doctrines of the Eighteenth Century," "Other Aesthetic Doctrines of the Same Period," "Immanuel Kant," "The Aesthetics of Idealism: Schiller, Schelling, Solger, Hegel," "Schopenhauer and Herbart," "Friedrich Schleiermacher," "The Philosophy of Language: Humboldt and Steinthal," "Minor German Aestheticians," "Aesthetics in France, England and Italy during the First Half of the Nineteenth Century," "Francesco de Sanctis," "Aesthetics of the Epigoni," "Aesthetic Positivism and Naturalism," "Aesthetic Psychologism and Other Recent Tendencies," "Historical Sketches of Some Particular Doctrines."

[43]Consider for example the following passage from *Scienza nuova seconda* [*The Second New Science*] cited by Croce (2005, p. 278): "Men at first feel without being aware; next they become aware with a perturbed and agitated soul; finally they reflect with an undisturbed mind. This Dignity is the Principle of poetical sentences that is formed by the sense of passions and affections; differing thereby from philosophical sentences which are formed by reflection through ratiocination; whence the latter approach more nearly to truth the more they rise towards the universal, while the former have more of certainty the more they approach the individual."

[44]At the same time, Croce refers repeatedly to Vico and de Sanctis — in the *Essence* and elsewhere. His friend and biographer Fausto Nicolini (1963, p. 83) writes, for example, that "all the philosophical-historical works of Croce are accompanied by bibliographical information, which in some cases takes the form of complete annotated bibliographies, among which we must remember that of de Sanctis and, in particular, Vico, whose bibliography, gradually updated with the collaboration of the present writer by means of seven supplements, was greatly expanded and totally redone about ten years ago."

In this way Eugenio discovered (if I'm not mistaken) a gold mine of ideas, and at the same time wondered, in all likelihood, about possible loose ends. Because it is true what Croce writes at the beginning of his "Disclaimer" — that is, "This volume is composed of a theoretical and of a historical part, which form two independent but complementary books."[45] And yet it is also true that, precisely for this reason, it is necessary to check whether those two independent books, in addition to supporting each other, actually interpenetrate.

5. Colorni is known to have had a "high regard for 'the great work of Croce'. He considered it important to immerse himself in this 'highly valuable' material, painstakingly collected."[46] But he concluded fairly quickly that the second part of the treatise could not be adequately "theorized from the first part." We do not know the details of the logic that led him to this conclusion.[47] But it seems likely that his careful reading of Chapter XV of *Aesthetics*, "Francesco de Sanctis," played a leading role.[48]

Indeed, after having discussed at length the contribution of Germany and having mentioned aesthetics in France, England and Italy in the first half of the nineteenth century, Croce opened the chapter by writing that "the autonomy of art found a strong supporter in Italy in the critical work of Francesco de Sanctis, who held private classes in literature at Naples from 1838 to 1848, taught at Turin and Zurich from 1852 to 1860, and in 1870 became professor at the University of Naples. He expressed his doctrines in critical essays, in monographs on Italian writers and in his classic *History*

---

[45]Croce 2005, p. ix.

[46]Colorni 2021a, p. 108–09; Meldolesi 2021, p. 27.

[47]And which undoubtedly were more complex than "The Philosophical Illness" leads us to imagine (Colorni 2021, p. 103–06) — if only because he had realized studying Croce, as he later wrote (1932, p. 1–2 and below p. 136), that the Neapolitan philosopher, having been the first in Italy to spark the movement on aesthetics through "a clear and precise definition of art," and having never failed "to follow the developments it brought about, the conflicts it aroused, or the innovations that [had] arisen alongside it or opposed it," trying "to take everything into account," had inevitably incurred the "the danger of not achieving true unity," which his own theory had promised.

[48]Croce 2005, p. 457–71. With regard to de Sanctis, for example, Colorni would later show an in-depth knowledge of his criticism of the *Divine Comedy* — cf. the letter to his wife Ursula of 21/9/1938 (now in Colorni 2019, p. 53–54).

of Italian Literature."

At this point, after having got to grips with a complex philosophical labyrinth of some hundreds of pages, it seems human to me that even the most industrious readers should wonder how the miracle of that "sure affirmation" of the autonomy of art claimed by this passage could have occurred and why it is so prominent in the treatise on *Aesthetics* (and more generally in Croce's work). What they would discover is that the Hegelian philosophical movement formed in Naples before the unification of Italy[49] influenced the liberal de Sanctis (who was, among other things, an involuntary guest of the Bourbon prisons), and that this dialectical-systematic way of thinking helped in shaping de Sanctis's famous *History of Italian Literature*.

"For de Sanctis," Croce had written, "the concept of form was identical with that of imagination, the faculty of expression or representation, artistic vision. This much must be said by anyone anxious to express clearly the direction his thought was taking. But de Sanctis himself," he added, "never succeeded in defining his own theory with scientific exactitude, and his aesthetic ideas remained the mere sketch of a system never properly interrelated and deduced."[50] Would it be wrong to assume at this point that Croce wished, in a certain sense, to complete his work? And that, in turn, the young Colorni intended to verify whether this operation had actually succeeded?

IV

6. Eugenio Colorni initially enrolled in the Law School and

---

[49] Today examined in Fernanda Gallo, ed., 2020.

[50] Croce 2005, p. 468–69. "The speculative tendency," the passage continues, "shared his attention with many other lively interests, the desire to understand the concrete, to enjoy art and rewrite its actual history, to plunge into practical and political life, so that by turns he was professor, conspirator, journalist and statesman. 'My mind inclines to the concrete,' he was wont to say. He philosophized just so much as was necessary for the acquisition of a point of view in problems of art, history and life and, having procured light for his intellect, found his bearings, and derived some satisfaction from the consciousness of his own activity, he plunged as quickly as possible into the particular and the determinate. To the immense power of seizing the truth in the highest general principles was joined a no less intense abhorrence for the pale region of ideas in which the philosopher takes an almost ascetic delight. As critic and historian of literature he is unrivaled."

then transferred (during the course of his studies) to the Faculty of Letters and Philosophy at the State University of Milan. He forged friendships and collaborated daily with young people and anti-fascist groups. He took part in specific actions in opposition to the regime (such as fighting with youngsters who attacked his professors during lessons, or attending the famous demonstration in support of Arturo Toscanini at La Scala).[51] He wrote his first essay while still eighteen years old[52] and presented it as a lecture on February 2, 1928 as part of the course taught by Giuseppe Antonio Borgese. At the same time, however (on February 10) Eugenio published a brief article entitled "Roberto Ardigò" in *Pietre*, a youth magazine inspired by Piero Gobetti.[53]

I would like to understand why he did so.

"To reconstruct as far as possible the history of *Pietre*, on the basis of documentation and testimony," wrote Giuseppe Marcenaro at the beginning of his interesting introduction to the anthology

---

[51]Gerbi 1999, p. 31–32 and 64–65. "A distraught Eugenio Colorni," wrote Gerbi (ibid., p. 59 and 60) "had rushed to Naples as soon as he heard of the tragedy [the sudden death of Enrico Sereni in early March 1931] and had watched over the body of his beloved cousin with Giorgio Amendola. They had know each other for years through the Serenis. Some time before — but the Communist leader is uncertain of the date — they had gone together to visit Benedetto Croce, who was more interested in hearing their views on the politics of the moment than in discussing Colorni's work on Crocean aesthetics (which would come out in '32 with a dedication 'to the memory of Enrico Sereni'). Recalling the hours passed with Colorni, Amendola stated that "that night we spoke to each other with due candor. The history of anti-fascism will not be understood if we do not appreciate the significance of a network of strong friendships, which will withstand even the harshest political clashes." (Cf. also Clara Sereni 1993, p. 270.)

[52]Eugenio was born in Milano on 22 April 1909.

[53]Piero Gobetti was "the only one, perhaps, who was recognized by all the editors of *Pietre* as a true and proper master" (Marcenaro 1973, p. 20). To the extent that in an introductory note to the February 1927 edition of the review, the first anniversary of Gobetti's death, Francesco Manzitti wrote: "On the 16th of February 1926, on a white cot in a Parisian clinic Piero Gobetti died. There is no stillness that moves us more than that of this restless young man who professed the religion of action with the ardor of a neophyte. We loved Piero Gobetti because he embodied in himself, in the acts of his daily life, all the heroic beauty of healthy idealistic youth, which moves forward without the corruption of utopias, without the hindrance of tinsel idols, without carnivalesque embellishments, in that voluntarism which is the truest reason for life. And Piero Gobetti, who did not want to be an educator, was a teacher to young people. He taught us the arid beauty of solitude, he educated us to fight and made us love the anguish of the struggle; he admonished us to live when everything falls and to believe again when, in the collapse of conscience, it may seem that ideals are shattered" (AA.VV. 1973, p. 166).

in the Genoese review,[54] "is to recount not only the political, social and cultural evolution of a certain period, but also to revive the distress of a group." *Pietre* developed " based not so much on the possibility of fighting openly — then nonexistent — as under the pressure of the will to persevere."[55]

In essence it was the search for a youthful cultural orientation alternative to the triumphant twentieth-century trends (from "D'Annunzianism" to the actualism of Giovanni Gentile) that had paved the way for Fascism and then facilitated its consolidation.[56]

As mentioned, the main inspiration for *Pietre* came from Piero Gobetti.[57] Another point of reference was undoubtedly Carlo Rosselli, who in 1924–26, as an appointee, taught Institutions of Political Economy (and in 1925–26 also Political Economy) at the Istituto Superiore di Scienze Commerciali in Genoa.[58]

---

[54]With its appropriate title: "*Pietre*: more than a review, an intention." Started in Genoa in 1926 by a group of students, the review was printed in the city until its suppression (following the noted raids of 12–13 April 1928). But due to economic difficulties (and the conscription obligations of the two editors), *Pietre* had interrupted publication after May 1927. A final issue in December 1927, however, announced its transformation into a four-page fortnightly periodical of which four issues came out. "By the time Basso took the initiative and responsibility for the magazine's new brief 'Milanese' series," wrote Marcenaro (1973, p. 27), "a network of relations, adhesions and sympathies had formed around *Pietre* that went beyond the original narrow circle of the Genoese setting and — though without giving rise to a true organization — constituted the fabric, albeit very precarious, of a broader movement of opposition to Fascism."

[55]Ibid. p. 8. "The immediate concern of the young people of *Pietre*," Marcenaro added further (p. 18), "was to find the strength within themselves to confront fascism from the vantage point of a civilized framework into which their own needs could be projected. It was basically an experiment that exuded the pretension of certain programmatic statements, an attempt to justify the publication of the magazine as a youthful educational initiative. But such forms could also amount to a naïve and approximate intellectual curiosity. Even the parts that might be construed as more homogeneous and better structured [such as the socio-economic and literary policy writings] sometimes induce this same sense of searching and tentativeness."

[56]Cf., for example, Salvati 2016, Ch. 1.

[57]Cf., above, n. 50.

[58]"Faced with the weakness and discouragement, however respectable, of so many well-known figures of the Italian intelligentsia, the appeal of moral resistance to the young people of *Pietre*, the Rossellian 'eulogy of character' that they were weaving, was a modest but positive act of courage." "Of all the 'illustrious' contributors,' the closest to the young editors" was undoubtedly Giuseppe Rensi, who sought to "keep the horizons in the world of philosophy open by indicating for Kant and the other classics of thought different perspectives from those prevailing in Italy at the time. Thus, for example, he gave prominence to objectivist interpretations of Kant, reacting against the idealist-actualist interpretation prevalent in our

Pietre was, as Enrico Alpino pointed out,[59] "a small magazine produced by young students who were openly non-conformist and not very sensitive to new developments in pure literature, being entirely caught up in the political and social problems of that crucial moment for our country [. . .]. But, despite their predominant political commitment, the young people of *Pietre* could not help but appreciate a new writer introduced by Piero Gobetti" — namely, Eugenio Montale. *Pietre,* Marcenaro clarified, "was an authentic testimony and tribute to a tormented and vilified culture. [. . .] From its first appearance its intention was to assume an austere and deliberately pedantic tone, its only bastion of defense against the uncultivated fascist machine."[60] As the editors of *Pietre* in fact wrote,[61] "We wanted at the outset to prove that the soul of young people can be found not only in empty and sensational words, but in serious and unassuming preparation, and (above all) in believing in ideals, be they utopian, and in building their future day by day in the name of these. We never proposed to offer number by number, author by author, an organic and complete edifice, but to create a building site where we could bring our bricks, so that those who deserved it and understood it would be able to build."[62]

7. "If the initiative was at first exclusively local and limited for the most part to young people," Marcenaro pointed out, "in 1927, after the May issue, it was characterized more by an interest [. . .] in promoting a kind of exchange between the anti-fascists of different Italian cities. The prominence of Lelio Basso in that period, became a fact of obvious importance, not least because of the work he did in organizing distribution, which contributed to the creation of a real anti-Fascist network, which was what he had intended."[63]

And it was precisely in that period of time that Eugenio Color-

---

culture" (Marcenaro 1973, p. 25, 22–23 and 24).

[59]Alpino 1966; cit. in Marcenaro 1973, p. 8 n.

[60]Ibid., p. 16.

[61]*Pietre*, a. I, n. 6, September 1926.

[62]Probably — as we discuss below — Eugenio shared such an intention.

[63]Marcenaro 1973, p. 9 (cf. above, n. 51). For the young Lelio Basso's numerous anti-fascist political activities, cf. also ibid. p. 28ff.

ni (who had met Lelio Basso at university), though prudently writing under the pseudonym of G. Rosemberg, decided to participate
in the common enterprise with an article, "Roberto Ardigò," which
occupied, one might say, the place of honor on the first page of the
journal's second issue of 1928.[64]

I come back to the question, why did he do this? Probably because — this is my hypothesis — mindful of "the respect for the past
that *Pietre* had sought to observe since its first issue,"[65] he intended
to suggest to these young anti-fascist intellectuals and their friends
that a careful rereading of the work of Roberto Ardigò would offer
them a path of interpretation of the history of aesthetic-philosophical thought that did not correspond to the idealistic, anti-positivist
"Vulgata" then prevailing. . . .

Colorni, as I have recalled elsewhere,[66] took an active (not
only intellectual) part in a "rebel" cultural circle and institute of
philosophy that included two prominent professors — Giuseppe
Antonio Borgese and Piero Martinetti. It was evidently at this point
that his perspective matured.[67] In a small CV written in German, in

---

[64]An occasion that marked (among other things) the second anniversary of the death of
Gobetti: cf. above, n. 53.

[65]As part of its anti-avant-garde logic: Marcenaro 1973, p. 19.

[66]Meldolesi 2021, p. 20–30. Within this institute (and more generally in the antifascist culture of the time) there was a double position regarding Croce. It was considered necessary
to criticize and move beyond Croce's philosophy while at the same time recognizing the role
Croce had played in the evolution of 20th century Italian humanist culture. "In our literary
history — to which in essence [Croce] belongs," wrote Borgese, for example (1934 p. 22)
" — he is the healthiest and most mature mind that has appeared since Carducci." "I believe
it my duty to recognize," Norberto Bobbio stated *post factum* in a letter to Rossi-Landi on
3 July 1955 (now in Quaranta 2018, p. 133), "that some important aspects of our culture
that we still believe to be valid and do not want to lose go back to Croce. Some that I recall
include his attitude of intolerance in the face of a frigid academic philosophy that is not
even philosophy but an occupation; a contempt for "amateurs," whom our cultural history
is full of, and whom Croce always treated harshly; a distrust of philosophers who are only
philosophers and have no *métier* [. . .]; a taste for well-done and well-written research that
goes hand in hand with an abhorrence of all improvisation; love for the general problem that
arises from particular research, and the general thesis that must be continually put to the test
by the results of particular research; devotion to the task of the educated man who must not
submit his search for truth to the flattery of the powerful."

[67]To get an idea of the Milanese philosophical-cultural climate in which Colorni's works on
aesthetics were conceived, it is useful in my opinion to consult *Poetica dell'unità* [*The Poetics of Unity*] — "Five preliminary essays for a poetics of unity," the result of thirty years of
work, which G. A. Borgese (1934, p. 9) would soon bring together in a single volume. (The

fact, (probably to compete for a scholarship),[68] after briefly recalling the main phases of his scholastic and university career, Eugenio
presented his works (which for the most part preceded the well-
known focus of his research on the work of Leibniz, which began
with his degree thesis). These consist of three texts on the aesthetics
of Roberto Ardigò, the aesthetics of Bergsonism and the aesthetics
of Benedetto Croce;[69] two essays — "Utility and Morality in the Political Philosophy of Tommaso Campanella" and "Some Relations
between Knowledge and Will" — that appeared in the *Rivista di
filosofia*; and finally, reviews and other reports on Italian and European publications that had appeared in numerous journals (*Leonardo, Civiltà Moderna, Il Convegno, La Cultura*) and displayed the

---

titles of the essays are "Personality and Style," "Thoughts on Eloquence," "Unity in the
History of Poetry and Art," "Figuration and Transfiguration," "A Summary of the History of
Literary Criticism from the Middle Ages to the Present"). A quick glance is enough to reveal
that a key point of reference in Borgese's teaching was, in fact, the aesthetics of Benedetto
Croce — both for the role it played in Italian culture and in the work of aesthetic-philosophical criticism that his students were invited to undertake. Hence the question — what
attitude did Colorni assume in his descent into the midst of that environment of thought? My
impression (to which I will return) is that he generally shared Borgese's point of view, but
that he tried at the same time to go beyond it by unhesitatingly pursuing the examination of
the proposed solutions — in his own interests.

[68]A sort of curriculum vitae [undated (but datable to 1933 or 1934)] which, thanks to the
courtesy of Eva Hirschmann, I was able to cousult in *Colorni Letters* (1918–1936), vol. 1, p.
12–13. Similarly, in an earlier "Curriculum Vitae" Colorni had written (in Italian): "During
my studies I focused especially on problems of philosophy and aesthetics, and under the
direction of Prof. G. A. Borgese, I drafted works on 'The Aesthetics of Roberto Ardigò and
Italian Positivism,' 'Bergsonian Aesthetics' and 'The Aesthetics of Benedetto Croce.' This
last study was later published in Milan by the publisher 'La Cultura.'" (Cit. in Gerbi 1999,
p. 52). In all probability these were papers to be presented at annual conferences organized
under the course in aesthetics. The first by Eugenio, as mentioned, carries the date of 2
February 1928, the second 'The Aesthetics of Bergsonism,' is dated 21 February 1929. The
third, "Saggio sull'autonomia e disinteresse dell'arte. Punti di partenza dal Croce" ["Essay on the Autonomy and Detachment of Art. Points of Departure from Croce"], has gone
missing, but probably it was later "absorbed" into the first part of Colorni's noted (and
only) monograph, *The Aesthetics of Benedetto Croce. A Critical Study* — 1932. (Cf. on this,
Cerchiai 2018, p. 51 n.)

[69]"At the university," Eugenio later wrote (in "The Philosophical Illness" 1939; now in
Colorni 2021a, p. 106) "the battle against Croce continues. Every week a student takes
the podium to debate his classmates and the professor [Borgese]. Pierino [alias Eugenio]
listens eagerly but understands nothing. He sees that each of them defends a thesis representing a side, but he wouldn't begin to know how to explain which side, or to take a
position himself." It is likely that the three writings on aesthetics cited in Eugenio's CVs
sprang partly from a desire to overcome this initial disorientation.

multiplicity of his intellectual interests (philosophical, philological, aesthetic, political, critical, psychological, etc.).

(In addition, this "author's selection" has made it easy to set up the first and second parts of the present collection, whose aim is to document the beginnings of Colorni's thinking. I thought it useful to add to this a small anthology of his literary criticism, since "there is nothing else. . ." — as he himself wrote at a certain point to his wife Ursula in a vein of self-irony[70] — along with two brief short stories.[71] Both the anthology and the stories exemplify in a particularly lively way the self-liberating consequences, partly unconscious, of the "Colornian revolution" then under construction in two specific fields — literary criticism and literature.)

8. As mentioned,[72] *Pietre* had two series of issues. The first was monthly, while the second consisted of "a more manageable fortnightly sheet with a four-page format, the same as that of *Liberal Revolution.*"[73] With this development, its center of gravity moved from Genoa to Milan, the idea being to transform a local youth initiative into an instrument of connection and coverage for various antifascist groups. But *Pietre* continued to be "a small avant-garde magazine kept alive by a non-homogeneous group of collaborators, all nevertheless equally sensitive to the Crocean idea of the 'conspiracy of culture,' — a magazine that was agile and accessible and which, with a more mature approach by comparison with the first series," accentuated its "generically literary and philosophical nature as opposed to the 'technical and sociological' character it had originally attempted to assume."[74]

The first issue of the new series opened with "The Death of the 20th Century" by B. D'Arzocco (pseudonym of Lelio Basso). "We are not alluding to Bontempelli's review [that is, to the literary review *900. Cahiers d'Italie et d'Europe* by Massimo Bontempelli and Curzio Malaparte]," the article begins, "which may perhaps even be

---

[70]Letter of 17.10.1938, in Colorni *Lettere* 1937–1938, vol. 2, p. 28: cf. below, p. 251.

[71]Probably written at Ventotene and datable, I would think, to around mid-1939.

[72]Cf. above, n. 54.

[73]Vigorelli 2011, p. 256–57.

[74]Ibid., p. 257–58 and Bianco e Costantini 1962, p. 469–70.

resurrected, thanks to the lucky combination of some young person in need of publicity meeting with a publishing house in need of great initiatives. We are referring to the myth of the 20th century [the '900'] as a homogeneous phenomenon of mental life. Nowadays there are very few who seriously believe in it, even if many still talk about it either out of habit or polemical convenience. Almost everyone has realized by now that the main feature of this quarter century is the total absence of any clear identification — it is the triumph of anarchism and spiritual confusion." And a little further on: "the idealistic revolution in Italy was certainly not a hard slog [. . .] The ease of victory aroused successive waves and cleared the way for the easy conquest of abandoned positions — and it was here that the noisy ranks of futurists, syndicalists, and pragmatists spilled out onto the scene. The rebellion of absolute activism against absolute passivity was the prewar mentality, it was the sudden hysterical crisis of the petty bourgeoisie that did not like the gray — oh, much too gray for them! — daily toil. The so-called spirits of the age were usually simply camouflaging some profound truth under the guise of adventurous rhetoric" and so on and so forth.[75]

In an editorial in the second issue (of 10 February 1928, in which "Roberto Ardigò" appeared), "Picture of the Times," Alberto Consiglio[76] takes up the same argument in a lighter tone in an arti-

---

[75]*Pietre* 3.1 (now in AA.VV., *Pietre* cit. p. 231–32)."In the place of honor," we read at the bottom of the page, "we are glad to open the new series with this article by a unique friend of ours [Lelio Basso], because we agree with the central thesis of his article, concerning the non-existence of a cultural current that embodies the needs of the new age, and the need to direct efforts in a direction completely different from the one desired by both the so-called Novecentists and their barbaric adversaries," *Il Selvaggio*. Vigorelli (2011, p. 260) commented that "it was an appeal to the rigor and seriousness of life (before that of work), in which Basso revealed an objective harmony with the self-criticism of idealism that Croce had just undertaken in the pages of the *History of Italy from 1871 to 1915* (which would be reviewed in the last issue of *Pietre* by Mario Vinciguerra)."

[76]In a letter from Naples written at the time the second issue of the magazine came out, Consiglio (who, Vigorelli tells us [ibid., p. 258, n.], had been introduced in the magazine by Vinciguerra) suggests adopting the literary inquiry as an instrument to liberate *Pietre* from "its somewhat Carbonaro aspect," which was hindering its distribution. "You should, in short, ask thirty young writers, between thirty and forty years of age (those who have shown that they are struggling in search of a spiritual and artistic path) to define themselves. In other words, you should ask each one of them for a moment of honesty and humility in which they share their torment and build a historical document of enormous importance."

cle entitled "Europeism." These two texts, along with "15 February" (the obituary of Piero Gobetti by Francesco Manzitti), sandwich Eugenio Colorni's article in such a way that the latter could be read as part of this political and literary framing.

It is perhaps useful to give a brief idea of the editorial. "For now," Consiglio begins, "faced with Verga, Leopardi, Berni, 'il Magnifi-co' defended by Malaparte, or with Giraudoux, Jacob, Mac-Orlan, Joyce or Ponson-du-Terrail as exalted by Bontempelli, Italian events are still small-scale, rather pretty and attractive, but at best nothing more than a promise that we will believe in depending on how our enthusiasms are oriented. But the two tendencies [of Malaparte and Bontempelli] take on a very different and considerably more im-portant meaning if we can manage to see them as states of mind, characteristics of our century, and to account for their origins. Es-sentially, what is Bontempellian *novecentism* trying to achieve? To be always and continuously contemporary. To proceed with the times, and even be ahead of them. It wants to break the boundaries of tradition. To go beyond the particular to reach the universal."

On the other hand, Consiglio later adds, "the small and paro-chial Strapaese, honored in the national limelight by the venturous Malaparte, wants something else. [. . .] He wants the field with its tight boundaries. The closed circle of tradition in which to govern, and since it is not possible to break out of the circle, the direction of movement will be depth, giving ever new meaning to old things." And again: "These notes will be enough for us to orient ourselves. Therefore, going beyond theoretical aesthetics, it is evident that these two tendencies in a part of our recent literature [. . .] are only two Italian phenomena among many in the gigantic crisis of con-temporary civilization, lingering tragically at a crossroads where it will not be able to survive for long."[77]

Hence the need for an alternative construction that would emerge from a "serene and firm moral reaction."[78] And an (im-

---

[77]Consiglio 1928. Note how between the opposing points of view of Bontempelli and Malaparte one glimpses, perhaps unwittingly, the possibility of a different path — that is, a way of thinking that, as we shall see, Colorni would develop shortly thereafter.

[78]Vigorelli 2011, p. 262. Naturally, this also reflects the article "Europeism" (Consiglio 1928a) where he argues, for example, that "we do not have a European literature because we do not

plicit) suggestion to carefully read Eugenio's accompanying article, which proposes a leap backwards — to the "Ardigoian" aesthetics and Italian positivism of the nineteenth century — as a way of helping us get back on track.

To return to my question — what sense did it make to publish Colorni's "Roberto Ardigò" in the second issue of the new series of *Pietre*? Is it sufficient to emphasize the obvious influence of his professors (Borgese and Martinetti) and perhaps see it as a sort of self-referential "clip" (which it certainly is) concerning his study of aesthetics? Or might the article represent, for both the review and for its author, "*una pietra*" — a stone in the foundation of the new building,[79] and be seen as an early attempt to start pointing out — stone by stone — another possible way?

Personally, I was pleasantly surprised by the free-thinking way Eugenio tackled the subject, by the very interesting and elaborate articulation (in a small typographical space) of the problem he derived from it, and by the positive, encouraging evaluation of the "ingenuous" ingenuity Roberto Ardigò demonstrated in his work. . . .[80]

We know how things went after that. Because he was so young and had used a pseudonym Eugenio was not identified by the regime, and he thus escaped the police raids that instead captured a large part of the intellectual circle of *Pietre* and consequently brought about the closure of the magazine.[81]

---

have an Italian one — one, that is, that senses and reflects the Italy of today. [. . .] This is the hour to finally begin our task of inhabiting our own time, feeling it according to our inclinations, being concerned with defining and rediscovering ourselves. Only in this way, with these qualities of honesty and deep passion [. . .] will Italy be able to initiate a European literature."

[79]For anyone who would like to get an intuitive idea of Eugenio's theoretical-political inspiration (which accompanied his entering the ring in the mid-thirties), it is worth recalling his writings of 1936–38 — the beginnings of the autobiographical and programmatic works that later would find full expression at Ventotene. Here we read, for example, "The author's profession is philosophy — and there is nothing he hates more than continually taking the pulse of his time, seeing brilliant prospects, and analyzing 'contemporary anxiety' [. . .] in order to express what is currently in the air." And again, "he considers philosophy [. . .] a concrete science that can achieve positive results, discoveries that constitute a gain for mankind. [. . .] This is the only way the author would like to do philosophy — to invent, to discover previously unknown explanations" (Colorni, July 1937; now in 2021a, p. 79).

[80]Cf. *Pietre*, year I, n. 6, settembre 1926; and above, sec. 6 and n. 59.

[81]Colorni of course continued with his philosophical-political work, although with greater circumspection.

V

9. Undoubtedly, in these reconstructions of mine (which some-times rely a bit on "hunches" . . .) I run a twofold risk: one is that the available information may be insufficient and the other is that, in spite of every effort, I may not succeed in adequately penetrating Colorni's reasoning. But I tell myself these risks are worth taking in the effort to get closer to the bottom of . . . how things actually were.

You were at ease, dear Eugenio, as a freshman (admitted to the second year), in the Faculty of Letters — especially in the aesthetics course. Not only was it a subject you had already dealt with in high school, but your professor of aesthetics, Giuseppe Antonio Borgese, was a volcanic and creative character endowed with extraordinary eloquence, who nurtured his relationships with students and even organized a sort of afternoon workshop to put his best students to the test. In all probability, as previously mentioned, this was the origin of the three manuscripts on aesthetics that you wrote "under the direction of Prof. G. A. Borgese,"[82] and then presented along with your CV to compete for scholarships.

The first of these — "The Aesthetics of Roberto Ardigò and Italian Positivism in the Second Half of the 19th Century"[83] — is of course contemporary with the *Pietre* article. It is a surprising essay in that it is hard to say whether it was written on the suggestion of the professor or simply accepted by him (but designed *motu pro-prio* by its author).[84] It is clear, however, that the broad and original exposition in this lecture corresponds to Colorni's political-episte-mological needs, and is revealing of his intellectual attitude — evi-dent from the very first stages of his scientific work.

In fact, this is the full-fledged debut (in the wake of *Pietre*) of the compelling need to reconstruct thought with reference to the past — as an alternative to the futurist cultural currents (ideal-

---

[82]Cf. above, sec. 6 and n. 68 and 69. (It is no coincidence, on the other hand, that on July 29, 1949, at the end of his American exile, Borgese communicated to Prof. Luigi Castiglioni, Dean of the Faculty of Letters and Philosophy at the State University of Milan, his intention to resume his teaching with a lesson on "Aesthetics and Politics," Riosa 2011, p. 268 and n.).
[83]It was in all likelihood part of the first volume (1929) of the official collection of these papers.
[84]Personally, I would lean toward the second of these.

ist, modernist, actualist, avant-guardist, Marinettist, D'Annunzian, elitist, supermanist, etc.) that had created the conditions for the rise and authoritarian (and adventurist) consolidation of Fascism. This took place, therefore, as a university exercise on aesthetics and nineteenth-century positivism, but with the intention of finding useful ideas to meet the pressing needs of the present. The theme, clearly indicated in the title, is laid out on the side of philosophy (rather than that of art). The undoubted theoretical fragility of Italian naturalist positivism thus saw, in this paper, a compelling (and unexpected) discussion of its greatest philosophical representative, Roberto Ardigò. In fact, in my view, this aspect of the text is where its interest primarily lies. In the documentation, that is, of Ardigò's various attempts in his argumentation to reconcile positivism and philosophy. At the same time, such a careful reconstruction of the history of thought has more than a merely philological purpose. Written by a sympathetic observer and therefore a "participant" (but not a very indulgent one), this essay, at times amusing and almost illusionist (like a conjuring trick), carefully detects, considers and ponders — this much is beyond doubt. But more than assigning itself a (too easy) judgmental function, its interest appears to be in remorselessly questioning the arguments successively considered, reconstructing Ardigò's problem, and learning from this the *ingenuity* of his attempts to find a solution, inconclusive as they may be in the last analysis.

One might say that the young Colorni was attracted to "philosophizing," to Ardigò's conjectural abilities, more than to what he specifically advocated — and that he manifests a breezy and wide-ranging interest that does not belong a priori to any school, but rather aims to bring to light, in a perceptive way, little known aspects of the entire intellectual output of the Mantuan philosopher. In this way he implicitly (covertly) privileges the search for interesting "seedlings,"[85] as an exercise in the midst of his own (antifascist) research.

---

[85]Cf., for example, how recognizing the psycho-physical "indistinct" and the need to contemplate it in order to be aware of it pushes Ardigò toward Bergsonian intuitionism.

It is as if, taking advantage of the opportunities offered at university (and the unexpected freedom of thought it permitted), Colorni had wanted to "test himself" to the point of concluding that "what matters to us today is the development of Ardigo's thought which, although no longer of vital importance to us is nevertheless supremely instructive. It shows us how the only real philosopher of Italian positivism, in seriously attempting to transform a method that was still on the philosophical sidelines into a true philosophical system, arrived at the high point of his philosophical investigations only to go off the rails, needing to support his thinking using resources that betrayed how very far from positivism their origins were."

10. All very well, the reader will be thinking. But what, more precisely, is the political purpose of Colorni's exercise? To understand this requires that we briefly revisit the opening of the essay (also in order to compare it with the *Pietre* article).

The main concern of the early Italian positivists, such as Cattaneo, Tommasi, Gabelli and others, Colorni says, "was to bring to the theory of knowledge the methods that had yielded so much progress in the science each of them was practicing." But through Hegelian premises and reminiscences from their youth, "these men had assimilated the immanentist and anti-dualist requirements of all post-Kantian idealist philosophy. In attempting to satisfy these requirements in the empirical study of facts they were faced with two pathways. One of these was the more coherent and courageous (even in its absurdity) way of materialism — which they hurried to reject, however, due to scruples remaining from their youthful education. The other [...] was a metaphysical agnosticism that turned its back on theoretical speculation altogether, reducing philosophy itself to an experimental science."

In such a way, according to Pasquale Villari, whose 1866 speech was considered a sort of manifesto, "positivism comes down to the application of the historical method to the moral sciences." And it is therefore "possible to establish a science of beauty while renouncing for the time being an understanding of its essence."

"It was natural," the young Colorni continues, "that this historical method, also faithfully and consistently applied in the field of philosophy, and especially aesthetics, should deal a death blow to any system or aesthetic theory, and reduce the science of art to a purely experimental and scientific level — a phenomenology or physiology of the artistic fact." [. . .] "All of Italian positivist aesthetics up to Ardigò is thus founded on a tacit dualistic-naturalistic premise. Assuming as a principle a natural reality acting on activities of the mind, and asserting the necessity for experimental research into the effects of this action, the solution of the aesthetic problem as such was hopelessly compromised."

Solid epistemological premises had to be found "before any research could begin in a specialized field of philosophy," which aesthetics definitely was. And consequently "the entire opus of Roberto Ardigò was dedicated to the search for these epistemological premises."

It was a starting point to which Colorni probably wished to draw the attention of young intellectuals when he opened his *Pietre* article, writing: "The last few days have seen the centenary of the birth of this forgotten figure [Roberto Ardigò]. After a period of glory and fame, when he appeared to be the founder of a new epoch and the father of a new approach to philosophy, the beginning of this century marked an abrupt [idealist] turning point in Italian thought — a period of demolition and ridicule followed by indifference and silence."

Evidently, Eugenio rebelled against the "unjust fate" that the philosophical establishment had reserved for Ardigò. He continued: "He was talked about as 'the father of positivism.' We instead believe that Ardigò was its last and most degenerate child [. . .]. It could indeed be said that the whole of his philosophy, all the force and meaning of his work, derives from the coexistence and attempted reconciliation of two great demands in his thought: positivist empiricism and the pursuit of unity." It is a key aspect of the question that Ardigò was in the final analysis unable to solve, but which Colorni considered it important to bring back from oblivion. Obviously he was not suggesting that young antifascist scholars should simply return to the past. But he did consider it very instructive to once again "take possession" of Ardigò's problem (and then compare it — not coincidentally! — with Bergson's intuitionism and Leibniz's monad) — as a useful reference point for open research directed towards new horizons.

11. In this essay, the passionate search for a way to effectively escape from positivism without falling into the (intellectually cogent) clutches of Hegelian idealism gradually becomes perceptible. In my view, this explains Colorni's interest in some of the little-known aspects of Ardigò's work and calls to mind what Eugenio would shortly afterwards write about Martinetti on the occasion of the reprinting of the latter's *Introduction to Metaphysics*[86] (as well as Borgese's typical approach, which I will discuss later). In my opinion, (and beyond any possible student artifice) Colorni here is already using "in a different way" what his (favorite) teachers were teaching him — so that in this paper, as in the two that follow it, it almost seems that he is in a certain sense, "making a virtue of necessity."[87]

This happens, as I have already mentioned, in a sequence. There is Ardigò, whom Colorni respects for his intentions and ingenuity, if not his solution, then Bergson, who he sees as a step away from a theory on the autonomy of art (which he is then unable or unwilling to take), and finally Croce, whom he appreciates for his industrious, vital, and continually evolving contribution, but whom he considers in the final analysis to be subject to the merciless logic of the dialectic of distinct forms derived from Hegel. Over and above their undoubted creativity, Colorni notes in all three of these essays the enormous difficulties encountered by the authors (and more generally by the aesthetic-philosophical thinking of the time) in their efforts to break free of classic German philosophy (as traditionally interpreted).

I would add, finally, that for an economist like myself, reading these youthful writings of Eugenio's was surprising from another point of view as well. Because they can be compared to the lengthy effort of critical economics to break free of the mental straitjacket of

---

[86]Colorni 1932. "Concerning all the classic authors as well as many others of lesser note [. . .]," he wrote, "Martinetti has ideas that are direct and profound. But he looks at them from a different point of view from the usual one [. . .] So that, even if the book does not offer a 'new philosophy', it introduces us into a new environment, it opens our eyes [. . .] it enriches. And this is what is needed most of all by young people, who are hampered by the pressure of celebrated doctrines from seeing outside the frameworks they provide; and who struggle to free themselves from their servitude" (now in Colorni 2009, p. 52–53; cf. also Meldolesi 2021, p. 23 and n. 33).

[87]So that the papers can be considered "proto-possibilist" (in hindsight of course).

"Economics." Colorni in philosophy and Hirschman in economics effectively freed themselves from these ways of thinking only when they advocated a kind of free thought that, while still taking account of their respective intellectual traditions (perhaps gradually reconsidering this or that aspect in its specific meaning), did not submit to their holistic, systematic, general logic — and therefore, by extension. . . to any system.

12. What can we learn or even glimpse in all this? I would say that it depends on how we look at it. My own position is twofold. On one hand I try to put myself in the shoes of Colorni as a student, in recognition of the daily aspect of his learning — with its inevitable inconsistencies, stumbling blocks, insecurities, etc. But on the other hand, I cannot help but also observe his work retrospectively, at a distance of over ninety years.

My reasoning is as follows. The importance of the rediscovery of the papers on Ardigò's aesthetics and on "Bergsonism" for understanding the first steps of this extraordinary intellectual is beyond question — also in order to "decode," as I will now argue, his little book of criticism of Croce's aesthetics, which might otherwise appear a bit excessive, almost obsessive even, at least to the non-professional eye.

On the other hand, the authority (not to say impudence) with which the very young Eugenio enters the debate at his Milanese institute in search of forgotten, unknown or little-explored aspects of the work of Ardigò in particular is evidently a response to a keenly felt need. Which is to say that there is a liberating intention that exists in him that leads him to focus on possible gateways, even though he evidently doesn't know why he behaves, even instinctively, in this way. This he would uncover later on, finally arriving at his famous argument against systems as such.

Once again we note Colorni's assurance as he moves through recent and contemporary aesthetics from the philosophical point of view, which had developed in Italy and France almost as if to counterbalance Hegelian dominance in general philosophy — to which both Croce and Bergson were ultimately tied. And again we observe Eugenio's surprising ability to utilize the small corner he found himself in to find enough space for fresh thinking — the pleasure of bringing the first results of his research to the young antifascists of *Pietre,* not least in the hope that others might share them. . . .

Of course, all of this is possible due to the constellation of objective and subjective circumstances Colorni found himself in — his time and place and predisposition. Think of the cultural, political and moral oppression of the regime, of how it affected Eugenio's microcosm, of his relationship with his "rebel" teachers and how they welcomed the freshness of his approach to the point of considering him, while still a student, a rising young star in philosophy. . . .[88]

Finally, it is notable how the authority he had by now acquired flows freely in the numerous reviews of the time that make up the second part of the present collection. Inevitably, these are brief contributions that are not homogeneous — either in terms of their subject matter, disciplinary reference or treatment (sometimes pleasant, sometimes tedious) — in which the interests of the literary critic alternate with those of the philosopher. Surprisingly, they sometimes reveal a degree of judgmental audacity toward much better established authors, and often contain, in a nutshell, useful and penetrating observations that reveal the still developing point of view of their young author. . . .

13. It is also true that this interpretation of the work of Ardigò undoubtedly reflected Eugenio's interest in the autonomy of art[89] and the "immediacy and individuality" of Bergson's "first theory of knowledge,"[90] and furthermore indirectly brought to light his need to free Benedetto Croce's laborious work, in aesthetics and other-

---

[88]Borgese (1931, p. 119) asserted that Eugenio was "nobly versed in philosophical studies." "In our university," Guido Povene wrote on 7 June 1944 in Rome's *Il Tempo* (now in Gerbi 1999, p. 296), "[Colorni] was the great hope in philosophical studies."

[89]A judgment shared by Borgese when he supported "the capital conquest of recent Italian aesthetic thought — which is the affirmed autonomy and non-transience of art, and the distinction of its means and ends from those of other activities of the mind" (1934, p. 134).

[90]Cf, below, p. 97 and ff., where art is intuition, sensation, non-reproducible inner flow ("durée"). This angle of vision in early Bergson should also be set alongside what Colorni writes about art as "pure representation, lack of distinction between real and unreal, and catharsis" at the end of his "Critical Study" of Crocean aesthetics (cf. below, p. 211). In fact, both points of view are part of the cultural horizon that Colorni refers to (also implicitly) in the numerous youthful reviews included in the second part of this volume.

wise, from the "Nessus shirt" of Hegelism (as well as Marxism).[91]

In fact, if we go through the aesthetics of "Bergsonism" — a very informative piece of writing that has among other things the merit of drawing aside the veil (of typical Italian provincialism) that covered this theme — we arrive at the key point of the entire question. And finally Eugenio's criticism of Croce's aesthetics appears to us in a new light. Here Colorni takes the opportunity to discuss Croce's work as Borgese wanted,[92] but without the latter's destructive intentions.[93] Because he also felt that he needed to do "precision work" in order to engage with a political-cultural "monument" like Croce on his own favorite subject (aesthetics) even at the cost of a certain tortuousness[94] — a patient process of "verifi-

---

[91]Conversely, it is understandable that the protracted non-availability of Eugenio's two unpublished conference papers on the works of Ardigò and on "Bergsonism" and the lack of attention given by the critics to the artistic and political aspects of the question (and therefore also to the article on Ardigò that appeared in *Pietre* and the essay on Campanella in the *Rivista di filosofia*) have up to now clouded any genuine perception of the youthful Colorni's intellectual development.

[92]In the conviction expressed by Borgese that "Croce's discoveries, meditations, and doubts are what is most important in these years in the history of taste and literary research," Alceo Riosa rightly argued (2011, p. 272), "there was a recognizable desire to keep a constructive debate on Crocean thought alive."

[93]Cf. above, n. 67. "For Croce," Piovene wrote in 1963, "there was [. . .] great respect, except for trying to demolish him in school exercises (as in fact Borgese's wanted)." Borgese had initially been a student of Croce's, but later, even while maintaining a considerate attitude toward his former teacher, he had gone so far as to write: "it turns out that Croce, over the course of a dozen years, and already eschewing a line of development from one thought to another in favor of an incessant process of contradiction, has declared at one time or another, with the same assertive energy: that the history of art needs the criterion of progress, that it must do without it, that it has cycles of progress, that it doesn't, that it cannot be separated from the overall history of human civilization, that it must be separated, that there are connections between one artwork and another, that there aren't, that works of art arise from tradition, and that every effort of artistic endeavor is faced with inert or rebellious material" (Borgese 1934, p. 97–98). Note instead Colorni's need to free himself, not from Croce's works per se, which he recognized as having an important educational role for whole generations, but from its forced systematizing.

[94]Another clear expression of this procedure is also found in "The Philosophical Illness" (1939: now 2021a, p. 108), where we find that Pierino [alias Eugenio] "is by now strong enough to absorb a shock or two, and he shrugs his shoulders at the accusations hurled at him of rationalism and moralism. What he looks for in every problem is not so much the solution [. . .] as the neatness, the cleanness, the honesty of how the problem is set. There should be no misunderstandings. What is intended should be clear, and the meaning of the words known. [. . .] Taking Croce apart with this method becomes a game of patience. Just test the whole system step by step, connection by connection. And the result is that the system falls to pieces. The circle of forms of the mind proves to be full of cracks and gimmicks.

cation" that allowed him to untangle the knots of reasoning a little at a time, and isolate the ideas on art that seemed to be in fact well founded — jumping-off points for possible future construction.

In this way, he inaugurated a way of proceeding that in a sense absorbed the positive aspects of the opposing judgments (for or against Croce) while leaving to their fate the aspects that he disagreed with. In fact, as the reader can verify, he was looking for a new path-way that would value "the great work of Croce" and "its precious in-sights," and at the same time free it from the restrictive confines of the dialectic of distinct forms, thus reopening the path of philosophical exploration — for the benefit, above all, of the new generations. It is an attitude of searching for the possible, which was to become typical of his thinking (and later of that of Albert Hirschman).

Looking back from our present vantage point, after so much water under the bridge, the rather difficult look of the monograph — the only one Colorni published — has fortunately been transformed so that it is possible to appreciate it wholeheartedly in a way can now be described following the unexpected finds of Mario Quaranta.

We can in any case deduce the decisive importance that Color-ni at the time attributed to art and to the need to fully understand its autonomy with respect to other forms of human expression.

All this probably created in him a protracted feeling of grati-tude concerning aesthetics and the arts,[95] if only because they rep-resented the primordial "breeding ground" of his elaborations.[96] It

---

The parallel between art and logic, economics and ethics comes down to an extrinsic need for symmetry. All that's left are individual discoveries and observations, with prejudices removed and appropriate distinctions made. Pierino could never go so far as to abandon all this valuable material just because the structure had been shown to be inconsistent. He has no iconoclastic urges; he is no triumphant destroyer."

[95]Consider, for example, what Hirschman said in 1987 (p. 41) about his own early writings: "those who write are often exposed, it seems to me, to a form of childish narcissism, which makes them turn a particularly tender eye to those unpublished or little-known writings they autographed in their youth."

[96]In fact, in the context of Professor Borgese's teaching, Colorni's exercises — of which the "Critical Study" of Crocean aesthetics probably represents (in its initial part) the development of the third lost manuscript — are very useful in themselves in their illumination of the author's formative processes. But they are also valuable in revealing the command already achieved of the subject by a student barely twenty years old (as the first reviews collected in the second part of this paper strikingly show). With this affirmation of his promise in the field of aesthetic studies, Eugenio seemed to have embarked on this specific career path. But this was not the

is probably from this appreciative viewpoint that he would today regard the youthful reviews included here — small way stations on a journey of liberation of thought through art, philosophy and politics. And probably, through them, such gratitude would extend to his having started right then the process of trespassing from one discipline to another (from art to philosophy and from philosophy to politics, and from the natural sciences to philosophy and back again). It is an attitude of mind that is already present in his study of the positivists, and then of Descartes and Leibniz, and is taken up again in great style in the research he did in his early maturity, as he tracked the great advances in mathematics and especially physics of the early twentieth century.[97]

It is true, in fact, that the political-cultural work undertaken by the young Eugenio already pointed to some of the subsequent steps of his intellectual trajectory — in a twofold sense. Firstly, his aesthetic-philosophical research could not fail to take into account political-cognitive necessities, and, conversely, the latter had to be able, in the final analysis, to suggest results that were actually convincing at the philosophical level.

Even while he remained, up to that moment, in accord with the teaching of Borgese and Martinetti, it seems to me that it was precisely that *leap backward* to retrieve Ardigò's problem[98] that

---

case. As we know, he decided instead to change the focus of his scientific interests and to earn his degree — under Prof. Martinetti's supervision — with a thesis on the "Development and Meaning of Leibnizian Individualism." In parallel, his initial interest in aesthetics, represented in the reviews collected here, began to transform into literary criticism. Later, after his arrest, this latter inspiration would be renewed, and would develop into almost daily discussions in his correspondence with his wife Ursula — and two short stories.

[97] And it is a theme we ought to revisit today — in order to better understand such relations in the interests of the indispensable abandonment of the nineteenth-century ideological constructions that they suggest, to learn from subsequent developments for the hyper-technological era in which we find ourselves, and even to further stimulate the latter by hunting down our own anthropomorphism — as was Eugenio's intention. It is a whole field in continuous evolution that is actually unfolding before our astonished eyes.

[98] A backward leap that, not coincidentally, was in tune with the political-philosophical inspiration of *Pietre*: cf. above, n. 62. While the essay on the work of Ardigò, starting out from positivism, goes in search of a real epistemological solution and thus introduces a problem that would engage Colorni at length, the pyrotechnic essay on Bergsonism alongside that theme (and focusing on intuition and the individual), also allows him to identify some features that he can agree with on the autonomy of art and on its nature — intuitive, cathartic, ahistorical etc. — which, however, Eugenio did not later transform into an aesthetics of his own.

paved Eugenio's way. This was an evolution that may appear incomprehensible if one fails to grasp the meaning of his political-philosophical background. In essence, Colorni was looking for his own solution to the epistemological problems that tormented him, and distanced himself from both positivism and idealism — instead trying to move cautiously in an open sea by means of learning that came from all directions (which he little by little sorted out), revisiting mainly the work of authors like Ardigò, Bergson and Leibniz, who together allowed him by degrees to unleash his thinking — in the direction of uncharted shores. . .

Bibliography

AA.VV. (1973) *Pietre. Antologia di una rivista (1926-1928)*. Ed. G. Marcenaro. Milano: Mursia.

AA.VV. (2011) *Eugenio Colorni e la cultura italiana tra le due guerre*. Ed. Geri Cerchiai and Giovanni Rota. Manduria: Lacaita.

Alighieri, D. (1308-20) *La divina commedia*; now Firenze: Le Monnier, 2002 and ff.

Basso, L. (1928) "La morte del Novecento." *Pietre* 3.1, (under the pseudonym D'Arzocco).

Bianco, G. and C. Costantini. (1962) "Un episodio dell'opposizione democratica al fascismo: la rivista *Pietre* (1926-1928)." AA.VV. *Miscellanea di Storia Ligure in Onore di Giorgio Falco*. Milano: Feltrinelli.

Bobbio, N. (1975) "Introduzione" to E. Colorni *Scritti*. Ed. N. Bobbio. Firenze: La Nuova Italia.

Bonetti. P. (1989) *Introduzione a Croce*. Roma: Laterza.

Borgese, G. A. (1934) *Poetica dall'unità*. Milano: Arnoldo Mondadori.

Campanella, T. (1951) *Campanella*. Ed. A. Testa. Milano: Garzanti.

___. (1953) *La Città del Sole*, with preface by R. De Mattei. Roma: Colombo.

Cavaglion, A. (2011) "'Il mio poeta'. Eugenio Colorni, Umberto Saba e la psicoanalisi." AA.VV. *Eugenio Colorni e la cultura* cit.

Cerchiai, G. (2018) *La filosofia di Eugenio Colorni*. Milano: Franco Angeli.

Colorni, E. (1918-1936) *Lettere*. Ed. Eva Hirschmann Monteforte. Vol. 1, mimeo.

___. (1928) *L'estetica di Roberto Ardigò e del positivismo italiano nella seconda metà dell'800*, mimeo.

___. (1928a) "Roberto Ardigò." *Pietre* 3.2 (under the pseudonym Rosemberg).

___. (1929) *L'estetica bergsoniana*, mimeo.

___. (1930) "Recensione a La giustizia di Max Ascoli." *Civiltà moderna* 6.

___. (1930a) "Recensione a Saggi critici di Giacomo Debenedetti." *Leonardo* (February).

___. (1930b) "Recensione" di L. Bandini. *Shaftesbury*, Bari: Laterza 1930; *Leonardo* (April).

___. (1930c) "Sviluppo significato dell'individualismo leibnziano." Bachelor's Thesis.

___. (1931) "Recensione a Estetica di Adriano Tilgher." *Il Convegno* 1-2.

___. (1931a) "Recensione a 'Parole all'orecchio' e 'Parliamo dell'Italia' di V. Cardarelli." *Il Convegno* 1-2.

___. (1931b) "In memoria di Enrico Sereni." *Israel* 13-20 March.

___. (1931c) "Recensione a 'La carne, la morte e il diavolo nella letteratura romantica di M. Praz." *Il Convegno* 5.

___. (1931d) "Utilità e moralità nella filosofia di Tommaso Campanella." *Rivista di filosofia* (July-September).

___. (1931e) "Recensione a Studi crociani di Guido Calogero e Domenico Petrini." *Il Convegno* 11-12.

___. (1931-36) "Lettere a Benedetto Croce"; now in Appendix to S. Miccolis "Eugenio Colorni" cit.

___. (1932) *L'estetica di Benedetto Croce. Studio critico*. Milano: Società Editrice "La cultura."

___. (1932a) "Recensione alla ristampa dell'Introduzione alla metafisica di Piero Martinetti." *La cultura* 3.

___. (1932b) "Recensione a *La scuola* di ballo di Arturo Loria." *Il Convegno* 7–8.

___. (1932c) "Di alcune relazioni tra conoscenza e volontà." *Rivista di filosofia* 23; now in Colorni 2009, *La malattia* cit.

___. (1933) "La filosofia giovanile di Leibniz." *Thesis*.

___. (1935) "Prefazione," "Nota bio-bibliografica," and "Esposizione antologica del sistema leibniziano," a Goffredo Guglielmo Leibnitz. *La Monadologia*, cit.

___. (1935a) "I problemi della guerra." *Politica Socialista* (August) (under the pseudonym Agostini); now in Colorni, E. 2017, *La scoperta* cit.

___. (1936) "La lotta all'interno del fascismo." *Nuovo Avanti!* (31 October); now in Colorni, E. 2017, *La scoperta* cit.

___. (1937) "La spontaneità è una forma di organizzazione." *Nuovo Avanti!* (12 June) (under the pseudonym Anselmi); now in Colorni E. 2017, *La scoperta* cit.

___. (1937a) "La funzione del maestro nella scuola fascista." 3 articoli. *Nuovo Avanti!* (July) (under the pseudonimo Agostini); now in Colorni, E. 2017, *La scoperta* cit.

___. (1937b) "Direttive per la costituzione di posti di frontiera e per il lavoro all'interno." (September); now in Colorni, E. 2017, *La scoperta* cit

___. (1937–1938) *Lettere*. Ed. Eva Hirschmann Monteforte. Vol. 2, mimeo.

___. (1939) *Lettere*. Ed. Eva Hirschmann Monteforte. Vol. 3, mimeo.

___. (1940–1942) *Lettere*. Ed. Eva Hirschmann Monteforte. Vol. 4, mimeo.

___. (1943) "Ultime volontà." (2 May); now in Colorni, E. 2017, *La scoperta* cit.

___. (1944) "Introduzione" to Spinelli A. and Rossi E. *Problemi* cit.

___. (1975) *Scritti*. Ed. N. Bobbio. Firenze: La Nuova Italia.

___. (1980) "Pagine di Eugenio Colorni." *Eugenio Colorni*. Ed. L. Solari, cit.

___. (1998) *Il coraggio dell'innocenza*. Ed. L. Meldolesi. Napoli: La Città del Sole.

___. (2002) *Il poeta e altri racconti*. Ed. L. Baranelli.

___. (2009) *La malattia della metafisica. Scritti filosofici e autobiografici*. Ed. Geri Cerchiai. Torino: Einaudi.

___. (2009a) "Libero arbitrio e grazia nel pensiero di Leibnitz." *La Malattia*, by E. Colorni. (2009) cit.

___. (2016) *Microfondamenta*. Ed. Luca Meldolesi. Soveria Mannelli: Rubbettino.

___. (2017) *La scoperta del possibile. Scritti politici*. Ed. Luca Meldolesi. Soveria Mannelli: Rubbettino.

___. (2018) *L'ultimo anno, 1943–44. Genesi di una prospettiva*. Ed. Luca Meldolesi. Soveria Mannelli: Rubbettino.

___. (2019) *Critical Thinking in Action. Excerpts from Political Writings and Correspondence I*. Ed. Luca Meldolesi and Nicoletta Stame. New York: Bordighera.

___. (2019a) *The Discovery of the Possible. Excerpts from Political Writings and Correspondence II*. Ed. Luca Meldolesi and Nicoletta Stame. New York: Bordighera.

___. (2020) *"La malattia filosofica" ed altri scritti*. Ed. Luca Meldolesi. Soveria Mannelli: Rubbettino.

___. (2021) *The Final Year: 1943–44. Genesis of a Perspective*. Ed. Luca Meldolesi and Nicoletta Stame. New York: Bordighera.

___. (2021a) *"The Philosophical Illness" and Other Writings*. Ed. Luca Meldolesi. New York: Bordighera.

___, and A. Spinelli. (2018) *I dialoghi di Ventotene*. Ed. Luca Meldolesi. Soveria Mannelli: Rubbettino.

___, and A. Spinelli. (2020) *Dialogues*. Ed. Luca Meldolesi and Nicoletta Stame. New York: Bordighera.

Consiglio, A. (1928) "Disegno di tempi." *Pietre* 3.2.

___. (1928a) "Europeismo." *Pietre* 3.2.

Croce, B. (1893) "La storia ridotta sotto il concetto generale dell'arte." commemoration read at the Accademia Pontaniana of Naples on 5 March.

___. (1902) *Estetica. Come scienza dell'espressione e linguistica generale. Teoria e storia*. Bari: Laterza.

___. (1907) *Ciò che è vivo e ciò che è morto della filosofia di Hegel. Studio critico seguito da un saggio di bibliografia hegeliana*. Bari: Laterza.

___. (1913) *Breviario di estetica*. Bari: Laterza; 22nd ed. 1988.

___. (1928) *Storia d'Italia dal 1871 al 1915*. Bari: Laterza.

___. (2005) *Estetica come scienza dell'espressione e linguistica generale. Teoria e storia*. 2nd ed. Ed. G. Galasso. Milano: Adelphi.

de Sanctis, F. (1870) *Storia della letteratura italiana*; now Milano: Rizzoli, 2006.

Elias, N. (1996) *The Germans: Power Struggles and the Development of Habitus in the Nineteenth and Twentieth Centuries*. New York: Colombia UP.

Franchini, R., G. Lunati, and F. Tessitore. (1990) *Il ritorno di Croce nella cultura italiana*. Milano: Rusconi.

Gallo, F., ed. (2020) *Gli Hegeliani di Napoli. Il Risorgimento e la ricezione di Hegel in Italia. Writings in Honor of Gerardo Marotta*. Napoli: La scuola di Pitagora.

Gentile, E. (2011) "'Tastare il polso della propria epoca.' La crisi della civiltà nell'epoca dei totalitarismi." AA.VV. (2011) *Eugenio Colorni e la cultura*, cit.

Gerbi, S., ed. (1999) *Tempi di malafede. Una storia italiana tra fascismo e dopoguerra*, by Guido Piovene and Eugenio Colorni. Torino: Einaudi.

Groenewegen, P. (1987) "Antonio Serra." *New Palgrave Dictionary of Economics*. Ed. S. Durlauf and L. E. Blume. London: Macmillan.

Hirschman, A. O. (1945) *National Power and the Structure of Foreign Trade*. Berkeley: U of California P. Third ed., with a new introduction, 1980.

___. (1971) "Introduction: Political Economics and Possibilism." *A Bias for Hope*. New Haven: Yale UP.

___. (1981) *Essays in Trespassing: Economics to Politics and Beyond*. Cambridge, UK: Cambridge UP.

___. (1987) *Potenza nazionale e commercio estero. Gli anni trenta, l'Italia e la ricostruzione*. Ed. P. F. Asso and M. de Cecco. Bologna: Il Mulino.

Hirschmann, U. (1974) *Rievocazione incompiuta*, mimeo.

Leibniz, G. G. (1935) *La Monadologia*. Ed. Eugenio Colorni. Firenze: Sansoni.

Lepenies W. (2006) *The Seduction of Culture in German History*. Princeton, NJ: Princeton UP.

Machiavelli, N. (1513) *Il Principe*; now e-book, Biblioteca di Alessandria, 2015.

Manzitti, F. (1928) "15 febbraio." *Pietre* 3.2.

Marcenaro, G. (1973) "*Pietre*: più che una rivista un'intenzione." AA.VV. (1973)

Pietre, cit.

Meldolesi, L. (2019) "Introduction." *The Discovery of the Possible,* by E. Colorni, cit.

___. (2021) "Introduction." *"The Philosophical Illness" and Other Writimgs,* by E. Colorni, cit.

___. (2020) *Eppur si può! Saggi e istruzioni autobiografiche e "filo-possibiliste."* Soveria Mannelli: Rubbettino.

Merker, N. (1974) *L'illuminismo tedesco.* Bari: Laterza.

Miccolis, S. (2011) "Eugenio Colorni e Benedetto Croce." AA.VV., *Eugenio Colorni e la cultura,* cit.

Nicolini, F. (1962) *Benedetto Croce.* Torino: Utet.

Piovene, G. (1944) "Ritratto di Eugenio Colorni." *Il Tempo* 7 June; now in S. Gerbi, *Tempi di malafede,* cit. 1999.

Riosa, A. (2011) "Giuseppe Antonio Borgese ed Eugenio Colorni tra letteratura e politica." AA.VV., *Eugenio Colorni e la cultura,* cit.

Quaranta, M. (2011) "La 'scoperta' di Eugenio Colorni nelle riviste del secondo dopoguerra. Gli scritti sulla relatività." AA.VV., *Eugenio Colorni e la cultura,* cit.

Salvati, M. (2016) *Passaggi. Italiani dal fascismo alla Repubblica.* Roma: Carocci.

Schumpeter, J. (1954) *History of Economic Analysis.* London: Allen and Unwin.

Scurati, A. (2019) *Il tempo migliore della nostra vita.* Milano: Bompiani.

Sereni, C. (1993) *Il gioco dei regni.* Firenze: Giunti.

Serra, A. (1613) *Breve trattato delle cause che possono far abbondare i Regni d'oro e d'argento dove non sono miniere con applicazione al Regno di Napoli.* Napoli: Lazzaro Scoriggio; now with preface by P. Savona. Soveria Mannelli: Rubbettino; English trans. by Sophus A. Renhert. Cambridge, UK: Anthem, 2011.

Testa, A. (1951) "Introduzione" to T. Campanella. *Campanella.* Ed. A. Testa. Milano: Garzanti.

Vico, G. (1725, 1730, 1744) *La scienza nuova*; now in G. Vico, *La scienza nuova. Le tre edizioni del 1725, 1730 e 1744,* Ed. E. Sanna and V. Vitiello. Milano: Bompiani 2012.

Vigorelli, A. (2011) "L'antifascismo tra i giovani: il caso di *Pietre.*" AAVV., *Eugenio Colorni e la cultura,* cit.

I: Young Eugenio

"Utility and Morality in the Political Philosophy of Tommaso Campanella," *Rivista di filosofia* 22.3 (1931): 230–48.

The difficulty of reconstructing the complex and multiform figure of Campanella lies entirely in finding the thread that reveals the unity of his thought while preserving the contradictions, that avoids splitting his character into a number of disparate and contrasting positions without undermining historical truth and without imposing a forced consistency on his opinions. The balance between respect for the genuine diversity of the data available to us and the single line that we want to find there is in this case — more than in many others like it — difficult to achieve.

And the difficulty is primarily a result of the contradictions between the medieval and the modern man in him, between what he believed he was and what he actually was, and between his commitment to orthodoxy and obedience to tradition on one hand, and a novelty of mind which unconsciously led him beyond its limits. But interpreting these contrasting elements can be of great interest to us, not only as a problem of historical criticism, but also because of the need to clarify ideas about the meaning of certain judgments, about the theoretical and doctrinal importance that the accentuation of one aspect rather than another of Campanella's ideas can have for current thought. Indeed, the problems that the interpretation of such ideas poses for us are a great incentive and aid in the framing of these same problems in the general field of research.

Following this impulse and analyzing and discussing mainly one of the most recent interpretations, that of Treves,[1] we have decided to organize and clarify some concepts regarding the significance of Campanella with respect to the political thought of the Counter-Reformation. These we will present only as points of departure for solving certain problems — as an example of the various ways in which the vast movement Campanella is linked to can be understood, and of various ways of conceptualizing the relationships between economics, politics and morality.

A fundamental problem with Campanella as a moral and po-

---

[1]Paolo Treves, *La filosofia politica di Tommaso Campanella* (Bari, 1930).

litical figure — already presented in various ways by Meinecke, De Mattei, Dentice d'Accadia and others, and again taken up and amply covered by Treves — concerns his relationship with Machiavelli and the contradiction commonly noted in him between his avowed anti-Machiavellianism and the Machiavellianism he actually practiced. The latter is seen as the reason for his considerable modernity, and we can recognize him as both the theorist of a universal and moral state — the supporter and celebrator of the Church, and the implementer of a utilitarian and particularist "Reason of State." These two sides and aspects of Campanella are hard to reconcile, and the problem of his spiritual unity is resolved by appeals to his human character, to the "ethical example of his personality and his faith."[2]

At the same time, attributing Campanella's modernity to his piecemeal use of the Reason of State and a "practical application" of his universalist ideas that reveals his gifts as an astute connoisseur of contingent political problems implies a concept of political activity and the relationship between economics and ethics that merits discussion.

Comparing Campanella's political doctrines (like all those of the Counter-Reformation) and the views of Machiavelli is now customary, and the degree of inconsistency of such doctrines is measured by their greater or lesser degree of affinity with the thinking of the Florentine Secretary. An apparently moralistic, universalist Counter-Reformation that is therefore profoundly anti-Machiavellian in its ultimate purpose and overall doctrine — but which is at the same time political, astute, and Machiavellian in the practical implementation of its aims, is the conception that, through various nuances, has taken shape in modern thought. Machiavelli, camouflaged in the guise of Reason of State or Tacitism, resurfaces, one might say, in practical precepts, despite endless condemnation. But it is interesting to note which elements of his doctrine, so complex and multiform beneath its apparent simplicity, were taken up more or less unconsciously by the Counter-Reformation.

The difference in tone between the mildly liberal and republican the *Deche* and the absolutist and vigorously amoral "The Prince" has already been noted more than once. Whether for psy-

---

[2] Treves, op. cit., p. 214.

chological reasons deriving from the environments in which the two works were written[3] or from the perceptions that the concrete politics of the Italian states provided daily to the careful observer,[4] it is clear that this difference ought not to be overlooked by those wishing to clarify their ideas on the true meaning of Machiavellian thought.

Treves makes a distinction, regarding relations with Campanella, between the real Machiavelli and what he calls "Machiavellianism" — that is, between the actual doctrine of the absolute and lordly state advocated in "The Prince" and "some of Machiavelli's suggestions," which, "removed from the rest of his work and transplanted into a historical climate that was not the one where they arose, took on a different life that led to the misrepresentation of Machiavelli that goes by the name of Machiavellianism."[5] It is clear and evident that Machiavelli's methodological teachings, more than his concrete political opinions, were taken up by Campanella's thought — even if it is also true that a fundamental aspect of Campanella is the application of the Machiavellian identification of the end with the means to the anti-Machiavellian principle par excellence of the universal theocratic moral state. But it is interesting to discuss whether these first lessons in method are really "secondary and minor concepts" and what in any case the relationship is between these two aspects of the Florentine's thinking.

Treves considers the relationship to be very close — close enough to consider one aspect as dependent on the other and to view political autonomy as a necessary consequence or the expression in another form of the principle that the end justifies the means.[6] Now, if it is indeed true — as he observes — that both these principles are characteristics of the same concrete and realist mindset, and express Machiavelli's mental makeup with equal clarity, it is however no less the case that — seen as separate absolute philosophical principles in their own right by the empirical personality

---

[3]Cf. Toffanin, *Machiavelli e il Tacitismo* (Padova, 1921) p. 25–36.
[4]Cf. Meinecke, *Die Idee der Staatsräson* (München-Berlin, 1924) p. 40–41.
[5]Treves, op. cit, p. 39.
[6]See also Treves, "Machiavelli e il problema della Ragion di Stato," *Civiltà Moderna* (December 1930).

that first expressed them with such admirable precision — not only can they be split one from the other, but they turn out to be fundamentally disparate.

Thus the accusation against Campanella of having taken up only some of Machiavelli's principles, which divorced from the rest of his doctrine show themselves to be sterile and empty, would be diminished in value if it could be demonstrated that two different lessons can be isolated in his doctrine, one representing a principle of methodology applicable to any type of practical activity (be it moral or economic), and the other indicating a certain content as typical of political activity. And if from a contingent historical and political point of view Machiavelli's modernity can be seen in the latter principle — that is, in his having perceived the need for autonomous, centralized states independent of any theocratic subjugation to the Church, it is not possible to invoke this need as an absolute criterion for judging historical and political facts or as a philosophical principle of universal validity. It is indisputable that in "The Prince" Machiavelli anticipated many aspects of later historical development — that in a sense he showed history the way. But that does not mean his principles in this field should be reduced to absolute norms. His shrewd eye showed him what political form was best suited to his times, and what in the near future would represent the best form of opportunity and, in a certain sense, of political morality. But it is not necessarily the case that by this he was indicating the essential forms and fundamental characteristics of politics.

His modernity as a historian is therefore not the modernity of a philosopher, and should be clearly separated from it. And what is usually considered his great philosophical discovery — that is, the autonomy of politics — does not find its expression here. The concept of the modern state whose theoretical basis is usually found in "The Prince" does not represent the explicit and conscious introduction of the criterion of utility as opposed to the criterion of morality, but is rather the solution of a specific historical problem. It constitutes the discovery of a new form of government that is more suited to the times and more moral, in the sense that it solves the political problems of the time more completely. But political realism — that is, staying abreast of current historical conditions instead of following some preconceived schemes, is still not political utilitarianism, let alone implying the introduction of an autonomous form of utilitarian and economic activity.

We have already noted the difference in tone between "The Prince" and the *Deche,* which is one more demonstration that the type of state advocated in "The Prince" is nothing more than a realistic proposed solution to the problems troubling the world in which the author lived. When applied to other peoples and other historical periods, this proposal might well give way to others more suited to the situation. And the fact that some of the problems that gave rise to "The Prince" are still with us today should prevent our being misled about that solution's timelessness.

But in addition to the concrete politics and the type of state he advocated, there is in the whole of Machiavelli's work that tone of concreteness, of connecting means to ends — that cold sense of the goal to be achieved at any cost — which has aroused hatred and love in so many generations. This is what Treves considers abstract if divorced from the context of his work and its concrete political doctrine. But it is precisely here that we believe we can see the "philosophical" modernity of our author, the serious and comprehensive awareness of the end to be achieved and the identity of this end with the means. It is here that his thought has provided one of the greatest incentives to our modern concept of practical activity. But that concept, precisely because it is universal and is the distinguishing criterion for any real act of will, is not connected with the doctrine of the autonomy of economic activity.

The identity of means and ends is a characteristic aspect of any activity — whether economic or moral — just as the identity of intuition and expression (to take two concepts that the Croce doctrine, which Treves evidently refers to, considers analogous) is valid for logical activity, as well as for aesthetics. It is not possible, therefore, to say that Machiavelli's "method" works only if it is applied to the ends he has proposed, because its greatness and universality as a method lies precisely in its applicability to any and all ends. It represents a clarification and broadening of the concept of ends without establishing whether they should be individual or universal, and it does not introduce an autonomous form of activity whose particular distinguishing feature is the identification of ends with means.

The lack of distinction between these two aspects, historical and doctrinal, political and philosophical, of Machiavellianism perhaps prevents us from resolving in the seemingly most plausible way one of the fundamental contradictions in Campanella's work — between his avowed anti-Machiavellianism and his practiced Machiavellianism. Treves judges the Machiavellian method inapplicable to anti-Machiavellian ends. But the discovery of Machiavelli's that establishes his greatness and modernity, and which Campanella adopted from him, is the affirmation that the attainment of an end must necessarily disregard any abstract and isolated consideration of the means required to achieve it. In this way the very concept of means is abolished. So that to pass judgment on the greater or lesser morality of the means is, in essence, to deny them as means and to transform them into many small ends, which will naturally be different from the overall end to which they were subservient.

To speak theoretically therefore of a morality of ends and an immorality (or amorality) of means, of an anti-Machiavellianism of ends and a Machiavellianism of means, is no longer possible — not after Machiavelli. At least not unless we want to see in this discrepancy some sort of deficiency in the evaluation of the contingent situation, an error of political tactics, which I do not think fits the present case, given Campanella's acumen in juggling problems of foreign and diplomatic policy.

Campanella's modernity, then, lies first of all in his methodological Machiavellianism, in which we seem to see the adoption not of a partial and isolated datum without value in itself, but of the Florentine Secretary's fundamental teachings. In this respect Campanella is fully within the current of modern thought, and we can even say that, from a strictly doctrinal point of view, he has assumed Machiavelli's legitimate and vital characteristics.

◆ ◆ ◆

So what is new about Campanella with respect to Machiavelli? Shall we appeal mainly to the medievalist, teleological, unwieldy

aspect of his concept of the state as a refutation of his entire political doctrine and relegate it among the old junk his thinking was
burdened with, or can we see some vitality there? Here again we
have to keep an assessment of the author's political wisdom separate from an appraisal of his doctrinal and philosophical clair-
voyance. On one hand, we can easily acknowledge that (the keen
insights on contingent and practical politics notwithstanding) the
ideal state that he gradually shaped, from the *The Spanish Monarchy* to the *The City of the Sun,* does not answer the needs of the
times and represents an antiquated and decayed ideal or an unreal
and utopian mirage. But our evaluation must necessarily be different if we intend to assign a meaning to this concept of a state that
is more doctrinaire than political, and want to see it almost as the
imaginative and allegorical manifestation of a philosophical concept — not so much an ideal of a perfect state as an expression of
the nature of the activity that leads to the formation of states.

The problem of the Counter-Reformation was not so much

Croce has observed[7] that, confronted with Machiavelli, the
Counter-Reformation had the merit of moving beyond the stage
of pure economic efficiency, rounding it out and making it and
more complete and active by establishing a connection with morality, which immediately superseded it. But he was quick to add
that only one of the writers of the period clearly mentions this distinction between the political (or economic) and moral situations.
This is a sign that in the minds of these authors the distinction was
not formulated in this way, and that they posed the problem in a
form different from the one Croce later attributed to it.

The problem of the Counter-Reformation was not so much
morality surmounting politics or a clear separation of the two activities, but rather what I would call an almost accidental reconciliation, a lucky coincidence or agreed compromise between the
two terms. Machiavelli had not been properly understood by these
writers. His methodological principle, applied to a particularist
end, led to consequences repugnant to their moral conscience,
which was still generic. Gifted with practical political minds sharp
enough to glimpse the historical inevitability of Machiavelli's solu-

---

[7]Croce, *Storia dell'età barocca in Italia* (Bari, 1929) p. 76–98.

tion, their moral conscience recoiled at the consequences its rigid and consistent application led to. And rather than decisively identifying the end as immoral and openly fighting it as such, or else resigning themselves to it as a necessity essential to the unfolding of history, they preferred to accept the end as desirable and useful, and to locate all the immorality in the means.

The theorists of the Counter-Reformation had by then abandoned the medieval conception of the universal and theocratic state and accepted the necessity of the formation of individual, centralized and autonomous political entities (even if they would still have liked to keep the Church above them as a weak and ostensible mediator of peace and symbol of unity).[8] But they turned away from the means that Machiavelli had shown to be necessarily connected with that political vision. They are amazed that the attainment of those ends must come at the price of honesty and conscience, not realizing that if the end is particularistic (as it inevitably is when a state is closed in on itself and opposed to other states for pure reasons of interest), the means cannot have any characteristics other than those of the end. "But what aroused me not so much to amazement as contempt," said Botero,[9] "was to see such a barbaric way of governing approved as not brazenly opposing the law of God — to the extent that it was claimed that some things are lawful by reason of state, others by reason of conscience. One cannot say anything more irrational nor impious because whoever withdraws from the sphere of conscience its universal jurisdiction over all that transpires among men, in public as well as in private matters, demonstrates that he has neither soul nor God. If all animals have a natural instinct that inclines them to what is useful and holds them back from what is harmful, should the light of reason and the dictates of conscience given to man to know how to discern good and evil be blind in public affairs and defective in important cases?" The problem is thus to reconcile the useful with the virtuous, showing that they are not in fact contradictory and that indeed they coincide perfectly.

---

[8] Cfr. Toffanin, op. cit., 92–104.
[9] Botero, *Della Ragion di Stato,* ed. Morandi (Bologna, 1930) p. 4.

But the discussion is taken onto the abstract terrain of actions that are moral and immoral in themselves rather than in the light of the purposes they serve, of means uprooted and separated from their end — "Reason of State is knowledge of *means* for establishing and expanding a dominion."[10] The state under discussion is not, as in "The Prince," or *The Spanish Monarchy* or even *The City in the Sun,* a specific kind of state that the author is advocating in support of a certain political conception, but an ideal, abstract state without specific features, where the concern is more with how to preserve it than with its inner structure. It is clear that Machiavelli had a particular form of rule in mind, and indeed, everyone knows the particular model that inspired him to sketch out his figure of "The Prince." Botero instead speaks generically of the state of his time, and if he places a Prince and the people in it, it is to give it the form that is most common and generic. "The Prince" is not a figure that he tries to model, opposing it to democracy or to the republic; it is for him an intrinsic element of political life — whether such a thing is possible or not is something he does not even stop to discuss. "Reason of State presupposes "The Prince" and the state (the former almost as creator, the latter as subject)."[11]

Botero's book is therefore not in any way a proposal for a particular type of political constitution, but rather a generic theory of government, intended to be applied to any form of state organization. The problem it sets out to solve is precisely to reconcile the useful and the good, and it solves it with a generic theory of the coincidence of the two principles. The entire book is dominated by this concept — that the best means of preserving a state and reaching a condition of profit is to operate virtuously.[12] Just as in the hedonistic doctrine of the Epicureans, for whom the greatest happiness is to be found in virtue. Thus, one of the chapters of the second book, having affirmed the importance of religion and the derivation of all authority from God, finishes with the observation that, besides being good in itself and a duty for reasons of

---

[10]Botero, op. cit., p. 9.
[11]Botero, op. cit., p. 9.
[12]Cf. Meinecke, op. cit., p. 86.

conscience, religion is also the most effective means of preserving the state, "because those who alter religion push many to the alteration of affairs, from which conspiracies, sedition and cabals arise; things altogether unsuitable for the principality."[13]

Doing what is best for itself, therefore, without going against the dictates of morality and conscience, is the fundamental nucleus of Botero's thought.[14] There is a notable passage explicitly theorizing this principle in the 1589 and 1590 editions which was removed from the reprints that followed: "First of all he must make a profession not of cunning, but of prudence. Prudence is a virtue whose office is to seek and find suitable means to achieve the end. While cunning tends to the same end, it differs from prudence in that, in the choice of means, the former follows the honest rather than the useful — the latter takes account only of interest."[15]

In Botero (whom we have taken as a typical representative of Counter-Reformation thought) Machiavellianism and anti-Machiavellianism battle each other and intertwine continually — and are reconciled in a compromise. In this form his need for morality actually represents a scruple, a remnant of the Middle Ages, an outdated preconception. It was not the universal aspect of Machiavellianism that he accepted, but the contingent one — as an affirmation of new particularist forms of the absolute state. Having accepted the principle, he backtracked in the face of its consequences in a way that is quite anti-Machiavellian, if it is indeed true that Machiavelli's great universal lesson is in the rigid and inflexible and impassive acceptance of the consequences deriving from any principle.

But Botero's consequences, despite his efforts, could not be completely moral in the sense of the religious and teleological morality he was trying to preserve. Accepting an end that was partial inevitably brought him up against that morality. And if a lack of clarity

---

[13]Botero, op. cit., p. 93.

[14]The phrase "I take it as settled that in the deliberations of Princes interest is what takes precedence over every other consideration" (p. 86) cited by Toffanin (op. cit. p. 103) to show Botero's Machiavellianism, should not be taken as referring to the ideal state Botero is talking about, but to the enemy states surrounding it. It is no more than an opportunity to advise prudence.

[15]Botero, op. cit., p. XLVI.

enabled him to mask the contradiction in the determining the goal, this contradiction emerged stronger and more evident in its application and concrete manifestations, and it was only avoided — as we have seen — through a compromise. The Machiavellian anti-Machiavellianism of the Counter-Reformation can thus be explained as a misunderstanding of Machiavelli — the acceptance of his concrete and contingent political teachings while rejecting the methodology that we have called his definitive and universal discovery. This position necessarily must lead to a discrepancy between the end and the means, because if we have seen that two doctrines may be distinguished in Machiavelli, one philosophical, universal and necessary, and the other political and contingent, it is clear that it is possible to accept the former and reject the latter, but not vice versa. In other words, while it is possible to rail against the state as proposed by Machiavelli and resolve concrete problems in a way different from his, we cannot at the same time reject his methodology and his lesson on the link between means and ends that is (and must be) valid for any and all forms of practical activity.

What is Campanella's attitude toward the problem when it is framed in this way?

We have noted that Treves (accepting the thesis of Dentice d'Accadia)[16] sees in the thought of the Stilese [Campanella] a contradiction between anti-Machiavellianism and Machiavellianism, between the theoretical conception of his moral, philosophical, universalist politics, and the practice of its purely positive, utilitarian, and unscrupulous application.[17] He is insistent in observing how "in practice — and politics is all practice — even the Stilese was not exempt from the inclination toward the dominant *reason of state* common to all writers of that time. Vigorously proclaimed by Machiavelli, it was opposed and yet covertly followed by the entire school of the Counter-Reformation." "But," he adds, "it is fatal — and even the philosophical politics of Campanella, placed in contact with the historical reality of the facts, could not resist the natural impulse of

---

[16]Dentice D'Accadia, "Tomismo e machiavellismo nella concezione politica di T. C.," *Giorn. crit. d. fil. It.* (1925): p. 1–16.

[17]Treves, op. cit., p. 87.

egotistical domination, and mutated into a very shrewd alignment with the hated *reason of state.*"[18]

But it is important to point out that if the contradiction we have noted in the Counter-Reformation lies in its having adopted purely economic ends unrelated to morality[19] without recognizing their full identification with their own means — in a sterile attempt, that is, to *moralize* the latter by softening their effects or by cleverly making them coincide with principles of conscience and religion — the position here is completely reversed. Campanella's main point of opposition to Machiavelli is the contrast in terms of *ends* between his philosophical, religious, universal and theocratic state and Machiavelli's, which is utilitarian and particularistic.

Treves does a good job of highlighting the unitary character of Campanella's entire political opus, and the leaning of all his writings, even the most concretely prescriptive, toward the ideal construction — utopian regarding its practical viability but rich in theoretical lessons — of *The City of the Sun.* Indeed, this is one of the most interesting and best argued theses in his book. But if this is the case, we will have to conclude that Campanella's objection to Machiavelli — unlike that of Botero and the Counter-Reformists in general — is aimed at the ends, even while accepting the means. In other words, to put it in terms of the distinction we have just made, it consists of rejecting the teaching of contingent politics with regard to the absolute and noble state, and fully accepting the theoretical and philosophical lessons, acknowledging that it is not possible to consider means except in view of the end they serve, and indeed that their value is tightly linked with that of this end. Or in short, to use the celebrated and oft-misinterpreted phrase, that "the end justifies the means."

It may be true — indeed, it undoubtedly is — that Campanella's concrete political doctrine and the type of state he advocated is a medievalist illusion, an unconscious visionary's dream concerning the political necessities of the hour. It is true that a moral

---

[18]Ibid., p. 80.

[19]On this feature of the Boterian political ideal, I think even Treves would agree. Cf. p. 64–65.

state like the one he proposed, entirely in the service of religion and with the false universalism that is theocratic universalism, would in his time have represented an example of regression and, in the end, immorality. It is true that the new Machiavellian concept (albeit carrying within itself the germs of particularism and setting as its supreme purpose an entity that is, in the end, not moral but empirical) based its political construction on elements that were more vital and less abstract, and that it anticipated the appearance on the political stage of forces that were more autonomous and conscious and, as such, more moral. All this is true. But we must not judge Campanella in the field of concrete politics. We know that history has shown he was wrong. And if history and the whole development of humanity are understood as the ongoing discovery of new truths and the continual formation of new moral values, then this distance of our author from historical reality kept him from participating in a fundamental phase in the construction of modern moral consciousness. But the essence and novelty of his doctrine should not be judged in this way. He was not a visionary in the field of politics — that is, he did not have a sense of how moral consciousness develops over time, how it progresses in ever renewed forms. But he was a firm proponent of the existence of a moral conscience and of its absolute validity in all fields — from the intimacy of the individual psyche to the complex and cumbersome organization of the state.

Treves noted that all his political writings come together and culminate in his most utopian and unrealistic work, which has value precisely as the exposition of a theory. We can use this observation to interpret all his concrete proposals, his sketches of constitutions, his own attempt to revolt — as allegorical terms in a great philosophical dispute.

And the dispute took place specifically between Campanella and Machiavelli concerning the nature of the purpose of politics.

We have observed how the state championed in "The Prince" represents more a proposal of contingent politics than a definitive theory on the essence of states, and how arbitrary and strained it is to credit the Florentine with the assertion that political activity is autonomous. But it is clear that if this proposal came to be accepted and developed — as we saw was the case in the Counter-Reformation — it also came inevitably to be imbued with a more absolute and essential value, and to be conceived as the theory of an ideal state. It was in this way that a picture of Machiavelli came to be constructed as theorist of a purely political and amoral state — a conception that, beyond not seeming to fit him, leaves serious doubt about its own doctrinal validity.

All Campanella's theoretical and political work is directed against this conception. There is no longer in him, as there is in Botero, an implicit but effective acceptance of the end and a rejection of its consequences — that is, of the means — but rather a clear and vigorous negation of the very Machiavellian end as such. Campanella's ideal monarchy certainly has no value as far as the possibility of its realization is concerned, but it affirms, in the face of any theory of politics as an autonomous and distinctive science, that the state has no meaning other than the moral one of achieving an absolute and religious end. "Politics, the science given by God to men."[20] "Therefore, since politics is dependent on ethics as well as subordinate to [it], from this whoever maintains that good itself is governed by ethics, knows good and otherwise through politics."[21] These celebrated and widely cited phrases indicate clearly the basic concept of politics behind all Campanellian thought — that is, politics in the service of Ethics, the divine science, the means given to humanity to reach a higher level of religious elevation.

Hence the invective against Machiavelli, and against any doctrine that places pleasure above goodness and moral health, and the temporal, transitory and empirical good above the spiritual and eternal good. "For which, Machiavelli, you rave 'without any established purpose' except for the utility of the Tyrant, harming yourself and others in coaxing men in the art of attaining and preserving tyranny for the pleasure of doing whatever they like, and not by the will of God. You might say that there was no higher cause, but

---

[20]*Monarchia di Spagna*, ed. D'Ancona (Torino, 1854) cap. XIX, p. 163.

[21]["Cum ergo politica dependeat ab Ethica tamquam a subalternante: ex eo enim quod bene se ipsum quis regere scit per Ethicam, bene et alios per politicam novit."] *Atheismus Triumphatus* (Parisii, 1636) p. 242–43.

if our counsels collapsed without our having weighed all causes, you would be proven wrong."[22] And this higher cause which must be weighed is God. Thus, if even in the refutation of Machiavellianism, the expressed purpose of the appendix of *Atheismus triumphatus,* the arguments all tend to show that those who have used Machiavelli's arts have perished,[23] this is only apparently a utilitarian argument similar to the one cited for Botero — the demise of tyrannical, utilitarian and irreligious states is not just an undesirable consequence, it is shown to be a divine sanction against sinful conduct: "Did not Caesar, by his mercy, defeat Pompey's superior arms? And the same for the magnanimous Scipio over the cruel Hannibal, whom you considered wiser and stronger than Scipio? And why? Because nothing holy, nothing pious, and no faith was in him, in Livy's testimony."[24] And just before this: "Are you a wretch who won't show your ignorance? Because you did not show this future wickedness in him you would say you did not know about it. Therefore your doctrine is foolish. And God who is in heaven shatters the counsels of men as he wishes. Well you know this and this is why your science fails three times."[25] The science that fails Machiavelli, however, is not a temporal doctrine of political expediency, but one from which we learn the designs of God.

Morality, therefore, must be at the base of any political constitution — not to purify (as in Bolero) and mitigate the wickedness of the

---

[22]["Quapropter deliras Macchiavelle, nullo praestituto fine, nisi Tyranni utilitate, tibi aliisque perniciosa, suadere hominibus artem arripiendi tyrannides et conservandi, et ad libitum omnia faciendi et non ad Dei voluntatem. Si nulla esset supra nos causa, aliquid diceres, sed cum nostra consilia corruant nisi et causas omnes perpendamus, falleris."] Ibid., p. 239. For the other relevant citations, cf. Dentice d'Accadia, cit.

[23]Cf. ibid., 332; "Certainly I would never have time to expose how many grasped at tyranny and were brought down, following Macchiavelli's art, and I see plainly that none of them transmitted the Principality to posterity." ["Tempus quidem deficiet, si narrare velim, quot arripuerint Tyrannidem, Machiavellistica arte, et corruerint: nec profecto video unum ex eis ad posteros transmisisse Principatum."]

[24]["Nonne etiam Caesar per clementiam vicit Pompeium, armis superiorem? Et Scipio benignus crudelem Annibalem, quem tu Scipione sapientorem et fortiorem facis? Et quare? Quia nihil sanctum, nihil pium, nulla fides erat in eo, teste Livio."] Ibid., p 232.

[25]["O miser, nonne sic tuam ignorantiam fateris? Quare tu non docuisti eum ista futura mala? Nesciebam, dices. Ergo tua doctrina stulta est. Et Deus est in Caelo dissipans consilia hominum prout vult. Hunc recognoscere oportet. Defuit ergo tibi triplex scientia in hoc."] Ibid., p. 230.

means, but precisely as an essential end in itself. What Campanella is fighting is tyranny and the particularistic state, which we have seen generally accepted in the Counter-Reformation. And his main political thesis proposes a state that is universal, religious, philosophical.[26]

Whether or not this ideal is well represented in the concrete project of *The Spanish Monarchy* and the ideal of *The City of the Sun* we will not discuss here. Possibly, we repeat, indeed certainly in the light of past history and the events that have followed, Machiavelli's project — which is more concrete and based on more dynamic and autonomous forces — is for us who have come later also ethically more elevated than Campanella's, which is instead permeated with a universalism that is now dead and obsolete. But at the root of this misapplication, this awkwardly sensitive manifestation, there was a very true and vital principle — that political activity, however it manifests itself, can have no value except in the light of a universal, that is moral, conscience.

Thus in Campanella we cannot speak of a conciliatory compromise between utility and morality, as in the Counter-Reformation. Consider this passage on the relationship between prudence and shrewdness, and compare it with the one cited from Botero: "It is given to know that prudence is in accord with the first cause which is God; but shrewdness aims at taste alone and at its own brain and calls it wisdom. . . . Prudence is magnanimous, and looks at things for great truths; shrewdness is pusillanimous and aims at the minutiae of the mind."[27] No longer, then, are there two activities aiming at the same end and differing only in their means. On the contrary, they oppose each other in their very structure and in the actual end that they are directed towards.

So Campanella vigorously rejects Machiavellianism, precisely in what we have called its teachings on contingent politics, and he rebels above all at this doctrine's being given an absolute significance, almost as if it were a general political methodology. The criterion that must guide any political action is for him necessarily and inevitably moral. Therefore any conception of the state that is

---

[26]Cf. Menecke, op. cit., p. 127–28.

[27]*Monarchia di Spagna*, ed. cit., p. 96.

not universal and religious, as his moral conception is, needs to be rejected and fought against.

How then do we explain the devious and utterly Machiavellian advice Campanella gives the King of Spain to achieve his ideal kingdom? How do we justify the utilitarian and unscrupulous political attitude he adopts as soon as the goal is to implement his ideal program? We have said that Campanella opposes Machiavelli's utilitarian state with his own moral state. But we have also seen that he accepts Machiavelli's more generic and universal lesson, applicable to all the ends of human activity be they utilitarian or ethical, particular or absolute — which affirms that means and ends cannot be separated, that means are not to be judged on their own, and that an end is not conceivable except as a function of the means by which it is implemented. In this concept, representing a universal lesson and shared by Machiavelli and the Jesuits, Campanella is very much a Machiavellian and a Jesuit.

Given a moral and universal goal, and given a perceptible manifestation of it, e.g. in *The Spanish Monarchy*, it is natural that this goal should be achieved using any means available to those who live in perceptible reality. And what is there about such means that is immoral, given that they are nothing more than the expression of the process leading to this highly elevated end? What are the enemies we are fighting, if not obstacles to establishing the Universal Kingdom? The use of Machiavelli's arts becomes reproachable and evil when "The Prince" who uses them has no more right to existence than his enemies — that is, when the state is separate and particularistic. But when the state is the germ of the Universal Kingdom or the Kingdom of God, what moral law can stop him from destroying anyone opposed to its development? Such obstacles themselves become reprehensible and sinful, and must be eradicated by any means possible. Thus virtue must be industrious and demolish with unflinching severity anything that obstructs its path. "We have seen how prudence must first accord with divine fate; it remains for us to speak of all the other parts of prudence, which includes every virtue, especially opportunity. Since it is characteristic of prudence to know how to take advantage of opportunity. . . . And it is evident that the opportunity of Spain consists in having its nearby enemies weak and fragmented in religion and state, and in having its powerful ones far away."[28] Here we see how Machiavellianism and Reason of State are tightly linked with the divine mission: "Therefore "The Prince" must be superhuman and almost God, as Plato says, as was Christ; or truly divine by the art given to him by God, as are the Pope and the bishops and Moses; he must be the divine legislator; or if this is denied him, he must at least be obedient to the divine legislator through human virtue, as was Charlemagne."[29] Thus some means of governance (e.g. divide and rule) are condemned as procedures undertaken for their own sake and as an end in themselves,[30] but are nevertheless accepted as means of combat.[31]

In this humanity of the divine therefore lies the whole meaning and justification of the contrast in Campanella between the anti-Machiavellianism of the end and the Machiavellianism of the means. This contrast derives, as we have tried to explain, from a rejection of the contingent and particularized proposals of Machiavelli, and an acceptance of his methodology, which has a truth value when applied to any form of practical activity. But in this relationship between the divine and the human, in this view of all the facts of the world in the light of a universal idea, and of religious law enacted and brought to life in all the world' s events, we seem to glimpse the relationship between the author's political conception and his philosophical and metaphysical thought.

It has been said that the philosophical substrate of Machiavelli's thought is the realism and naturalism of Humanism,[32] the entirely empirical view of human events that in another climate of thought led to the great construction of the Leviathan. And if a mechanistic and empiricist vision of the world was also able to lead to a conception of politics as a game of action and reaction between utilitarian and self-interested pursuits, it is evident that Campanella's theological-political moralism must have had a com-

---

[28]*Monarchia di Spagna*, p. 106.
[29]Ibid., p. 103.
[30]Ibid., p. 129.
[31]Ibid., p. 176.
[32]Cfr. Toffanin, op. cit. p. 79–81.

pletely different philosophical basis. This is not the place to analyze his philosophy even in a summary way. But it must be noted
in passing that his concepts of practical politics and the clumsy
application of an absolute and transcendent purpose to human affairs have a direct philosophical counterpart in the relations that
exist between his epistemology and his metaphysics. Here again it
is customary to point to the former as his element of philosophical
modernity, and to reject the latter as a remnant of the Middle Ages.
But it is important to observe how Campanella's sensualism is kept
closely bound to the religious conception, to that "sense of things,"
to that panpsychism — as it has been called — which allows the
sensory process (the source of power, knowledge, and will) to be
attributed to things themselves and to constitute that "Soul of the
world" which is the basis of all Campanella's theology. "This bless-
ed Soul sees in the primal mind what it has to do and according to
these ideas it works in particular matter and form; and it is the first
instrument of primary wisdom; and the world has the spirit which
is heaven, and the body has the earth, and blood the heart, and the
mind this soul."[33]

In these coarse analogies we can trace Campanella's dead
ends — the less rigorous, more fantastical and arbitrary sides of
his doctrine. But in this attribution of human cognitive processes
to the whole universe, and in this manifestation of the universal
soul in the concrete — in this panpsychism that resolves itself into
pantheism — we can find an analogy with his political conception
which is theological, abstract, and universalist, and at the same
time concrete and Machiavellian. And we can suppose that he intuited, though still in a rudimentary way, that there is no universal
that is valid if it is not implemented and lived, and that in the concrete and perceptible there is no perceptible and concrete life if it
is not illuminated by a universal light.

---

[33]*Del senso delle cose e della magia* (Bari, 1925) p. 161.

"Roberto Ardigò," *Pietre* 3.2 (10 Feb. 1928). (Published under the Pseudonym G. Rosemberg.)

The last few days have seen the centenary of the birth of this forgotten figure. After a period of glory and fame, when he appeared to be the founder of a new epoch and the father of a new approach to philosophy, the beginning of this century marked an abrupt turning point in Italian thought — a period of demolition and ridicule followed by indifference and silence.

He was talked about as "the father of positivism." We instead believe that Ardigò was its last and most degenerate child. If his starting point was positivist, and if positivism provided the first incentive for his philosophical work, what followed was certainly influenced by tendencies and needs that went beyond positivism and in the end overwhelmed it, leading him unconsciously to a position that bore scant resemblance to where he had started. It could indeed be said that all his philosophy, all the force and meaning of his work derives from the coexistence and attempted reconciliation of two great demands in his thought: positivist empiricism and the pursuit of unity.

The intellectual environment that Ardigò found in Italy when he began his work had a character of pure methodology. Devoid of truly original thinkers, Italian positivism was entirely reduced to attempts to graft onto philosophy the experimental methods that had led to so much progress in the natural sciences. Absorbing the teachings of Comte from France and Spencer from England in support of its position, it had taken on a purely empiricist character, settling for a comfortable agnosticism in the field of philosophy proper. The principal interpreter of this state of mind is Pasquale Villari, in his essay on the *Historical Method and Positive Philosophy*, which made such an impression in the ambiance of the time and which Ardigò mentions as a strong influence on his embarking in a positivist direction.

This experimentalist tendency founded on tacit dualist and naturalist premises thus constitutes the immediate precedent of Ardigò's thinking. But in him, the roots of a strong unitary need are deeply grafted onto the dominant empiricist base.

Accepting the methodological postulates of the previous positivism, he felt he needed to build onto them a system that takes the epistemological problem more seriously, and avoids the non-philosophical agnosticism deriving either from Comte or from the mystical Spencerian theory of the unknowable. Because of this need for unity and immanence and his struggle against dualism, which led him to associate Spencer's Unknowable with Kant's Noumenon, it may be said that Ardigò, even in his philosophical isolation, felt the basic demands of post-Kantian thought more deeply than other positivists and belongs in a more vital way to its history.

But let us review the history of this attempt to adapt empiricism to the demands of a monism devoid of transcendence.

The nominalist position that characterizes all empriricism is made here to assume a particular aspect. It is no longer possible to deny abstract formations and representative concepts and go back to the pure data of experience, which necessarily supposes a perceiving subject. Nominalism has to be reworked in a way that allows it to set aside the opposition of subject and object, of matter and mind. The monistic orientation requires a system in which this split does not exist, and in which the negation of *a priori* formations can lead to a concrete principle of absolute evidence that does not require the passive receptivity of the mind. Ardigò's principle discovery, which appeared to answer this need, was his law of distinction, his strongest logical tool and one that he retained throughout the entire course of his thought. This law, by which reality is a continuous process of distinction from a previous indistinct state and by which the distinct of today becomes the indistinct of tomorrow, constitutes for Ardigò not only a necessity of thought, but also the rhythm of reality, which, proceeds according to this law in all its manifestations and phenomena, from the formation of the solar system from the original nebula to the act of cognition.

We will see later how Ardigò justifies this duality of origin and application, and his degree of philosophical coherence in doing so, but what is certain is that he made use of this law as something absolutely real, apodictically certain. It provided him with the anti-dualistic system of nominalism he was looking for, and which was necessary for his philosophy.

With his theory of distinction it was no longer necessary to go looking for primary cognitive data in anything "perceived," upon which the mind was supposed to exercise its powers of abstraction, and it was possible to think of this abstraction as the effect of the process of distinction inherent in the real, which meant that primal and original reality was to be sought in the primordial indistinct, anterior to all distinctions. In the cognitive field, this primordial indistinctness is made up of what Ardigò called "the psycho-physical element."

It was natural that the original element, the "fact" from which all experience derives, should be prior to the distinction of subject and object.

Ardigò, moving by the aforementioned process from the most complex distinctions to the elementary formations of ME and NON-ME, is forced to conceive even of these formations as abstract, as distinct from a previous indistinct, and in a further logical step he reduces them both to the original activity of the psycho-physical indistinct. In this indistinct lies the true essence of the "fact," which according to Ardigò constitutes the primal cognitive element. It is prior to the formation of the subject and object — these are distinct forms [distinti] deriving from the psycho-physical indistinct and have the character of mere abstractions without true cognitive value.

In this way, the initial problem of Ardigò's philosophy appears solved. Positivist nominalism seems now to have acquired a new look, freeing itself of dualistic constraints and achieving a true monism founded on a truth which is neither the product of thought nor a simple datum of experience, but goes back to the primordial moment in which thought and experience are one and live indistinctly in their original unity. But at this point are we still in the domain of positivism?

In assessing Ardigò's position, it is interesting to examine the justification he gives for the grounding of his law of the distinct and the indistinct. He attempts to combine the a priori with the a posteriori, and to give the resulting "law of intelligence," as he is obliged to acknowledge it, a real and positive value, supposing it to be derived from pure fact.

"The Infinite is found to exist as a function, i.e. mental law, and mental law in turn has an absolute value because it is determined in its existence and form not *a priori* but *a posteriori* — i.e. by the fact, by what we apply it to" (*Formaz. natur.,* p. 71).

Here there is an obvious vicious circle, which Ardigò strives in the pages that follow to explain away. The fact to which we apply the law cannot then in its turn influence the same law that produced it. The two principles, matter and mind, cannot sustain themselves here except by presupposing one another in turn, and therefore paralyzing each other — and it is not logically possible to get out of this difficulty except by positing one or the other of the two principles as primary and real, and thus lapsing back into either materialism (with its contradiction, which Ardigò knew well) or idealism.

This initial contradiction undermines the foundation of the Mantuan's entire philosophical system. The psycho-physical principle that claims to resolve the antinomy is itself a consequence of the law that lives and feeds on this same antinomy.

This principle, meant to mark the glorification and victory of the *a posteriori,* is itself an *a priori* derived from necessity and an apriorist method. In addition, its elementary atomistic character, universal in its representation of the entire knowable world, perhaps brings to mind Leibniz's monad.

It remains abstract and sterile as long as it is conceived intellectually, and to be fully grasped it requires a living extra-rational activity: "To think of it in such a way as it thinks of itself, one must contemplate it in its very indeterminacy, which alone makes it what it is" (op. cit., pg. 39).

So here we are with this impossibility of thinking of the indistinct according to common schemes, and with the necessity of an activity of contemplation, a kind of intuitionism that makes us think immediately of Bergson. And it is to Bergson that many other developments in Ardigò's thinking lead, as do the continuations of it pursued by the best among his students. And we may consider the extreme point of his thinking to be the doctrine of individuality, one of the last and most interesting requirements, where it is quite easy to notice points of contact with the Crocean "individual as institution" (*Il Vero,* p. 366 ff).

Idealism thus crops up on all sides, and the Ardigò's positivism, at the end and culmination of his system, is routed and annihilated by requirements that transcend and destroy it. The empirical method, in the light of a strong monistic imperative, is obliged to negate itself; and nominalism, considered rigorously, leads to consequences the author himself would not have wished to reach — the same consequences French intuitionism was led to by a similar nominalism. But if in Ardigò the consequences are very far from the premises — so long was the road his thinking traveled — we still cannot speak of any real evolution in this philosopher's thought. His system is sketched out in its basic lines starting in his earliest works, and those that followed are nothing more than developments and clarifications of the principles presented earlier.

In this way the path is complete right from the start, and the consequences follow immediately from the premises. But all this without any awareness of having gone too far, nor of the internal contradiction between the point of departure and the point of arrival.

In all of Ardigò's work there is a strange naivety that leads him to believe he has never deviated from positivism — indeed, that he has established a solid and unshakable foundation for it. And next to the most daring and unorthodox developments we nearly always find a repetition of positive experimental premises. Nearly every book or argument starts with an affirmation of the methodological principal, which is empiricist, objective, and *a posteriori* — and then during the course of the discussion, philosophical inspiration and ardor get the upper hand and lead him further than he wanted to go.

This naivety perhaps prevented Ardigo from reaching clearer conclusions and from speaking his mind in a louder voice.

But his value lies precisely in what he said to us unintentionally or did not realize he had said. It was this that led the only true philosopher of positivism to end up very far from positivism. He was the only one, or perhaps the greatest, who tried to transform a method into a system and was forced by the method to build a discordant system. It was a demonstration — if method and system (as we have all by now memorized) are the same thing — that positivism, being depleted the moment it becomes a system, is for this reason not even a proper method — I mean a philosophical method.

"The Aesthetics of Roberto Ardigò and Italian Positivism in the Second Half of the 19ᵗʰ Century," Conference 2 Feb. 1928 (Unpublished).

The first look Italian positivism presents is distinctly methodological. Among its first proponents (none of whom was a philosopher by profession), such as Cattaneo, Tommasi, Gabelli and others, the principle concern was to bring to the theory of knowledge the methods that had yielded so much progress in the science each of them was practicing. And almost all of them were grounded in youthful Hegelian premises and reminiscences (some of them had attended the school of De Sanctis, while others had been in close relationship with Spaventa), and even in their activities as scholars and scientists they retained the sort of philosophical aspirations that always led them, sentimentally at least, toward philosophical activity. Once the initial enthusiasm for idealism had been redirected into the positive sciences, at the time making great progress, these leanings suggested to them that they ought to adapt their theoretical activity to the systems and methods of those sciences.

In this almost propagandist position they adopted, we can of course note all the uncertainties and contradictions typical of dilettantes. We see Marselli, for example, perhaps the most cultured among the thinkers of the period and already the builder of an aesthetic based on Hegelian philosophy, shifting with great caution and uncertainty to positivism and the study of the *fact*, and contradicting himself from one moment to the next by appealing to the strictures of idealism. With Hegelism these men had assimilated the immanentist and anti-dualist requirements of all post-Kantian idealist philosophy. In attempting to satisfy these requirements in the empirical study of facts they were faced with two pathways. One of these was the more coherent and courageous (even in its absurdity) way of materialism — which they hurried to reject, however, due to scruples remaining from their youthful education. The other, which had been pointed out by Comte and in a certain sense Spencer as well, was a metaphysical agnosticism that turned its back on theoretical speculation altogether, reducing philosophy itself to an experimental science.

The main proponent of this trend, which has the character of a method rather than a system, was Pasquale Villari, in his introductory 1866 text *Positive Philosophy and the Historical Method,* considered to be the manifesto of positivism in Italy. Its new requirements are clearly stated: "Positivism comes down to the application of the historical method to the moral sciences." And elsewhere, regarding aesthetics: "It is possible to establish a science of beauty renouncing for the time being knowledge of its essence." A complete abandonment, that is, of all philosophy — the abolition of any sort of speculative activity and the reduction of philosophy of mind to a natural science or to experimental psychology.

The statement made a deep impression in the scientific and cultural circles of the time. Ardigò declared that it had given him his first push toward a belief in positive science. The so-called "historical method" became the banner of the age and its rapid application in the various sciences and to political and literary history gave rise to the proliferation of philological and erudite critical studies that characterized the end of the 19th century.

It was natural that this historical method, also faithfully and consistently applied in the field of philosophy, and especially aesthetics, should deal a death blow to any system or aesthetic theory, and reduce the science of art to a purely experimental and scientific level — a phenomenology or physiology of the artistic fact. Many of the so-called psychologists of art worked on this basis, first of whom was Lombroso with his studies on Genius and Madness.

But anyone starting from this basis who wanted to observe various artistic manifestations and arrive at a theory of art was unconsciously compelled to produce the theory before completing the historical work of observation, almost as a guide and support for it. This was the case of Taine, who at the beginning of his *Philosophie de l'Art* [*Philosophy of Art*] announced his empiricist methodological intentions, declaring that he wanted to do aesthetics using the same methods that might be used in botany — simply considering artistic facts and "looking for their causes."

Searching for causes, however, meant doing aesthetics in the most traditional and least positivist sense of the word, so that Taine, after a few pages devoted to some examples and a sketch of inductive research, sets out his theory in a clear and explicit definition: "The purpose of a work of art is to manifest some essential or salient feature, conveying some salient idea more clearly and completely than real objects do."

An assertion of naturalism, then, but still the affirmation of a principle and so scarcely experimental and objective — and so immune to discussion — that Villari replied, believing he too was offering a solution based on experience (and in turn contradicting his own empiricist promises) in stating that "art, on the other hand, is a creation of the human mind," that "art always changes with our spirit," and that "an idea that has not yet become form or color for the artist is a vague ambition that is still powerless," statements that clearly reveal the subjectivist requirements and concerns of the author.

But unlike Villari, who did aesthetics and philosophy as a dilettante, and whose positivism was continually interrupted by idealist requirements, Taine, in presenting his aesthetic system, keeps himself steadily within the positivist stream. His position, important to our present subject because of its great influence on early Italian positivist aesthetics, derives in part from Comtian philosophy, in which epistemological problems are not only left unsolved, they are not even dealt with, and in which real nature external to the spirit is postulated without discussion.

This position absolutely outside philosophy, this agnosticism that does not even know the concept of the Unknowable, was introduced into Italy, at least in the realm of aesthetics, by Taine. And here it ran into the methodological tendency mentioned above and gave rise to empirical, positivist aesthetics and to the positivist philosophy that prevailed up until Ardigò, about which Gentile rightly declared: "Positivists are sleepwalkers passing before and through the real, vigilant world of philosophy, asleep. And they are perfectly correct in protesting that the true and absolute reality is in facts — that is, in their dreams."

All of Italian positivist aesthetics up to Ardigò is thus founded on a tacit dualistic-naturalistic premise. Assuming as a principle a natural reality acting on activities of the mind, and asserting the necessity for experimental research into the effects of this action, the solution of the aesthetic problem as such was hopelessly compromised. In the hands of physiologists and naturalists, aesthetics moved further and further from the mind, and while Taine had spoken of art as imitation of the truth, still leaving a certain part of it to the action of the subject, this action disappears completely in his successors. Already Guyau, who denied the Schillerian doctrine of play (without understanding its value as an affirmation of catharsis), in order to give art a totalitarian value and to see the true purpose of art in life and reality, begins to consider *natural beauty* per se — things or actions, that is, that are aesthetic in themselves, such as the curved line, action accomplished without effort, etc.

Among Italians, this tendency is even more pronounced, so that art becomes a single chapter in the great book of aesthetics. That this was the spirit of the times is demonstrated in this passage from Bergson: "One considers the beauties of nature as previous to those of art, the processes of art are then only means by which the artist expresses the beautiful, and the essence of the beautiful remains mysterious."

Determining what was beautiful was left to the discretion of the researcher, and indeed, discussions in this area intertwine and doctrines overlap. Absorbed in their own experimental research, it is clear that each of them drew from it their own definition. Thus Pilo, after defining beauty as "what is pleasing," ends up establishing a series of degrees by which beauty successively takes on a character of somatic sensation, corresponding to goodness, then to truth, and finally to the ideal. Mantegazza is seen almost to reach an agreement with Mengs in defining beauty. But differences in theory have minimal importance in the face of the one method. The definition of beauty begins to look like a naturalistic classification, which may or may not be desirable. What is common to all is the method, which frames art as something experimental.

But this confusion in the definition of beauty displays the insufficiency or lack of seriousness of the school.

Starting from dualist premises not based on a solid doctrine of transcendence but derived from simplistic agnosticism, and armed at the same time only with the experimental method, it is reduced, in attempting to provide systematic doctrines of the facts of the mind, to reverting to traditional forms of hedonism, intellectualism, moralism and even mysticism. Its failure demonstrates yet again (and demonstrated even then) the need for solid epistemological premises before any research in a specialized field of philosophy can begin.

◆◆◆

The entire opus of Roberto Ardigò was dedicated to the search for these epistemological premises.

In this author the roots of strong unitary and immanentist requirements are grafted onto the dominant empiricist base. But rather than stemming from juvenile idealist reminiscences easily silenced by the accommodation of the Unknowable, this tendency derives from an intimate spiritual need, which makes the problem a dominant motif in all his philosophy and is its greatest source of interest.

From the very beginning of his work he steers clear of the dominant positivist current. While accepting its methodological presuppositions, he has a very clear picture in his mind of the particular task that the history of philosophy expects of him — to unify what was divided, to bring back monism to take dualism's old place. We will see how he went about it and whether he succeeded, but in this sense we can certainly say that Ardigò, despite his philosophical isolation and his distance from the other great positivist currents, felt much more deeply than others the fundamental demands of the thought of the last century and experienced its history much more actively.

Empirical methodology, brought into the basic field of epistemology, assumes an initial aspect that is nominalist. It was obvious that naturalism, forced to anchor itself in a doctrine, tended to deny the value of all constructs that were not immediately derived from experience. And already in his earliest works, in which the author makes his entry into the field of positivism — that is, *Pietro Pomponazzi* and *La psicologia come scienza positiva* [*Psychology as a Positive Science*], there is alongside the affirmation of the inductive method, a clear statement of the *a posteriori* character of laws and concepts, and the exclusive cognitive validity of the *fact* as such.

"The law is the fact itself," he says. "The law and its idea are generalities and abstractions formed on the basis of particular facts, or — the same thing — are likenesses of them and serve to classify them."

This was his fundamental position, the source of all his developments and the foundation on which he built his system. But in him nominalism, when it meets the doctrine of unity, takes on certain features and presents particular requirements. And if Locke, for example, presents the problem as a simple negation of innate ideas, (a negation founded on dualistic needs that leads to skepticism and sensualism) here, on the other hand, the monistic requirement constrains the philosopher to seek an organization of nominalism in which this split does not exist, and in which the negation of *a priori* formations leads to a concrete principle of absolute evidence, in the face of which it is not necessary to suppose the passive receptivity of the mind.

This requirement implied the need for an instrument, a means in the hands of the philosopher which could be used to reach the reality sought. Ardigò built this tool with his law of the distinct and the indistinct, which is both the conclusion and the organization of Ardigò's nominalism.

According to this law, the process of abstraction to be invalidated is derived from a subsequent movement of distinction between original 'indistincts,' which must be revisited in the search for the pure fact, without any successive elaboration. Thought then proceeds in continuous distinctions by which one moves from an 'indistinct' to subsequent 'distincts,' which are in their turn indistinct with respect to the distinctions that will follow.

For Ardigò, this law of thinking, which also embodies its logic, is also valid as the law of reality. It constitutes the actual rhythm of reality, proceeding by successive distinctions in all its manifestations and phenomena — from the astro-physical formation of the terrestrial nebula to the act of cognition.

But this conception of the law of distinctions as intrinsic to reality itself, along with considering it a requirement of thought, offers the author a way of responding elegantly, though not exhaustively, to the most obvious question for anyone considering this system, namely: "How is it justifiable as a *"law"*? What is it derived from? From the necessities of reason or from experience? Ardigò's answer to this question seeks to reconcile the two solutions and to demonstrate the groundlessness of the antinomy — it is best to read the original.[34]

The principle that any fact has its cause in a previous fact is, because of the experience which established it, a law of intelligence. And intelligence always applies it, for every fact, whether moving forward or backward. That is, it applies it without end. And it cannot do otherwise. To suppose that the mind, which is guided by this law — i.e. is formed to function in this way — would close down, stopping at the beginning — that is, at a fact to which the same law is not applied, is to suppose that the law of the mind is not its law, which is absurd. In the same way, the mind, having been trained to function within a concept of time, must conceive of any moment in time as preceded by another, and this without end.

Which is the same as saying that the infinite is found to exist, like this function, this mental law, which operates in every instance — is stimulated to do so — without end, for as long as the mind can remain active. And the mental law, in its turn, has an absolute value because in its existence and form it is determined not *a priori* but *a posteriori* — that is, by the fact, by that very being to which we apply it, a being whose mind is itself a special distinction formed by the same system of production, common to all nature.

Nor does science therefore turn out to be a circle. Only *a priori* science is a circle. It assumes the law as the reason for the fact, thus conceiving not only a precedent to the fact, but a prime fact in a series of facts, one that is at the head of the series itself. But if the law is a fact and this is a consequence, then the law cannot at the same time be adopted as a principle. And if the law is a repeating fact — and a repeating fact is not the original fact (which, as such, does not repeat) — then the law cannot at the same time be invoked for the purpose of establishing the first fact — i.e. that which is not the repetition of another fact.

A posteriori science, on the other hand, is not circular. It is an on-

---

[34]*Opere filosofiche*, vol. II, p. 70–71.

going straight line. But with an infinite beginning and end. Given two consecutive facts, the second is distinct from the first, and the one is taken to be the reason for the other. The beginning is infinite because every preceding fact leads to yet another before it that explains its existence in the same way. And the end is also infinite, by an analogous process. And by obvious and sound logic, since reason is the law, and this is experience, and experience is neither the beginning nor the end.

It is easy to see that the vicious circle that the author was trying to avoid still exists. It is stated at the outset that, framed in this way, this is a law of intelligence. Therefore what is real — the fact — is determined by the law, which is a mental law. And how then can the law itself be suggested by the fact, if the fact is a function of it? Here the grounding for a construction is missing because the two principles, matter and mind, cannot sustain themselves except by presupposing one another, so that the real exists as a function of a mental law which, in its turn, is nothing more than an expression of the evidence of the fact. This contradiction nullifies the validity of the law and undermines Ardigo's entire system.

But if the disagreement appears irremediable in the eyes of the idealist critic who starts from the Kantian formulation of the problem, which is based on the initial opposition of thought and experience, it must not be forgotten that in the general spirit of his work (and the passage read is a rare exception) Ardigò ignores that formulation and seeks, as we will see later, a starting point where thought and experience are not distinct. And perhaps it is precisely because the author ventures in this way into another field, because he solves problems by other means, that viewing him in the light of our problems of today may lead us to overlook the value of his formulations and lose sight of the very approaches that constitute his originality.

And besides, our task today is not to refute Ardigò (also because a refutation on idealistic grounds has already been undertaken by Gentile in his 1909 *Critica*) but to trace his history and critically examine the development of his thought.

Therefore, having considered the law of the distinct and the non-distinct as real *tout court*, real in the sense of the reality in which there is no subject and no object, let us consider its application to the field of knowledge, where the author has made his most interesting observations and which can be used to explain his aesthetics.

We have seen how the empiricism of his premises led him to the formulation of a law constituting the rhythm of reality, and therefore encompassing all of experience. The validity of this law is absolute — real — since, like all of experience, it derives from "*fact*." Fact alone can give absolute certainty — truth without intellectualism and abstraction.

But what is this "*fact*"? This is the problem Ardigò now sets himself. Naturally he could not solve it based on common methodological empiricism which, unable to do without an actual perceiving subject, is forced to set this subject in opposition to the experiential datum. And nor could he indulge in a Spencerian position (which he likened to Kant's doctrine of the noumenon), being unable to accept its mystical dualism of the Unknowable. His requirements here, as always, are unitary. Pure fact, which by its premises must be the first and only cognitive datum, must also be immune to any transcendence.

What helps him here is the method of distinctions, the very method that the new solution was meant to support and justify. Through this method, a powerful tool at the disposal of his logic for analyzing mental formations and getting back to their causes, Ardigò arrives, following the usual process, at the two original formations of Me and Not Me. Faced with these two elements and the problem of their unification, he believes he can get past them via a further step in his dialectic, positing them too as an abstraction and reducing their formation to the reality of an original "*psycho-physical*" activity.

This psycho-physical element contains the true essence of the *fact*. It is anterior to the formation of the terms *subject* and *object*. These are distinct forms derived from the psycho-physical indistinct and from it they derive their only reality — without it they are mere abstractions devoid of cognitive meaning and reducible to each other. The only truth is in this primordial element that we must return to to have a unitary vision of the world. With this the problem of the unification between mind and matter appears solved, and it would seem that all knowledge comes down to the simplicity of the primordial indistinct.

The light shed by this principle also solves the problem of the origin of the law of distinctions, the law that itself was of service in revealing this solution, which Ardigò sees as the basis of his entire philosophy. He believes that by means of it he can solidify his positivism and bring it out of the restricted field of methodology and agnosticism. He believes that it will enable him to reconcile his opposition to the *a priori* with his aspirations to unity.

But we have seen that more than a premise and a foundation, this is a conclusion following from Ardigò's philosophical premises. It represents the end point of his speculations, the final consequence of positivism understood monistically. But it must be observed that it also marks its end, its collapse and liquidation.

From the moment Ardigò sets the psycho-physical principle as the basis of his philosophy, he ceases to be a positivist. The objection already mentioned against the basis of the law of distinctions, if it temporarily did not prove fatal to Ardigò's whole philosophy, clearly demonstrated the impotence of this philosophy to solve its problems purely through elements provided by experience.

If positivism means objectivity, empiricism, nature, and *a posteriori,* then the doctrine of the psycho-physical indistinct cannot be called positivist inasmuch as it is derived from needs strongly felt by the mind, based on and closely linked to a method we have shown to be *a priori* in nature. The path followed by Ardigò from positivism to his psycho-physical component may perhaps afford a summary glimpse of the road linking Bacon and Leibniz. The great attempt of the latter to unify empiricism and rationalism, matter and force, the individual and the universal, are perhaps echoed in the efforts of the Mantuan philosopher, whose psycho-physical indistinct may correspond to some of the needs addressed by the Leibnizian monad. Consider for example the following passage from *Monadology* in comparison with the elementary, atomistic and even universal nature of Ardigò's indistinct.

Every portion of matter is not only divisible to infinity, as the ancients realized, but is actually sub-divided without end, every part divided into smaller parts, each one of which has some motion of its own. Otherwise it would be impossible for each portion of matter to express the whole universe.

And from this we can see that there is a world of creatures — of living things and animals, entelechies and souls — in the smallest fragment of matter.

Every portion of matter can be thought of as a garden full of plants or a pond full of fish. But every branch of the plant, every part of the animal (every drop of its vital fluids, even) is another such garden or pond.

But Leibniz was not a positivist — he based himself on *a priori* elements.

And nor is Ardigò, whose principle, though abstract and sterile when considered intellectually, is nevertheless open to far-reaching and vital developments when it is experienced — when it is united with a lively and active mind. Take for example this passage:[35] "This indistinctness cannot be explained because the explanation is a distinction and this, as such, is the negation of the indistinct; but it can nevertheless be thought about and it is thought about — indeed it is the implied condition of determined thoughts. It is only that in order to conceive it so as to be able to think about it as it is, one must *contemplate* it in its very indeterminacy, the only way it is what it is."

Already in this concept of the psycho-physical indistinct's being unthinkable according to standard patterns, and the necessity of contemplative activity in order to be conscious of it, we can see the tendency of Ardigò's position to move closer to Bergsonian intuitionism, with which he also shares a nominalist approach. And the fact that Ardigò's positivism leads to an affinity with the French philosopher is demonstrated by Ardigò's best students, Tarozzi and Dandolo for example, who, as Gentile observes, follow the tradition of the master in this sense.

Once Ardigò had reached this point, even without any awareness of having exceeded positivism, it was natural that the new position should give rise to new problems and new manifestations

---

[35]Vol. II. p. 39.

unknown to positivism. And first among them was the problem of the forms of the mind, the explanation and placement of aesthetic, logical and practical activity within his system.

But it is not possible to speak of Ardigò in terms of true chronological evolution, since his entire system is sketched out in his first writings and is only developed and filled in with details in those that follow, without any notable evolution in the thinking. It thus happens that next to positions marked by the most straightforward empiricism, we often find developments that reflect needs that emerge from the final consequences of his system. There is a strange ingenuousness in this thinker resulting in a complete lack of awareness of the excesses he has committed, and even in the face of conclusions that are blatantly remote from positivism, he is convinced that he has always worked in favor of it and that he is strengthening its foundations.

He saw his entire opus as a justification of initial empirical and experimental premises, and even when, having started from these, the vigor and coherence of his explorations carried him very far from the point he wanted to arrive at, he lacked the courage and strength to look back and compare the point of departure with the point of arrival. Having established that the one must justify the other, he does not investigate whether this purpose has really been achieved. This explains why the methodological postulates of positivism are insistently and vigorously repeated in all his works from the first to the last, and why the same problems are very often treated in two different ways depending on the principle illuminating them.

In Ardigò we may thus speak of two distinct types of aesthetics. One is conducted on the experimental basis of a physiological psychologism, while the other is determined by the fundamental need to build a philosophy of the mind based on the primal indistinct, the original element of consciousness.

We have very few fragments of either of these types of aesthetics. Regarding the former, which is certainly the least interesting, some data can be found in the exemplifications and references concerning the world of art scattered through the author's work, and it is discussed *ex professo* only in the essay "Il meccanismo dell'intelligenza e l'ispirazione geniale" ["The Mechanism of Intelligence and the Inspiration of Genius"].

Here the science of art is based on the methodological premises characteristic of Italian positivism that I spoke about at the beginning of this essay, only the author adheres more closely to them and, unlike other aesthetics experts, does not contradict the premises by immediately issuing a theory of the artistic phenomenon. Here art is treated purely as a subject of experimental psychology, as a documentation of how people react to certain stimuli, or as a physiological phenomenon to be studied. And when conclusions are drawn and the time seems to have come for an explanation and evaluation of the phenomena, this is always kept in the inductive field — the artistic fact as such is always seen as given beforehand, and only the effects are considered. "Art requires two things: natural aesthetic taste perfected by educational training aimed at challenging artistic thought and stimulating the integrative and substitutive work of the artist's imagination to its satisfaction — the copying of aesthetic mental formations which are already there in the artist's mind, ready to be recalled in the work of integrating and replacing spontaneous accidental representation."[36]

He is speaking here of aesthetic taste and aesthetic training. But what this taste and training might be is not expressed, and solving the problem requires recourse (and the author himself often sends us there) to the passage from *Morale dei positivisti* [*Morality of the Positivists*], almost the only documentation of Ardigò's second type of aesthetic, derived from the extreme conclusions of his thought.

We have said that having achieved the unity of the psycho-physical indistinct, the philosopher turned to the further problem of explaining the forms of the mind. This, I would almost say, is proof of the idealistic urge inherent in Ardigò's doctrine. All the problems that he was unable to solve using an *a posteriori* method and by experiment are brought here for their solution. And so we see the psycho-physical indistinct, after having been the conclusion and arrival point of a certain empirical construction, break away from its previous path to lead an independent life and lay the foundations of a new edifice of which it is no longer the consequence, but

---

[36]Vol. VIII, p. 164.

rather the base.

For this new edifice, which is barely sketched out and rather indistinctly displayed in Ardigò's work, morality and aesthetics had to be essential elements. The primary need to justify morality in a non-deterministic and non-utilitarian way was what gave Ardigò the initial impulse to set himself on this path, and his book on the *Moralità dei positivisti* documents this. But aesthetics made its contribution in determining it and gave rise to one of the most interesting developments in the author's thought. In short, it is at this point that the problem of the distinct arises.

The need for an immanentist solution to the new problems prevented Ardigò from accepting any mystical or religious explanation in moral and aesthetic problems, and the same need understood in a different sense made him refuse content-based solutions. On the other hand, scholastic necessities and his positivist and psychological tendencies obliged him to adopt a certain classification of this activity, and precluded the possibility of annulling such solutions in the single original element.

From the unity of the psycho-physical foundation, it was necessary to generate the reality of art, thought, and action, while at the same time preserving the validity of both the former and the latter three. As a more logical solution, consistent with the premises, a quantitative distinction was presented so that these three mental forms were considered produced by a differentiation in intensity of the primitive sensation.

In considering this sensation as *impulsive* and thus reducing practical activity to something not especially distinct from theoretical activity, a process is conceived in which an individual passes from one form to another based on successive gradations of intensity. In the middle of this process between practical and theoretical energy is the place of beauty, of aesthetic form, which thus in the end is not determined in its particular essence, but is conceived as just one of the manifestations the initial sensation can give rise to, and is by definition affective — that is, involved at the same time in the practical and the theoretical.

And in this way art too comes to be part of both the practical and theoretical, marking the point of transition between these two activities.

The different affective states are also distributed on a scale analogous to that of chemical affinities. It is a scale of affective states, along which one goes from the most grossly and brutally sensual to the most frankly and humanly naive. The first represents the ignoble satisfaction produced by the lowest of physiological functions; the second, the sublime satisfaction of hard evidence in the highest function of abstract cognition.

Here again the scale is continuous, and the most distant extremes are part of it — the purest evidence and the coarsest pleasure, which are therefore not irremediably separated from one another. They are not identical when it comes to evidence or sensuality, but nevertheless, starting from above them, in successive and descending states of affect one increasingly loses the naivety of the higher extreme and acquires the brutality of its opposite. And *vice versa* by starting from the bottom.

In the middle of this scale of affective states are the aesthetic states, or states of beauty. This is therefore the connecting link between the evidence or truth of one part, and the sensuality or goodness or pleasure of the other.

And so the evidence, the beauty and the will are not three entities utterly unlike one another, and belonging, as common vulgar opinion would have it, to three different metaphysical regions.

And evidence is not just one thing — there are many different kinds of evidence. And the same for will and beauty.

Beauty as well — there is not just one, there are many different kinds of beauty. And in the last sentence we have the fundamental concept of the positivist philosophy of art, which regrettably I am here unable to do more than hint at.[37]

A distinction of degree, therefore — quantitative, which must necessarily rule out the possibility of aesthetics as an autonomous and original form. Indeed, in speaking of *different degrees,* it is unable to give beauty, or any of the other forms, anything but a purely empirical explanation, taking them all back to the prime and orig-

---

[37]Vol. III, p. 28–29.

inal activity of the substance of impulse, which alone would have a true character of totality.

But the importance of this position is mostly historical, and as a documentation of the extreme point Ardigò had reached.

Earlier we traced this philosopher's doctrine back to Leibniz's monad. And now it is to Leibniz and through him to Baumgarten that we must trace him in connection with aesthetics. What they have in common is the unity of the primal element, and this leads them also to share the need not only to derive from this element the forms and activities of the mind, but to derive them with quantitative distinctions. And if the terms and modes of distinction do not correspond exactly, the type of distinction has the same character and is animated by the same spirit.

With aesthetics, an advanced position in his system, we thus see Ardigò arrive at a formulation that is clearly Baumgartian, a formulation still infected with the intellectualism which — just as it kept him from more clearly and consciously achieving Bergsonian intuition — now precludes what would be the most natural development of his aesthetic position — that is, the dialectic of 'distincts.' We dare not accept this here as a true and final solution, but it cannot [but] be considered as the most vital development and end point of the above-mentioned position. And another thing not without significance for our argument is the story that has been set out here of the development of Croce's aesthetics as a successive move to more coherently idealistic positions and away from formulations affected by initial residues of positivism.

But what matters to us today is the development of Ardigò's thought which, although no longer of vital importance to us is nevertheless supremely instructive. It shows us how the only real philosopher of Italian positivism, in seriously attempting to transform a method that was still on the philosophical sidelines into a true philosophical system, arrived at the high point of his philosophical investigations only to go off the rails, needing to support his thinking using resources that betrayed how very far from positivism their origins were. And he shows this in his need to build his aesthetics aided by and based on these resources.

"The Aesthetics of Bergsonism," 21 Feb. 1929 (Unpublished).

If by Bergsonism we mean the entire complex of attitudes and intellectual tendencies directly or indirectly influenced by Bergsonian thought, then to speak of Bergsonism is to speak of all, or almost all, of contemporary French culture, and of a good part of world culture — such is the influence his thought has exerted, in scope as well as in depth. But even to exhaustively study all the currents that directly and immediately trace their origins to Bergson would be a task beyond not only my powers, but the available time as well. I shall therefore limit myself to considering, through the thought of the author himself and of those who have more specifically studied his work, some of the many directions in which Bergsonian thinking has developed or could develop, trying to draw conclusions about current problems in the field of aesthetics. And since such thinking is mobile and dynamic as never before and its history from beginnings to final conclusions is long, it is worth noting that there are consequences and directions of thought that arise at each stage of this journey — so that Bergsonians find themselves scattered like milestones, so to speak, along Bergson's road.

But this road is not straight and regular. It has twists and turns. And a basic and decisive one of these was the moment, toward the end of the century, when Bergson moved from the psychological formulations of the *Essai* [*Essay*] and of *Matière et Memoire* [*Matter and Memory*] to the ontological and mystical formulations of the *Evolution créatrice* [*Creative Evolution*]. That will be the point that divides this presentation into two parts.

But this division will be all the more striking in its particular concern with the aspect of Bergsonism that was the first to arise and had the good luck to provide the system with its liveliest and most conspicuous feature. This is irrationalism and the denial of the theoretical value of logical frameworks, a denial common to all of French contingentism, but which perhaps took a specific characteristic from Schopenhauer — the attribution of validity to these frameworks as practical, utilitarian activity.

It is this feature that led many to see Bergsonism as related to the doctrines of pragmatism — whose main exponent was James, in America, and which sought to reduce truth to an instrument of action, something that was only valid in the light of its practical results. Except that Bergsonism is if anything an inverted sort of pragmatism, and its recognition of the practical significance of logical patterns opened the way to the negation, rather than the affirmation of the value of such patterns. And if Bergson was later able to look sympathetically at James's thought, this was either because of the pluralism it vigorously affirmed or because of its conception of reality as tension, action — volition, in short — of which Bergson, in his later work, became an advocate. Two conceptions, then, the first of which indeed belongs to James but is extraneous to his pragmatism, and the second to Bergson, but at a much more advanced stage of his thinking, and applies to James only insofar as it lends a certain strength to his thought.

Thus the more intimate and intrinsic of these affiliations do not properly and in the most precise sense concern pragmatism and Bergsonism in its primary meaning, and are in any case a result of developments that would be interesting but not at the moment opportune to study. And if we want to make comparisons in the more strictly methodological field we will always find superficial similarities along with a substantial divergence of attitudes and purposes — derived, I repeat, from opposing assessments of the practical function of logical activity.

It would therefore be difficult to understand how *Georges Sorel*, despite some reservations, could bring the two doctrines together in his book *De l'utilité du pragmatisme* [*Utility of Pragmatism*][38] if it were not for the fact that in Sorel what might be called applied pragmatism is merged with the historical materialism deriving from his Marxist[39] experiences, and the fact that the dialectic of the economic moment inherent in these doctrines, well reconciled with pragmatist utilitarianism, leads him to a sociological consideration of philosophical systems that makes one think of Taine (and it would be interesting to study the relationship between Taine and Marx, perhaps in the light of their common Hegelian roots).

---

[38]*De l'utilité du Pragmatisme* (Paris: Rivière, 1913).
[39]*De l'utilité du Pragmatisme* p. 393.

But in the work of Sorel, rather than being explained and justified, systems are judged and evaluated on the basis of sociological considerations, so that the thesis of the *Evolution créatrice* is accepted essentially because it corresponds to the times and economic conditions of the society in which it arose, and there is no hesitation in rejecting a doctrine and an opinion if by chance they do not correspond to those conditions. In this way, according to Sorel, the history of art would refute Bergson's theory of the non-existence and negativity of disorder since, for Sorel, art actually presupposes a state of disorder into which order is introduced "with great difficulty following a long process of civilization," and is always threatened "by the arbitrary and the academic."[40] Art consists, in short, of the vital overcoming the academic. But, (leaving aside the fact that this doctrine is not, as it claims to be, contrary to the guidelines of Bergsonian thought, and that it is a very sustainable doctrine) art is considered by Sorel as a given fact of social need — so that its definition does not begin with the words "Art is" or "Art presupposes" but with "Artists say or demand that."

This utilitarian account of any theoretical framework would later find its vitality and purpose in Sorel's doctrine of the Myth,[41] which has been widely applied in politics and economics. But in the purely theoretical field it appears worthless and — as long as it takes the practical to mean utilitarian and economic rather than vital and fluid — it can be clearly contrasted with Bergsonian doctrine, which has always strictly denied the utilitarian and economic.

Against this denial, not because it opposed practicality, but insofar as it identified it with logical schemata, *René Berthelot*[42] spoke out in the more strictly philosophical camp, and *Julien Benda*[43] in the more journalistic. Despite differences in tone and pretension, their arguments are in substantial agreement, and consist of rejecting Bergson's substitution of intelligence with intuition in the field of cognition. But this criticism is not, as it at first appears, a simple re-

---

[40]*De l'utilité du Pragmatisme* p. 429.
[41]*Considerazioni sulla violenza*, introd. Croce (Bari: Laterza, 1926).
[42]*Un Romantisme utilitaire Vol. II: Le pragmatisme chez Bergson* (Paris: Alcan, 1913).
[43]*Le bergsonisme ou une philosophie de la mobilité* (Paris, 1912). *Sur le succès du bergsonisme* (Paris, 1913).

habilitation of intelligence in the form in which Bergson denied it — indeed, his denial is often simply viewed as an old and now benign truth which it is ridiculous to advocate with such pomp and fanfare. It is certainly not Bergson's version of intelligence that Benda puts back on the altar. "If we use the term Intuition for what we call Intelligence, and Intelligence for what we call Foolishness,"[44] then of course intelligence is going to come out badly. But for Benda, true intelligence is living and conscious, not schematic — a sort of intellectual intuition. And intuition that is not intellectual, like Bergson's, is relegated to the purely artistic: "It is not a poem that we are asking you for; explain yourself without categories; we are waiting."[45]

This is not the place for a study of Benda's aesthetics, but it is clear that it is entirely based on a fundamental distinction between art and philosophy, a distinction that reveals the rigidly rationalist position of this author and his detachment from idealism despite the "advances" made in it with the concept of an intelligence that is vitalized and made subjective. Because the accusation made against Bergson at the end of both his books, of being a man concerned with moral rather than theoretical problems — of being a "layman," in short, and not a "cleric"[46] — is an accusation made against Bergson the idealist whose intuition is conceived as practical reason, as opposed to pure reason. And what, ultimately, is all of idealism, from Kant and Fichte, even through Hegel and down to Gentile, if not a predominance of the practical in the form of conscious perception, the absolute "I," etc. over the theoretical?

But if in Benda rationalism remains abstract and incapable of assuming forms of concrete universality, it achieves these forms in Berthelot, whose severe and pointed criticism of Bergsonism leads to a clear affirmation of idealism in what I would call its most orthodox form. For Berthelot as well, Bergson's opposition to logic applies only to classical, abstract, immobile logic, not to the concrete, dialectical logic that philosophy has known since Descartes and Kant — the only kind alive today, the kind recognized by serious opinion.

---

[44]*Une philosophie de la mobilité*, p. 63.

[45]*Une philosophie de la mobilité*, p. 98.

[46]See *La trahison des clercs* (Paris, 1927).

So that here again, lashing out at the other kind amounts to breaking down an open door. Berthelot, through a meticulous analysis and refutation of Bergsonian theories and demonstrations, arrives at a denial of the validity of intuition as a substitute, so to speak, for logical knowledge. This denial and refutation, which we will not dwell on, is mainly based on the best known problems and dubious points of the Bergsonian system — i.e., the contradiction in rationally justifying intuition (which then becomes a problem of the relationship between intuition and language), and the contradictions in the problems of individual reality and absolute reality, individual life and absolute life, etc. These are problems that Bergsonism undoubtedly struggles with, and disparate if not contradictory solutions for them appear in the successive stages of Bergsonian thought. And it is on this divergence of Bergsonism from itself that Berthelot sometimes bases his accusation and his rejection of the doctrine of intuition.

Intuition exists for him, certainly, but as true knowledge that the mind arrives at "prior to discursive and reflective knowledge"[47] by which it will then be revealed and demonstrated — or at least this happens in the case of *genius,* which perceives a truth before giving a demonstration of it. What specific activity of the mind is indicated by the word *genius* is not specified, but it is certainly a cognitive activity, destined to be followed by the logical form, as in the case of Crocean intuition. And all thought (which is true knowledge for Berthelot) is "the passage from the momentary and the individual to what is supra-momentary and supra-individual,"[48] according to the well-known dictates of rational idealism in which, despite the numerous explanations given, knowing how this momentary and individual knowledge arises is still a problem.

But if Bergsonism has a particular characteristic, it lies in having given to the problem of the negation of formal logic a solution other than presenting thought as the sublation of the individual. It is certainly to Berthelot's credit that he saved from the critics, as a true Bergsonian original, the concept which for us constitutes our

---

[47] *Un romantisme utilitaire*, p. 151.
[48] Op. cit. p. 204.

author's most important discovery and truly great affirmation —
the concept of *durée* [duration].

◆◆◆

Without delving for the moment into an analysis of this idea
and an interpretation of its meaning and origins, I think we can
say that for Bergson, at the beginning of his studies, i.e. in the formulation of his *Essai sur les données immédiates de la conscience*
[*An Essay on the Immediate Data of Consciousness*],[49] it has a value
that is purely psychological and intimate to the mind, rather than
being absolute and inherent to the external reality of things. It represents quality as opposed to quantity, the intensive as opposed to
the extensive, freedom as opposed to necessity. But this quality is
wholly intimate, for now, wholly inherent to us and our states of
consciousness — belonging, you might say, to our internal sense.
It is no accident, perhaps, that this principle of inner consciousness for Bergson takes on a temporal form, however adjusted and
revitalized. This is a sign that Kant's determination of time, as the
form of an internal sense (and opposed to space, the external) is
not yet dead as a human need. And while it may be true that in
Bergson, Kant's homogeneous time is superseded and corrected
such that "duration" might in some respects be rather closer to
"transcendental conscious perception," it is also true that in Kant
himself relations between an internal sense and transcendental
conscious perception may be more intimate than they appear at
first sight.[50] This shows how the absolute Ego that dominates all
idealism arises from various quarters — of which one, perhaps,
is practical reason (hence Fichte and the current that takes its cue
from him) and the other could be this primitive internal and personal experience, sublating itself in a universal experience. This
passage from personal to universal experience, from psychology

---

[49]*Essai sur les données immédiates de la conscience,* 21° ed. (Paris: Alcan, 1921).
[50]See, in this regard, *Critique of Pure Reason,* p. 7 of sec. II of *The Transcendental Aesthetic*; the theorem regarding the "Refutation of idealism" in the *Analytic of the Principles,*
and the last note in the Preface to the second edition.

to ontology, is the route taken by "la durée," from the *Essai* [*Essay*] to *Evolution créatrice* [*Creative Evolution*]. But, once it has reached the universal, it will have nothing or almost nothing remaining to distinguish it from the idealistic universal, which arose, to put it crudely, from the will — apart from its origins. And our interest lies precisely here, in these origins. Therefore, we will have to try to stop the process halfway in order to take from it what is new, before it flows back into the common current.

In any case, at first this duration has an internal character, and the argument it deploys against logical forms happens entirely within the limits of consciousness, from which it rarely emerges to take a position before the external world. And this explains how this first Bergsoian attitude seems to be, but isn't, dualistic. For although it may seem to be the sharp opposition of space and time, of design and intuition, of matter and memory even on somewhat closer inspection, the dualism will turn out to be only apparent, concealing beneath it a special form of multiplicity.

The formations of space, the intellect, etc. are not contrasted with mental duration the way one reality is contrasted with another reality (and this would be the true dualist formulation). They are considered only as superstructure. Space, frameworks, etc. are falsities — arbitrary formations that the mind constructs to facilitate its action, but they are not in any way (at least in this first formulation) realities, whether or not they are real to the mind. They are essentially "phenomena" in the negative sense of the word.

The position here is decidedly Schopenhauerian, from the Schopenhauer who denies any representation subject to the law of causality and to the *principium individuationis* (and the third chapter of the *Essai*, on freedom and against causality and the law of conservation of energy, is a luminous proof of this). But if Schopenhauer is a dualist, his dualism certainly does not appear in this aspect of his doctrine, concerning this denial of intellectual formations, but rather in connection with his concept of a will as the essence of all things, the object of artistic knowledge — of a will that has, in short, all the characteristics of transcendence. Schopenhauer's dualism is found only in this transcendence, which doesn't exist in Bergson, or in early Bergson. And I would say that it doesn't exist and is not expressed precisely because of the author's initial anti-idealist concerns — an idealist conception would perhaps have brought him nearer than it might seem to transcendence. And what is the Schopenhauerian will if not a hypostasis of Kantian practical reason or Fichte's productive imagination — of the absolute and transcendental self, in short, that is intrinsic to idealism?

Schopenhauer's will, I would say, represents the exact extreme point at which idealism, at the apex of its development, dissolves into transcendence. And there is a slight contradiction between the negation of logical schemata — of the basic mediating activity of the mind, that is — and positing this will as reality, objectified in Platonic ideas and in essence a synthesis of all mediation. Whether this contradiction represents the greatness of Schopenhauer and the responsiveness of his doctrine to needs that may be conflicting, but are all alive in modern culture, it is not the case here to investigate.

In Bergson, in any case, the negation of "form" is more constant and radical; and *aesthetic activity* (which is for him, as everyone knows, recognition of the real in the "durée") does not have a real object, or at the very least, it is an object in itself. Art, more than an activity involving knowledge or some kind of relationship between intuitor and intuition, between representative and represented, is an emotion, or rather a feeling, the very feeling of duration as it flows — manifested, for example, in the feeling of grace. "The object of art is to numb the active or resilient powers of our personality, and to bring us to a state of perfect docility in which we take in the idea suggested to us, or sympathize with the feeling expressed."[51] "Art aims at imprinting feelings in us rather than expressing them."[52]

Not, therefore, the apprehension of an object, but the lived life of an inimitable personal experience — inimitable, certainly, and such that it will never be repeated, but universal, felt by the mind as its own, and above the particularities of empirical and logical frameworks.

Mediation, therefore? Not yet, because mediation presuppos-

---

[51]*Essai*, p. 11.
[52]*Essai*, p. 12.

es a mediating (or self-mediating) subject and a mediated object (even though this object is nothing more than a position of the subject), while here this object to be sublated, this particular to be universalized, does not yet exist — nature has not yet emerged. "The beauties of nature are considered as prior to those of art. . . . But one might wonder if nature is beautiful except through the happy meeting of certain processes of our art, and whether in a certain sense, art does not precede nature."[53]

So art precedes nature, and it precedes it because nature is not yet there, it has not yet arisen as a degeneration of the mind and as an object of the mind itself. For now, art is a kind of inner monitoring, whereby we feel in us the flow of our consciousness in the form of "durée."

But this inner monitoring is essentially already a form of knowledge, even if it is knowledge of ourselves. And the need to attribute a cognitive value to art, or to actually introduce generic cognitive activity, is already felt in the *Essai*, even before taking on a predominating tone in the works that followed. Already in the *Essai* there is a strong need to set something against the mind that will serve as a substrate and on which the mind can work. And this something is matter — but matter considered as the schema of the mind, as homogeneous multiplicity, as space: "All unity is that of a simple act of the mind and . . . as this act consists of uniting, it is necessary that some multiplicity of units serve as its material. Undoubtedly, when I think of each of these units in isolation, I consider it as indivisible since it is understood that I think of it alone. But as soon as I leave it aside to go on to the next one, I objectify it, and by that very fact I make it a thing, that is to say a multiplicity."[54] The thing, the material, thus consists of this objectifying carried out by the mind through its forms — its frameworks and abstractions. But is this material really the object of intuition, the reality that we apprehend in the "durée"?

If it were, we would be falling once again into idealism. But Bergsonian thought — let us say it once and for all — has in its

---

[53] *Essai*, p. 10–11.
[54] *Essai*, p. 61.

first manifestations the admirable virtue if skirting idealist formulations without ever falling into them. In Bergson, one of the most literate, perhaps, of contemporary philosophers (if by literacy we mean taking in a great number and variety of currents and intellectual approaches, and living continuously with them), idealist requirements and formulations are deeply felt and relived. And to us, vastly less educated than him and immersed up to our eyeballs in idealism and almost nothing else (I speak of course of us very young people) it seems easier and more comfortable to reduce Bergson to idealism, especially since inner developments in his thinking would later lead him to positions much closer and more similar to idealism itself. But if we would like to obtain what is most intimate and novel in Bergsonian thought, if we would like to have a genuine lesson from him, we have to seek in him not what is most consonant and coherent with our own thinking, but what, if anything, departs from it. And all the more so if we begin to find ourselves (as some do) incapable of deriving new satisfactory conceptions from his thought, and most of all (this is paramount) if the extraction of this thought of our Author's were partly arbitrary and not conforming to his original intentions.

Parentheses closed, we can thus see that the "matter" of the *Essai*, the multiplicity of spatial forms, can by no means be the object of intuition, and if we speak of the mind as if it were an activity that "posits things," that objectifies, even this objectivity is placed on a level completely opposite that of the subject. And the contrast between these aspects of the self is such that one of them can never become the object of the other. The two multiplicities, one of objects in space and the other of the purely affective states of the mind, live parallel to one another, without meeting or interfering with each other — and indeed, one belongs to true reality, and the other to appearance, falsity, the superstructure.

At this point, therefore, it would seem that the only relations of the mind with the external world — that is, the only relations of knowledge, should come about through the medium of space, in discursive form, and it is clearly stated that the process of numbering the quantitative multiplicity "is nowhere . . . accomplished as easily as in the perception of an external phenomenon, *unknow-*

able in itself."[55] Knowledge of the external world is thus a monopoly of the framework, of the language of the 'mot brutal', and even that gives us apparent and phenomenal knowledge.

But as for the reality of our own selves and our inner stream, it comes to us only from the "Durée," and if some dashing novelist comes along and tears away the Veil of Maya of our conventional self, we can thank that person for having "known us better than we know ourselves."[56] So here art starts to be knowledge, even if only knowledge of our interior, and the only true, real, non-arbitrary and schematic knowledge. In short, philosophy — and right here, in a nutshell, is all of Bergsonian aesthetics, which would culminate, in the essay *Rire* [*Laughter*], in the view that a specific objective of art is "putting ourselves face to face with reality itself."[57]

But it is necessary, in order to better understand what this reality is, and therefore also what this art is that is a direct vision of it, to have seen how this intuition arises from the pure sensation of an intimate and inexpressible stream; and it would also be interesting, if there were time, to follow the whole process by which this stream passes into known reality. An essential stage of this process is marked by the "images" that form the foundation of the construction of *Matière et Memoire* [*Matter and Memory*] and are a sort of compromise between subject and object, an elementary and indivisible datum that we operate on.

Postulating these "images," which I cannot go into now, certainly does not take one out of the field of the mind, and ensures that "Matière et Memoire" or "Souvenir-habitude" and "Souvenir pur" are still essentially states of consciousness. At the same time, attributing to them, as a substratum, formations endowed with a certain reality, such as the "images," gives them a character of greater concreteness and corporeality. If we wanted to make diagrams, we could say that the antithesis between logic and intuition, (or whatever we want to call the two terms) is presented, essentially unchanged, at three different and consecutive levels in the three

---

[55]*Essai*, p. 94.
[56]*Essai*, p. 101.
[57]*Le Rire*, p. 160.

subsequent works: the *Essai, Matière et Memoire,* and *Le Rire,* and that the process it accomplishes takes it from mind to reality or, in Bergsonian terms, from the "Durée," through images, to intuition.

◆ ◆ ◆

What remains to be said is what this intuition is and what meaning it has for us and our aesthetics. And it remains to be seen whether it can be framed in our models or whether it represents a new and different experience. Because its affinities with the new idealist aesthetics appear at first glance to be notable. The sublation and elimination of abstract logical schemata (or pseudo-concepts), the name itself of intuition and the clear-cut cognitive position of the artistic fact, making it difficult even for philosophy to distinguish them, would suggest an affinity of attitudes and conclusions. This seems even clearer considering that in both theories the concepts of the universal and the individual appear as essential elements.

But the contrast between them seems clear if we move beyond their actual formulation and take into account the directions in which the two doctrines are aimed. If the concepts of the universal and the individual are seen as two open roads, it will be observed that the aesthetics led by Croce is directed toward the former, and Bergson's toward the latter.[58]

---

[58]As a clarification of this and what follows, I would like to say that I am fully aware of the one-sidedness of this interpretation of both Croce and Bergson, since it is evident that in the former the need for individuality is also very strong, just as the need for universality is in the latter. But perhaps the utility of the above juxtaposition is that it indicates the opposing directions of the two philosophers' thinking. Because although Croce is still today a resolute proponent of individuality, it does not fit in well with the line of thought that he follows and with the principles that inspire him, and with respect to that line it remains an extraneous element that is difficult to assimilate. This is why the places where it is introduced (correction of the Hegelian dialectic and, in substance, the entire dialectic of the distinct) appear to be the most questionable in Croce's work. While in Bergson individuality is instead the main avenue, and the transition from it to universality, as we shall see, is if anything a degeneration.

Now, it seems to me that we should accept any of a thinker's ideas that seem good and in keeping with the essential needs of our own position, but mainly those that answer fundamental needs and find harmonious and logical justification in the system. Otherwise systems would become jumbles of disparate conceptions and to solve a prob-

If it is true (as I believe it is) that the Crocean dialectic of distinct forms is produced by the intersection of two dialectics of opposites, the practical and the theoretical, on one hand, and the one and the many, on the other (which, like all dialectics of opposites, in essence identify each other); if it is true that the substantive element of Croce's aesthetics is that of spiritual elaboration and catharsis, (hence the *Saggio sulla liricità* [*Essay on Lyricism*] and the one on *Totalità* [*Totality*]); if it is true that a necessary consequence of Croce's thought is Gentile's, in which art and philosophy are united and undifferentiated (in spite of attempts to distinguish them) in the single concept of the pure act; if all this is true, we must conclude that the principal and particular characteristic of Croce's aesthetics is mediation. How, in fact, can we justify the universality and immortality of a work of art, essential requirements of all serious thinking, if not with *mediation*? How can we think that a work of art can be experienced anew in its original peculiarity by the whole of humanity, unless we admit that the artist, in making it, freed himself and his material from their empirical individuality, in an attempt to express an essential element, an eternal attitude of the spirit?

If this is the essence of Italian aesthetics from Croce on, then we have to say that Bergsonian aesthetics is from this point of view its polar opposite. Starting in fact from different premises and requirements, it presents itself with all the characteristics of immediacy. Arising from a negation of logical schemes (Boutroux), its ongoing journey is continually dogged by this negation, which is the dominant motif, the only one that never leaves Bergsonian thought. And its constant concern is with finding that truth which is concealed behind the veil of space, mechanism, or language; and finding it first in psychological duration, then in the apprehension of a continuous and uninterrupted series of images, then in the very flow

lem or reconcile an antithesis it would be enough to accept its terms and make them coexist in a doctrine. So we all recognize Croce as our great master because of his strenuous affirmation of the value of individuality; and if in him it appears to us as a mere residue and an addition irreconcilable with his idealist leanings, we look to Bergson (who is perhaps less conscious of the importance of the matter, and started from a completely different place) for that framework that we had sought in vain in idealism.

of reality, does not bring a change in the method of gaining knowledge which, instead of catharsis or liberation in a higher synthesis, is a method of dispossession, as it were — of abandonment of the external superstructure in an effort to achieve a primitive purity and spiritual virginity, which will lead close to true reality.

Now, if we want to call the mediated universal *Apollonian*, and the universal "in itself," so to speak, *Dionysian*, we will have to recognize that the aesthetics of idealism is clearly Apollonian and that of Bergson Dionysian; but it is a Dionysian that keeps universality and excludes (or at least should exclude) transcendence. It is a point of equilibrium where Bergson stood for a single instant and fell from immediately. But it is precisely here, in this doctrine of art, that he appeared to have unified universality, immanence and immediacy. This intuitive activity that penetrates the individual so that they merge into one (reminiscent of the "images" of *Matière et Memoire*) is at the same time not particularized because, as truth, it carries within itself "a power of conviction, of conversion even, in which it (the truth) recognizes itself."[59] This "contemplation" which, to use Proust's words, "although eternal, is fleeting,"[60] evokes the orientation of a current which can perhaps solve many problems and satisfy many needs — a current which does not yet have its own character, or in which everything is still to be done; whose name would be *pluralism, individuality, multiplicity,* but which naturally would not be satisfied with the fleeting flashes of a Bergson, or the vague formulations of a James; in which the need for universality, inherited from idealism, should still have a preponderant part; and which should recognize as its progenitor Leibniz, in that body of needs that led him to the great doctrine of the monad.

This way is uncertain in its direction and results, but following Bergson's indications it could be tried by anyone who is not willingly resigned to transcendence, is free of idealism's inability to solve the problem of the individual, or the multiple, or nature (or whatever you want to call it), and sees in idealism's prioritizing of the practical over the theoretical an intrinsic inability to give firm

---

59*Le Rire*, p. 166.
[60]Proust, *Le Temps retrouvé* (N.R.R.F. 927) vol. II, p. 19.

moral guidelines.

In any case, the fundamental difference between the Bergsonian and idealist conceptions is clear. But it is interesting to note it because from the substantially identical cognitive function both attribute to art, one could easily be drawn to a fictitious affiliation of positions. In this regard, it should also be noted that, if it is true that the denial of formal logic is common to Bergsonism and idealism, the idealist transcendental, precisely because it is mediated, appears to represent a strengthening of logical and intellectual frameworks and has consequently been able to call itself an "Intellektuelle Anschauung" [Intellectual Viewpoint]. At the same time, intuition excludes everything intellectual as a matter of principle, so that the characteristic that distinguishes it from other transcendental principles is that it is, if such a thing can be said, *anti-reason*.

And if *Marcel Proust* was on occasion able to identify the artistic process as generically rational, this means either that he gave the term "reason" a meaning that was anything but precise, or that he is anti-Bergsonian. But Proust's entire "oeuvre" along with countless observations apparent to even the casual reader argue for the former hypothesis and, without any need to appeal to incoherence (always possible and not at all offensive to an artist) we can spontaneously observe that "raison supérieure, une et infinie"[61] means *reality* in the highest sense that this word has in Bergsonian philosophy, or at least in the mystical and Plotinian sense that it comes to assume, as we will see later, in *Evolution créatrice*. But what is the *content* of intuition? What is this reality that is immediately grasped in its intimate essence and its value beyond ourselves, whether it be good or bad, mobility or immobility, Schopenhauerian will or "élan vital" — this is the problem that will come up next, when the immediate process of intuition splits into an intuiting subject and in an intuited reality or life force, and when it comes to replacing the primitive "real intuition" with an intuition *of the real*. But then "reason" will have a mystical or absolute meaning very different from the reason we were talking about here, which is reason as a means of gaining knowledge.

---

[61]See *Pastiches et mélanges*, p. 45.

But for now what interests us is the method — if what is meant by method is philosophy in the process of its construction, a mental fact that has not yet been immortalized or dogmatized into a system of reality — (and, may we say in parentheses, if this is method, then method in philosophy is everything). Here we are interested in what seems to me the only essential method of Bergsonian philosophy — which is in essence Freud's method turned upside down. Again proceeding somewhat schematically for the sake of brevity, we can say that if Freud's *Unbewust* is perverse instinct, imperative — in short, *evil,* then Bergson's *durée* or *mémoire* — comparable to *Unbewust* as a subterranean, flowing, "trieben" [drive] — is instead truth, freedom, *goodness.* And since art is for both the strengthening of the ethically positive side of these antitheses, it will be in one case the sublation of the *Unbewust* and the reduction of this to the conscious, and for the other liberation from false consciousness and the discovery of true consciousness in the *Unbewust-Mémoire.* And since in both this original tendency has the character of the primordial reality of the mind, the art which, as Freud says, supersedes this reality will have a predominantly ethical character; whereas the art that is immersed in this reality, a la Bergson, will have a predominantly cognitive character.

Now, if Proust's problem is posed in these terms — that is, as a problem of the relationship between *Matière et Mémoire,* between unconscious and conscious, even for someone like me who only knows Proust's work partially — it seems clear that "temps perdu" is precisely time that is alive, not fixed, and is fed by everything in its past and "gnaws at the future." It is the "durée" that we find in "pure memory"; and finding that memory again is an inverse process with respect to the rational, a process of dissociation of associated elements in order to arrive at those pure sensations, free of elaboration, which alone, like the taste and smell in Aunt Léonie's cup of tea, "alone, more fragile but more enduring, more immaterial, more persistent, more faithful, remain poised in time like souls, remembering, waiting, hoping, amid the ruins of all the rest; and bear unflinchingly, in the tiny and almost impalpable drop of their essence, the vast structure of recollection."[62]

This seems to me the essence of Proust. And if there is something else, something different (and no doubt there is), we must see whether it is not just fringe or ornamentation around the fundamental skeleton of his work and thought. Which once again demonstrates that Bergsonian art is immediate and un-mediated knowledge. And if we have seen mediated art, or art that is "form" or catharsis, answer the need for universality, eternity, immortality, we find in this immediate art the satisfaction of another fundamental need — the need for a particular, individual kind of art, so that we ask the artist for images and not ideas, intuitions and not concepts, for art that is special, you might say, rather than systematic, illogical rather than organically deduced. This need, like the other, is essential and inherent, I believe, in the consciousness of anyone who produces or enjoys a work of art. But at times this need is in sharp contrast with the other, and leads to completely opposite conclusions. So that in idealist thought the one comes close to the identification of art with philosophy, and the other to the distinction between them. This problem of the relationship between the two activities is very important in all aesthetics, and perhaps at present it is one of the most vital and least understood. Because, though we all feel deeply that there is a substantial difference between artistic and investigative activity, it does not occur to us to formulate this distinction in clear and definitive language. And the individuality that we wish to attribute to artistic knowledge in contrast to the universality of logical knowledge has proved to be more empty words than true and meaningful thought.

How is it possible, in fact, to speak of individuality in connection with an activity whose very essence is "formal," such that the subject has been freed of its singular particularity? If this individuality were meant to be located in content rather than form, and if art as *knowledge of the individual* were to be postulated, rather than *individual knowledge,* the answer would be that in view of the subjectivist premises, this individual cannot be a *given,* a presupposition. The individual will be, if anything, a position of the

---

[62]Proust, *Du côté de chez Swann,* p. 73.

subject, an attitude of the universal that is realized and embodied in a particular evaluation — in history that is, or, following the well-known identification, in philosophy. So idealism also resolves the individual into a universal. And Gentile is right in wanting to deny the distinction, made on this basis, between art and philosophy. But perhaps he is wrong when he seeks to maintain the same distinction on other equally unsound bases and save the autonomy of art by introducing the new form of "feeling,"[63] which is, so to speak, the immediacy that accompanies every act of mediation, the activity of the mind in its subjective moment before it recognizes itself as an agent or a thinker or anything else. It is, in short, mediation itself at the moment when it happens, before we can say it has happened. It is not the case here to deal with this doctrine; but it is certain that art cannot be "feeling" as understood in this way, as a simple constant accompaniment to any and all mental activity which, precisely because it is an activity, is an unfolding, a striving — in short, a passion. If the idea is to arrive at this identification of feeling with art based on the so-called involuntary nature of artistic activity, it ought to be noted that this involuntariness and lack of reflection is characteristic of any autonomous attitude of the mind as it occurs, that when it happens it is entirely single and undifferentiated — an act of thinking or wanting, or of intuiting artistically — and has not yet split into wanting and wanted, thinking and thought, intuiting and intuited. This is a trivial observation and typical of the most elementary psychological experience, and it could be said that in a certain sense even an act of will is involuntary in its execution and even thinking is done without thought. But just as the immediacy and subjectivity intrinsic to every act does not exclude mediation as the distinctive meaning of the act itself, so from this constant accompaniment by immediacy one cannot infer the existence of an immediate activity for its own sake — that is, one with immediacy as its particular content.

And so the involuntariness of the artistic fact will indeed serve to identify it as an autonomous and original activity not derived from any other — a producing and not a product — but it cannot

---

[63] *Il sentimento, Giornale critico della Fil. It.,* January 1928.

be attributed to it as a trait that distinguishes it from other original activities. The distinction must again be, as in all idealism, a distinction of degree.

This very brief digression is intended to show how, for anyone taking idealism as a basis, distinguishing between art and philosophy is clumsy. It is a distinction, however, that is strongly felt by everyone, and a vague indication of it comes in the clear and precise awareness of a fact that to me seems incontrovertible — namely, that art cannot be given a history. Perhaps one of the most useful and vital features of modern thinking is to make the so-called history of art a history of artistic contents, of the underlying life and culture belonging to the artistic sphere, but not of the work of art itself, which appears to live its own independent life closed in itself, outside any nexus with past or future. So that if coherent thought leads us to identify the two activities with one another, when this identification goes so far as treating one as if it were actually the other, or making even art a dialectic, our consciousness draws back and refuses to follow. This feeling is of course not enough to give us the criterion of distinction, but it can serve simply as an indication of the direction in which the distinction will be sought.

Now, in this sense anti-historicism means *multiplicity*. In this sense, I say, because it is not out of the question that the term *history* can be given connotations that are actually the opposite of this. If, for example, in the face of the closed and almost transcendent fixity of the absolute self, one wanted to highlight the particular or dynamic concreteness of life in its variety of forms and aspects, then it seems evident that this very inexhaustibility of life is what history would amount to — in other words, multiplicity. But if history is understood in the Hegelian sense that characterizes it in philosophical theory — that is, as dialectic, a necessary and coherent link between events and between ideas such that their succession in time is the unfolding of a universal and single process — then multiplicity, which means the dissolution of this historical link, will be a requirement of anti-historicity. In the latter sense, therefore, art is anti-historical and multiple, and in this sense the requirement that art should have no history is at the same time what distinguishes it from philosophy and what makes it an immediate activity and a pluralistic mode of knowledge.

Thus we have come once again and by a different route to Bergson. But we have learned from this new route that the necessity of the distinction is not specific to idealism, and that it is something general and felt by everyone, to the extent that it actually leads idealism off its usual rails by imposing an individuality on it which, as long as it stays alongside the mediated universal, is an accessory that can be postulated without being accounted for. Bergsonian individuality, on the other hand, arises coherently from a robust denial of mediation. And art would in this way appear to be saved — although it may be that saving art means losing philosophy.

Remember that if idealism's artistic individual arose out of the necessity to distinguish between art and philosophy, the primitive accent of the Bergsonian individual, whose origins are different, represents true and real knowledge in the face of the falsity and superstructures of science. So true philosophy will be found precisely in this intuition, which by another route we found to have an aesthetic character, and instead of finding the true autonomy and independence of art in Bergsonian individuality, we are forced to see even here a substantial identity between art and philosophy.

Indeed, the identity appears much more marked and manifest here than in the idealist formulation. So much so, in fact, that it is one of the problems most widely addressed and discussed in systematic expositions of Bergson's doctrine. We can pass over *Gillouin*,[64] the most pedestrian of commentators, who gets by with a few quotes from the master. *Parodi,* who dedicated two chapters to Bergson in his book on contemporary philosophy in France,[65] attributes to intuition, the source of our knowledge of reality, a predominantly aesthetic character, and uses this as a reason to deny it the cognitive value it would like to claim. *Le Roy,* perhaps the most authoritative of Bergsonian interpreters, addresses the problem starting at the outset of his book[66] where, after noting that "the instrument of choice for philosophical thought is the metaphor,"[67]

---

[64]*La philosophie de M. Henri Bergson* (Paris: Grasset, 1928).

[65]*La philosophie contemporaine en France* (Paris: Alcan, 1919).

[66]*Une philosophie nouvelle. Henri Bergson* (Paris: Alcan, 1919).

[67]*Une philosophie nouvelle. Henri Bergson* (Paris: Alcan, 1919).

he immediately attempts to avoid falling into error by introducing the distinction, stating that "art is in a way philosophy before analysis, before criticism, before science: aesthetic intuition is nascent metaphysical intuition, limited to dreams, not going as far as a test of positive verification," which is instead applied to philosophy, "the art that takes over from science and takes it into account — the art that takes analysis as its subject matter and submits to the demands of rigorous critique."[68]

A compromise solution, this, which is not satisfying because it does nothing more than make philosophy participate in scientific activity, which had previously been categorically forbidden. But given the way the problem is posed, making it insoluble, this may seem ingenuous. In essence, Bergson himself appeals to it when he contrasts philosophy, with its "deliberate, reasoned, systematic detachment" with the "natural, innate detachment" of art.[69]

Thus the problem has not been resolved, and other critics, Höffeding[70] and Segond[71] for example, identify Bergson's philosophy with art even more explicitly, the former with a reproachful tone, the latter with approval. But if in his reply to the former Bergson made another attempt, posing a new and equally sterile distinction of content in which philosophy "captures the vital before its dispersal, while art deals with images,"[72] the latter is the subject of a citation from an interview that appeared in the 11 December 1910 issue of the journal *Paris,* where Bergson said: "Philosophy as I conceive it, is closer to art than to science. . . . Art and philosophy meet . . . in intuition, which is their common base. I would even say: philosophy is a genus of which the different arts are species."[73]

So we see that in spite of some doubt and indecision he himself was drawn into issuing this identification. Given this formulation, its character is a reduction of philosophy to art, rather than vice versa, and art is thus given the privileged position. This way art comes

---

[68]*Une philosophie nouvelle. Henri Bergson* (Paris: Alcan, 1919) p. 50.
[69]*Le Rire,* p. 151.
[70]*La philosophie de Bergson* (Paris: Alcan, 1916).
[71]*L'intuition bergsonienne* (Paris: Alcan, 1913).
[72]See Höffding, op. cit. appendix, p. 159–60.
[73]*Intuition bergsonienne,* p. 14.

to be the spokesperson and marker of reality for the entire course
of Bergsonian thought, so that from the changes and evolution of
aesthetics all the changes and evolution of its metaphysics may be
deduced. We have seen an example of this in the passage of art from
the inner feeling of the stream to the actual act of intuitive knowing.

In any case, this identification and reduction of philosophy to artistic forms is closely related to another of Bergsonism's famous problems and may in part originate from it, one which also stems from a
primitive anti-intellectualist concern — the problem of language.

That language should be identified with intellectual schemata
and thus eliminated from forms of intuition is one of the principles
that is most often repeated, if not most essential, in Bergson's work
— and if even he admits that some artists can construct "rhythmic
arrangements of words that manage to organize themselves together
and come alive with an original life," he has to recognize however
that by this means they "tell us or rather suggest to us things that
language was not made to express."[74] Language as an expression of
intuition is therefore an exceptional tool that is itself reducible to
rhythmic movement — to music, which has been affirmed many
times[75] as the only form of artistic expression that is saved in the
Bergsonian system, or the one to which all others must be reduced.

But will we then have to reduce philosophy to music as well?
This is the absurd and almost grotesque solution that the principle
of the inexpressability of intuition leads to. And it makes us feel
once more, in the harshness of its consequences, the need for a
distinction between art and philosophy. Because if the *universal*
and *one* locked art in the grip of dialectics and history, here the
particular and multiple dissolve philosophy in the fantastic and inexpressible. On the face of it a devastating conclusion, that might
lead some to declare the failure of Bergsonism. But perhaps we
should not leave it at this contradiction, but should look instead
at whether it necessarily derives from the premises that he started
with, or whether it is a partly arbitrary illusion for which some

---

[74]*Le Rire*, p. 159.
[75]For example, by Raffaello Piccoli in his essay "Il Bergson e l'estetica," published in
Cultura Contemporanea of 1911.

explanation can be found in a study of the origins of the two concepts of intuition and art or the relationship between them.

It is worth noting in fact that the individuality and multiplicity that had appeared to be the main avenue in early Bergson toward solving many of the theoretical and moral problems left open by idealism had arisen as an attribute of a faculty that was distinctly theoretical, with a decidedly cognitive nature. So that the alogical and asystematic form that had been sought and was then found in intuition was meant to have only one main and essential function — to provide immediate knowledge of reality in its essence. Only later on (in an ideal sequel, of course) was it observed that such an activity, with its immediate, intuitive character, had certain characteristics in common with artistic activity. And it was identified with art, which gave it a more normal aspect that was perhaps more acceptable to common thinking. In this way, therefore, art has become the authentic bearer of knowledge and truth.

This is where the identification of art with philosophy originated. But we mustn't forget that intuitive activity arose independently of art and that art was joined with it almost as a symbol, as its manifestation and voice — so that it might almost be said that a true Bergsonian aesthetic in which art is situated and defined doesn't exist, and that the references to art in his books almost always come in the form of exemplifications of intuitive activity.

This immediate and individual knowledge, then, is a fundamental and primitive characteristic of Bergsonism — a multiple knowledge that has proved very valuable in our present spiritual climate. Inexpressible knowledge, of course, but which an alogical consideration of language (in no way contrasting with the principles and essence of Bergsonism) would immediately render into speech. And indeed, in certain rare moments there is already in Bergson a notable need to revitalize language — to give words a closer adherence to the thing signified: "One would have to be very naive," he said one day *ex cattedra*, "to ask a philosopher for an unvarying definition of the words he uses. . . . Words that designate real things cannot always have the same sense. . . . In any particular passage, the context influences the meaning of the words."[76]

As I have said, this knowledge, which can also become express-ible, is such that it has much to commend it and solves many of our problems. What we cannot accept is the reduction of it (as phi-losophy, in essence) to art. The difficulty here, like the analogous problem in idealism, may lie in the concern to give the artistic fact a cognitive character. From the day when the autonomy of this es-sential form of mental activity was discovered, attempts have con-stantly been made to fit it into and graft it onto the two forms we already know — theory and practice, and attempts to distinguish them met with no success except as differences of degree. We have seen how attempting any other sort of distinction boils down to postulating two forms of philosophical knowledge — individuality and universality, forms that cannot coexist because they are mutu-ally exclusive and presuppose a subjectivist and an objectivist con-ception of reality. So that even this distinction has to be reduced to a difference of degree. And from here, because of the impossibility of giving preeminence to one of these activities, or rather because of repugnance at making one or the other subordinate, we arrive at a complete identification.

But is the nature of art really cognitive? Or has it rather been assigned to this category because of a sort of false analogy? And aren't the psychological elements that constitute artistic emotion very different from those that distinguish cognitive and volition-al activity? And that sense of expansion that animates the artist during the act of creation, whereby he believes he is at that mo-ment the whole world — is it the same as what someone feels who has seen an indubitable and universal truth whereby the whole world may well open up before him like an unveiled abyss? And the certainty and the impossibility of contradiction that are char-acteristic of the known truth, drawing us to divulge and dissem-inate it as if it were an inexhaustible possession to be shared with everyone — is this also characteristic of a work of art? And on the other hand, unlike practical activity, does not a work of art have its own aloofness and purity from all interest, its own "visibility," that

---

[76]Thibaudet, *Le Bergsonisme* (N.R.F., 1923) p. 136.

distinguish it plainly from something practical?

It is difficult to characterize artistic activity, but it is clear to everyone (since everyone is an artist of sorts) that art is substantially different from knowledge and will. And if knowledge is perception and ascertainment, and the will is externalization, art will have points of contact with both, but it can never be reduced to them. And that vision that is inherent in the artistic process, that act of making oneself an object to oneself, will not be knowledge because of the indifference to the content that makes it an activity of contemplation and not of observation, much less of discussion. And the joy of artistic creation is not going to be the will, because of this same indifference, and because of the absence of that movement of outward expansion and extroversion that is a peculiar characteristic of the will. These distinctions are in part obvious and in part confused and obscure. But I think the independence of art from other forms of the mind is clear to everyone.

And so why not attribute an autonomous place of its own to this activity that everyone recognizes as autonomous? Why not free it from the yoke of theory and forget art as knowledge (whether individual or universal) in favor of art *tout court,* containing within it its own reason and explanation? And could not that very form of catharsis whereby life is seen but not known, created but not willed, be its distinctive character? Then one could still do philosophy of art, but without any longer making it a preparation or aid, or the conclusion and synthesis of philosophy.

Once again, this is just one direction in which further study is needed. But perhaps this route would allow more consistent conclusions to be drawn from the principle of the autonomy of art.

◆ ◆ ◆

This is where we have arrived in the attempt to justify and keep alive and viable in Bergson the principle of individuality, abolishing the repugnant identification of art with philosophy. But Bergson did not follow this route, and the same problems that led us to these conclusions — the problems of language, history, and the relation between art and philosophy, along with many others left open in the formulation of the *Essai, Matière et Memoire,* and *Le Rire,* still call for a solution. And it was in searching for this that the author was led to abandon the route of the individual and to fall into that of mediation, creating his own version of the transcendental with what might be called an ontological character. Being transcendental and mediation would make it history as well, but the sort of history that is inherent in all natural realities — that is *Evolution.*

II

We have already seen how the essay *Le Rire* interprets intuition as the apprehension of a reality, knowledge of the real; and we have noted how this immediate apprehension brought together elements of concreteness and immanence, and at the same time of universality, which could meet many needs left unsatisfied by the overly abstract idealist universal. But we have also seen that this was a point of equilibrium where Bergson would not remain for even a single moment.

And indeed the first problem he set himself at this point was: What is this true reality that intuition is knowledge of? What does it consist of?

The answer to this from someone who wanted to continue along the route of intuition would be not to answer, or not to set the problem in these terms — because, if we are dealing with true intuition, then it is an indivisible act in which there is no longer any difference between subject and object, intuiting and intuited, knowing and known, so that reality would be in the intuition itself, not in the purported object it is supposed to apprehend.

But we need to keep in mind that this way we have of understanding intuition is simply an attempt to draw on Bergson's teachings and to put his discovery to our own uses. And it should be remembered that Bergson's own needs were certainly different, and that his scientific and empirical origins led him to focus on *data* and to presuppose a natural reality. For this reason he is led to apply his discovery of "durée" to all the spheres science works in, from the inorganic, biological, or social — or moral, as his followers (e.g. *Le Roy*) would attempt to do — to the psychological. And if the fact that his point of departure was the psychological (or as we say, mental) world doesn't look like a coincidence to those of us who see "durée" as a principle arising from the mind, such that its raison d'être is there alone, perhaps to him this anteriority of the psychic did seem coincidental. Perhaps it seemed to him that the psychological deduction of the "durée" was an application for which any other phenomenon of the natural world could have served equally well as an example. So it is easy to understand how this problem of the content of reality could have arisen for him once intuition had been posited as the means for understanding it. And true reality would also have the form of duration and would also be opposed to something fixed and spatial — this is the source of *élan vital.*

Without doubt, "élan vital" in its original meaning was one of the many manifestations of the principle of intuition. But it is also true that attributing a mental form to natural reality (which for the empiricist is all of reality) gives this reality an immaterial character that it would not otherwise have. "Je dure, donc je suis; le monde dure, donc il est" says Thibaudet, paraphrasing the famous principle. And in fact Bergson's passage from the self, even if it came from a different place, is very similar to the transition from the empirical self to the absolute Self that all idealism is based on. And if at the beginning we found a certain similarity between Bergsonian and Kantian self-awareness, here we see that this similarity continues and is strengthened in the passage of self-awareness from the individual to the universal.

And so we arrive at a "world with duration" by a process of externalization of the "durée" from the recesses of personal feeling — and it is immediately clear that this formulation completely loses the multiplicity and individuality that we had established as our most vital message from Bergson. But perhaps this about-face was fatal — for there is no doubt that idealistic models have such solid construction and such power of assimilation that it is almost impossible for anyone who has not yet experienced them and paid the price to know their deficiencies not to fall for them. Idealism, in short, is an experience that has to be lived, even for someone who wants to go beyond it or follow other paths. Otherwise there is the risk of being captured, when you least want to, in its web.

And perhaps "élan vital" or the universality of duration is exactly the painful and necessary tribute that French contingentism has to pay to German thought.

An indication and first appearance of this passage from the individual to the absolute universal is found in the *Introduction à la Métaphysique*,[77] which many consider Bergson's small masterpiece and which, because of its central position in Bergsonian thought (it dates from 1905), brings together many of the author's basic positions. In fact, along with the affirmation of intuition as the "integrating experience," and as an identification of the mind in reality and of reality in the mind, it is stated that "There is a reality that is external and yet given immediately to the mind. . . . This reality is mobility. . . . All reality . . . is tendency, if we agree to call tendency a nascent change of direction."[78]

Already here, intuition, which is duration in the mind, becomes the apprehension of a duration that is in things — and the entire journey of science is marked not by deductions and analysis, but by successive immersions in this mobility, by probes into the ocean of becoming.

From here it is easy to arrive, and by a road that we will not follow, at "élan vital." And from here we will also arrive at that kind of parallelism, so odd in Bergson and so repugnant to our way of thinking, between intuition and "élan vital," or correspondingly, between intelligence and matter. Hence intelligence, the subject of much controversy, will nevertheless have its own domain, a field in which it will be true knowledge — the field of matter, so that the inferior aspect of the mind will be legitimate and justified when it is applied to the inferior aspect of the world, which is to say, to matter; through a kind of affinity that we find a bit difficult to understand.

We can already see from this example that the ontologization (so to speak) of the principle of duration brings new and unforeseen problems. A very important example, which gave rise to new directions in the field of aesthetics, is the problem of the rise of

---

[77]Italian translation in the book edited by Papini: *La filosofia dell'intuizione* (Lanciano: Carabba, 1913).
[78]*Filosofia dell'intuizione*, p. 61.

the individual and of matter in general. The character of the problem is purely idealist and shows once again how Bergsonism falls into such patterns. Because if the whole world and universal life is flux and becoming, how can we explain the rise of individual consciousness within it? And if the "élan vital" is the overcoming of the fixed and the material, where does this materiality arise that opposes it as in the form of an obstacle to be overcome?

In order to resolve this difficulty we need to look more closely at a feature of "durée" which perhaps, and not without reason, was somewhat obscure in the early formulations — namely, the nature of *action,* which is inherent in the primitive "durée" as a flowing, tending mobility. It was natural that this immersion in the "durée" or participation in it, this continuous instability and continuous change should be active and not passive — a doing and not an incurring. But this aspect of action had been from the beginning obfuscated by that of knowledge. In this way intuition had the function of apprehending reality. But now that this intuition is transported into reality itself, its dynamism is exposed in all its force and violence — and behold "élan vital," action, *will.*

Here too, the comparison with Schopenhauer comes spontaneously to mind. Here too there are two forms of will, two types of "practice." One is false and apparent, from the utilitarian scientific framework, while the other is true or representative of the inner essence of reality. In this second sense as well, Bergson has been linked by some to pragmatism, and in this second sense even he found similarities between himself and James,[79] but here we are dealing with a pragmatism interpreted very broadly (and perhaps not it at all) such that even Blondel's "Action" could be reduced to it, as could, in short, any doctrine (and they are countless) that puts the practical before the theoretical.

Once these two types of practical activity were established they remained in sharp opposition, like principles of good and evil. But given the need to unify them and establish an origin for the degeneration of matter, it was natural that it was precisely in their practical character that their unifying point was found. "Èlan vital" would be a

---

[79]In the introduction to James's book: *Le Pragmatisme* (Flammarion, 1906).

tending, an acting which, as such, must manifest itself in some thing
— it must create objects that identify it and determine it. And things,
matter, all the forms of the universe would be stops or "coupes" that
necessarily formed along the journey of the "èlan vital."

In a 1902 study entitled *L'effort intellectuel,* revisiting the problem of memory that he had resolved in his early work with a clear
distinction between memory for practical use and pure disinterested memory, Bergson introduced the new figure of the *schéma
dynamique,* intended to represent, among psychic formations,
a pregnant image containing in itself at the level of implication a
whole multiplicity of other images, a "simple representation that
can be developed into multiple images."[80] This dynamic schema is
given great importance in memory function, so that "the effort of
recall consists of converting a schematic representation with intertwined elements into a pictorial representation whose parts are
placed side by side."[81] Now what could be more *practical* than this
schema? How was it formed if not through the concentration of
images inherent in "souvenir-habitude"? Yet this dynamic schema
is part of the motion of reality, and "l'effort intellectuel," occasioned
precisely by the passage from this schema to the images, is an operation analogous to that of life, which consists "of a gradual passage
from the less realized to the more realized, from the intensive to the
extensive."[82] In it we have witnessed "this increasing materialization
of the immaterial that is characteristic of vital activity."[83]

This is the definition of life that supports all of *Evolution
créatrice,* in which all aspects of nature — the inorganic world,
plants, animals, people and the forms of the mind itself, intelligence and instinct, are "coupes," interruptions in the process of
"élan vital," which then proceeds in divergent directions. "The way
the wind rushing through a crossroads is divided into diverging
air currents, all of which are one and the same breath." And in this
process the action itself, just as in the case of Fichte's self, creates its

---

[80]*L'énergie spirituelle* (Alcan, 1923) p. 171–72.
[81]*L'énergie spirituelle* (Alcan, 1923) p. 178.
[82]*L'énergie spirituelle* (Alcan, 1923) p. 202.
[83]*L'énergie spirituelle* (Alcan, 1923) p. 202.

own object. But in Fichte the agent is the Ego — that is, an objective activity, albeit absolute, and in Bergson, although the "élan vital" derives by analogy from a subjective activity, the consciousness of this subjectivity is lacking; so that his "*evolution créatrice*" could be called an ontologized transcendental principle. Therefore the individual, the subject, is no longer the source and starting point, but will also arise as one of the many manifestations of the vital process.

As the highest of them, however, and thus able to reproduce within himself the process itself. It should not be forgotten that there is a certain oscillation at this point between the naturalness of evolution and its psychological origins, which cannot be completely discounted. And "élan vital" always has to resemble an activity of the mind. Thus, if in previous works, examples were drawn from the art world, here it is no longer examples, but comparisons that Aesthetics will provide. It will no longer, however, be the primitive aesthetics of purely cognitive intuition.

In *L'effort intellectuel* we read that originally, in the mind of the artist, "there is something primitive and abstract — I would like to say incorporeal" and that art is the realization of this "incorporeal," so that "literary and poetic invention thus goes from the abstract to the concrete, which is to say, in short, from the whole to the parts and from the diagram to the image."[84] So art participates in the "élan vital," and in *Evolution créatrice* we again find art that "lives on creation"[85] or that, like life, develops and expresses itself in different directions through successive bifurcations. In this way, "the author puts a lot of things into a hero at the beginning of a novel that he is obliged to give up little by little as he goes along."[86] And he gives them up because the process of art is one of determining, fixing: "These original lines drawn by the artist — are they themselves not already a fixing, like the freezing of movement?"[87] Understood in this sense, "creation of matter would be neither incomprehensible, nor inadmissible, because we seize from within,

---

[84]*L'énergie spirituelle*, p. 186.
[85]*Evolution créatrice*, p. 49.
[86]*Evolution créatrice*, p. 109.
[87]*Evolution créatrice*, p. 260.

we constantly experience creation of form, and it would be precisely there, where form is pure and where the creative current is momentarily interrupted, that matter is created."[88] *Thibaudet* latches onto this second aesthetic of Bergson's, basing his entire interpretation on the principle of "élan vital," the universalized "durée." He reduces it to Cartesian cogito and Kantian morality, if not for its content, for the form of self-awareness and *a priori* principle — which, according to him, "bring about . . . communication by the interior with the absolute."

So that this "élan vital" that Bergson wanted to give a rigorously scientific demonstration of, bringing to its defense even a controlled principle from the natural sciences, Carnot's law, ends up being mainly valued as an intimate experience of the mind. I don't know how valid Bergson's demonstration is for a biologist or for science in general, nor whether his interpretation of Carnot's principle is legitimate; what is certain is that other scientists, for example Meyerson,[89] have arrived by means of that principle at similar conclusions. Nevertheless, the fact is that starting out with this scientific demonstration can give "élan vital" nothing more than the status of a hypothesis, plausible perhaps, but such that it can always be disproved by *a posteriori* observations. Bergson does not claim or affect to claim any more than this, and his statements are often qualified by the opening caveat: "everything happens as if. . . ." Not admirable modesty, this, as it strips his principles of all philosophical value — that is, as necessary and definitive. But Thibaudet, like many other critics, claims a philosophical origin for the principle of "élan vital," and while Le Roy, for example, still speaks of a simple analogy between mind and nature, in him the transcendental character of the principle of duration bursts from every part of his exposition, so that the direction of Bergsonian philosophy he indicates is toward distinctly extra-natural principles: "durée," "changement," "qualité," "tension," "action," etc., and matter is no longer opposed to mind, but a position of it, *mens momentanea seu carnens recordatione* [thought, a reflection of the moment].

---

[88] *Evolution créatrice*, p. 260.
[89] *Identitè et réalité* (Paris: Alcan, 1909).

Understood in this way, philosophy should be knowledge of the flow, the tending, the action — but how to position such knowledge when it presupposes something external to what it knows, and this exterior is not possible given that "élan vital" is everything, that nothing can be outside it, and that it cannot be seen except from its own interior? Philosophy thus struggles with two opposing needs. "It must be an action and it must go beyond action."[90] The antinomy is resolved with the placement of philosophy within the "élan vital" and so that it takes part in it. "Philosophy . . . is . . . reaction, and if this reaction exceeds action, it is not by becoming contemplation, but by becoming creation."[91] "We experience the creative impulse within us the moment we act freely."[92]

Thus philosophy is also creation, and its logical and rational designs are no longer just a simple escort and a mere tribute paid to the science of time, as Bergson would like, but normal explanations of its flow — simply stopping points in the eternal journey of thought. In this sense, Thibaudet reintroduces history and reproaches Bergson for having spoken, in his communication at Bologna on *Intuition philosophique*,[93] of a philosophy done as if by intuitive leaps and strokes of original genius whereby "a philosopher worthy of the name has never said more than one thing, and what is more he has only tried to say it rather than actually saying it."[94] Thibaudet sets against this the fact "that the philosopher and his philosophy have developed in "durée," above all an individual "durée," that no intuition can reduce or abridge."[95] It might be observed that the opinion of Thibaudet is perhaps more consonant with the spirit of *Evolution créatrice* than with Bergson himself. There is in Bergson a natural reduced awareness of the revolution accomplished by his philosophy as well as a lingering indulgence, even in later years (*Intuition philosophique* is from 1911) for the formulations his thought has surpassed.

---

[90]Thibaudet, op. cit. I, p. 194.
[91]Thibaudet, op. cit. I, p. 194.
[92]Thibaudet, op. cit. I, p. 195.
[93]*Revue de métaphysique et de morale* (1911) p. 809.
[94]*Revue de métaphysique et de morale* (1911) p. 809.
[95]Op. cit. II, p. 181.

In Thibaudet, in any case, this conception of everything as action is clear. It is a conception that also resolves the question of language — for what is it, if not another manifestation of practical activity, one of the many divergent directions of "élan vital"? The practical nature of all these formations is maintained, but the judgment of it is reversed, becoming positive instead of negative. In this way pure knowledge assumes a subordinate position: "To conceive of this 'élan vital' in its reality, which is called the Will, is to renounce living it."[96] Maximum emphasis would be given to the words that Bergson let slip in one of his very rare mentions of moral problems, "Great and good men are illuminators of metaphysical truth."[97]

And so action is everything, and all the essential activities of the mind are reduced to it. This is no less true of art, so that in Thibaudet the myth of the contemplative artist is replaced by the artist-creator. In him the position and dignity of art in the hierarchy of human faculties is unchanged — it still gives us reality in its true essence: "If reality is creation, it is in the moments of creation that we will grasp reality: such as the act of generation, maternal love, the work of art." But if art is creation, as is philosophy (and once again the identification of art with philosophy cannot be avoided) "it implies a need for matter. . . . We cannot be artists without being to some extent craftsmen."[98] And this craftsman's work is manifested in the individual: "art imitates nature in so far as it expresses itself in individuals, it creates organisms."[99] "The purpose of art is to coincide with the productive nature of being."

It is a process of evocative objectification, therefore, whereby from the most universal art, music, we move on to those that are more concrete and more involved in corporeality, such as, for example, dance. This opens the possibility of a hierarchical scale of arts, and the division of literary and artistic genres that Thibaudet would continue to uphold in his criticism. But what interests us here is the *active* character of his aesthetics, so that in the preface

---

[96]Op. cit. II, p. 94.
[97]*Energie spirituelle*, p. 26.
[98]Op. cit. p. 53.
[99]Op. cit. p. 55.

to a book on the novel he mainly sees the reader as someone who relives the situation narrated, and if the novelist who reads novels reads them differently from the ordinary reader, it is because "he has enough to do living with his own creations."[100]

◆◆◆

Having reached this point we can observe how art, this form that requires autonomy but is so difficult to collocate, has come to be an integral part of practical activity, as witness the constant comparisons and analogies Thibaudet makes between art and love. But here again actual identity repels, and Thibaudet tries to find the distinction by opposing the virtual nature of art with the reality of love — art as the possibility of action, faced by love as the effective force of action. But this, too, is an artificial distinction, and once again we see the impossibility of reducing art to either of the two forms, knowledge or will.

But this aesthetic of Thibaudet's, Bergsonian without doubt — which can be legitimately deduced from the author's thought, can be considered here again as documentation of the long journey this thought has taken, from primitive psychological "durée" to absolute and universal "élan vital."

If we want to think of this road as a passage from the negation of rational forms to a union with them, we come to the same conclusion as *Segond*[101] (close to Thibaudet in this sense), who reduces all Bergsonian philosophy to a dialectical conciliation of antitheses. Having established a certain number of antinomies (quality-quantity, duration-uniform time, art-science, etc.), he seeks to move from an abstract view of them to an intuitive consideration that reduces them to a concrete unity. But what is intuition according to Segond? It is individual duration through which we conceive the duration of the entire universe — it is "the immediate intuition of our 'durée'" that lets us "grasp in truth the progress of life."[102]

---

[100]*Le liseur de romans* (Paris: Crès, 1925) p. XXVI.
[101]*L'Intuition bergsonienne* (Alcan, 1913).
[102]*L'Intuition bergsonienne* (Alcan, 1913) p. 58.

This is the principle that resolves the antithesis through "the implication of the generated term in the generating term." In this way
the antithesis of thought and language and even of art and science
will be resolved. "It is the aesthetic achievement, limited by narrow
intuition, that completes, intellectualized and universalizable, the
metaphysical act of vital intuition — open, expandable and unlim-
ited."[103] But what is this intuitive principle, creator of unifications,
if not a dialectical principle? And to what is all reality reduced by
the implementation of this antithesis, if not to a transcendental
reality — that is to say, to the reality of idealism?

So Segond also reduces Bergsonism to idealism, and this fact is
particularly significant for the study of the development of Bergsonian doctrine if we recall that at the beginning of this study we encountered an author, Berthelot, who fought Bergson on the basis of
idealism, and now we find two who celebrate him on the same basis.

But this "élan vital" is, we have said, natural reality. It is the
process of becoming, but transformed into an entity, a real and
positive formation. And it is a first principle, the animator and
generator of the whole world and all the creatures that live in it —
so what is the difference between this and a divine principle?

Bergson himself mentions divinity in *Evolution créatrice*, immediately adding, however, that it "has done nothing at all."[104] Especially in the two letters to the priest of Tonquédéc,[105] he makes
significant concessions in this direction, so that even if official
Catholicism (*Maritain*) and the followers of neo-scholasticism are
against him, he gains the approval of those close to the modernist movement. And the *Annals of Christian Philosophy*, under the
direction of father Laberthonnière, have made no secret of their
deference to him.[106] But if Blondel, for example, in order to arrive at
his "action," started from the powerful critique of science made by
Boutroux (a critique that then passed almost entirely into Bergson),
and if even in Le Roy, the extreme representative of modernism, a

---

[103]Op. cit., p. 107.
[104]*Evolution créatrice*, p. 270.
[105]Published in *Etudes* 2 February 1912.
[106]Vedi Parodi, op. cit. p. 194.

direct dependence on Bergson leads to what I would call an almost pragmatic consideration of dogma in which a purely practical value is attributed to the rational element of faith[107] (and *Péguy* also refers to a conception of this kind[108]), a religious vision of life could also be arrived at directly from the doctrine of "élan vital." This is the position of *Chevalier,* for whom the author of Evolution, the great creator of the world and its forms, is God. In *Evolution créatrice* Bergson speaks of a "center from which worlds would spring like fireworks from an immense bouquet." But for him this center is not "a thing . . . but a continuous outpouring. God, thus defined, has nothing ready-made; he is incessant action, freedom."[109] It is with this dynamic and mobile God that Chevalier tries to reconnect.[110] But all transcendence presupposes dualism, and the positing of a principle outside ourselves that is eternal and in essence immutable — so that even if this principle is "durée" and mobility, it will be, in a way, a hypostatized duration, no longer flowing in the intimacy of things, but known as external, and therefore, with respect to these things, static. And this is what Chevalier's God comes down to — not so much a movement as an actual principle.

Bergson, he says, posits "an unbridgeable abyss between matter and life, between animal and man — unbridgeable, except by the creator." And so the creator is no longer life itself but intervenes from outside to unite life and matter. And intuition will then be the knowledge of this mystical and absolute creator.

Chevalier's intuitionism and therefore aesthetics thus turn towards a conception that moves art close to God, that posits it as knowledge of the absolute. But this immediately raises the question of matter. How to justify the use of the forms and means of the senses to express what is beyond them? Chevalier, who has a refined artistic awareness, feels the impossibility of making a distinction between form and material in works of art, and indeed sees how in such works the representative element is everything,

---

[107]See "Le miracle" and "Le concept de Dieu" in *Annales de phil. chr.*
[108]See "Note sur Mr Bergson," *Œuvres* (Paris, N.R.F., 1924).
[109]*Evolution créatrice,* p. 270 (vol. IX).
[110]J. Chevalier, *Bergson* (Paris: Plon, 1926).

and he therefore seeks to save sensory expression by posing it as a necessary obstacle to the development of the idea, as a means of liberation, as the "vehicle" of the mind.[111] But he is then always obliged to place matter as an inferior element, and after having affirmed that "art is born of a union and close interpenetration of matter and form," he then comes out with the naive statement that this union expresses itself in "the subordination of matter to form."[112] As if the subordination of one principle to another were the perfect sort of union. And indeed, matter is seen as the cause of imperfection, so that artistic expression will never be adequate to the ideal reality of its subject.

But this inadequacy and imperfection is dear to Chevalier, and what humanity there is in a work of art tending towards the divine moves him and seems to him to constitute the greatness of art. Thus instead of Greek art, perfect in its completeness, he prefers the unfulfilled striving for perfection inherent (according to him, of course) in medieval art.

But this takes us beyond the field of Bergsonism. It should only be noted that this contrast between the sensory and super-sensory, carried into another field, is the what upsets Bergson about the inexpressability of intuition and its relationship with language.

In any case, this religious and mystical interpretation marks the last stop in Bergsonian thought. It can teach us once again what a desire to take a principle of individual knowledge into nature and the absolute leads to, if by means of these degenerations, as they might be called from a certain point of view, we have had the opportunity to perceive the vastness of Bergson's thought and the richness of its development. Nevertheless we should perhaps go back to his initial teaching, where the immediacy and individuality of his first theory of knowledge gave us a glimpse of the truly new message that Henri Bergson was able to offer the world.

---

[111]*In Art vivant* (1928) p. 579.
[112]*In Art vivant* (1928) p. 622.

The Aesthetics of Benedetto Croce. A Critical Study"[113] ("La Cultura"
Publishers, 1932).

PREFACE

*In some ways talking about an author is talking about oneself. All
the more in the case of Croce, who has given the entire Italian world a
basic set of concepts and definitions that is by now part of the substrate
of the culture, and whether you accept or reject it, it is impossible not to
take it into account and make use of it. What has been written about
him has in most cases emerged as an examination of conscience, stemming from the need to come to terms with something that makes up an
integral part of our own personality, and to establish what parts of it
should be kept and strengthened as essential for further progress. And
at the same time, many examinations of conscience take the form of
writings about him, or else draw on his formulations of problems and,
I would say, his terminology of the mind.*

*This booklet is not intended as either a defense or a refutation,
but rather an investigation seeking to capture and extract the living
elements provided by Crocean thought and to eliminate what is superstructure. It is an attempt to create possibilities for work that draw
sustenance from its spirit, while not accepting some of its formulations and its systematic organization. The rejection of the latter is not
at all an admission of the general possibility of isolated data without
a system of their own, but only an assertion that Croce's system is
extraneous to his most vital data and derives from other improperly
superimposed requirements of his thinking.*

*In Croceanism, what lies beneath the exterior organization is the
real system, not yet clear and formulated, but agile and rich with multiple possibilities. Looking for this richness under a largely dissatisfying
framework is the task at hand for whoever experiences his thought as
part of their own life. And following the possibilities it offers for contin-
uation and development even beyond the form it has given to itself is I
think the highest tribute that can be paid to a philosophy.*

— E. C.

---

[113]To the memory of Enrico Sereni.

I. Preliminaries on the Method

It is safe to say that the considerable competence in aesthetics acquired by Italian culture in the last thirty years has served to delay rather than hasten the solution to the problem it poses. As always, the questions that provide the most data are the most difficult and intricate to resolve. On the other hand, the high level of maturity that has by now been reached works to promote an urge to arrive at a synthesis quickly, so that anyone with well-honed tools, in a rush to build the edifice, in most cases manages only individual annotations, interesting and lively perhaps, but partial and insufficient. We therefore find ourselves facing numerous manifestations, tendencies and movements, valid mostly as indications of directions to follow and ideas not to be overlooked — an ensemble of data with no unitary justification.

Benedetto Croce, who was the first to stimulate this movement and who set out with a clear and precise definition of art, has never failed to follow the developments it brought about, the conflicts it aroused, or the innovations that have arisen alongside it or opposed it. He has always sought to take everything into account; enlarging, modifying, and clarifying his points of view with such sensitivity to the new thinking in the field and with such a desire for completeness, that his work, in addition to being an edifice of thought continually under construction, could almost serve as a reflection of all the lines of inquiry that, whether following his own impulses or others, have developed in Italy. Hence its great interest but also the danger of not achieving true unity — because the newly introduced concepts and new requirements do not always fit with the previous ones or with the system they are meant to be grafted onto. And Croce, who does on occasion explicitly abandon his old positions, sometimes aspires to present these new developments as a confirmation or at least an extension of what he had stated previously. This way what seems at first sight a unitary and well-conceived system turns out to be less rigorous in its linkages, although richer in its variety of data. And it appears as a great collection of notes, precious observations, aspects of truth illuminated, prejudices removed, problems more clearly formulated, and experiences of life brought together in a curriculum vitae that can be considered exemplary, if it is true that for Croce living has always meant (as it must) continuous philosophizing.

Our purpose here is to sort through these multiple truths, to analyze the true and the obsolete aspects of the various superimposed doctrines — or as Croce would put it, what is alive and what is dead — and to put these data explicitly in mutual contact, raising in this way the issue of their coherence and conciliation. If the possibility of a solution and a unitary panorama were to emerge from these juxtapositions, it would mean that the aesthetic question had reached a certain maturity, and that we have nearly reached the point when we can draw conclusions.

It should be noted immediately, however, that this multiplicity of data, this pluralism inherent in Croce's investigative practices, if in contrast on one hand with the organic and systematic requirements he absorbed from idealist philosophy, corresponds perfectly on the other to the *transcendental empiricism* intrinsic to his doctrine of history and his basic concept of philosophy. Framing aesthetics in a system deduced from *a priori* principles and following inevitably from a determined series of premises is necessary only for someone who has a corresponding conception of all of reality and only sees the world as the deductive or dialectic development of initial positions. In such a case, art is one of the essential forms by which these principles unfold, an ever-repeating aspect of the process whereby the universal becomes particular and manifests itself in the world. But anyone who begins with the world itself and, by making all its data eternal and universal, seeks to build a science of the possible forms of this universalization and from there arrive at an overall vision of the eternal modes of reality and their reciprocal reactions — does not posit the system at the outset, as the premise of their research, but arrives there at the ideal end of the journey, when connections, relationships, and mutual links can be tested once again. This way, rather than forcing a multiple reality into a presupposed and determined coherence, we can observe such coherence in the things themselves, so that the logical justification will be almost a proof of the truth and universality of what is observed.

Thus Croce does not want to introduce any new factors into his dialectic of mental forms, unless he has repeatedly ascertained and tested their reality and autonomy in the life of the mind.

It is true that in this construction of an organism of relations we may note a certain pressure exerted on particular observations by the taste for the symmetry of the whole. But this is not his intention. And in any case, if by system Croce means the organization of elements of the mind according to the dialectic of distinct forms it can be said that this dialectic aims more than anything else (not that it always succeeds) to be the end result of a complex of observations — that it comes last in the ideal succession of ideas and concepts that this philosophy consists of, and instead of being a premise, is a consequence. Croce does not use *ex professo* facts deduced *a priori* from the dialectic to demonstrate his assumptions of transcendental psychology. If this happens at times, it is done unconsciously and without a precise purpose, by accident we would say, in moments of the least explanatory vigor, and it leads precisely to those formulations that we believe to be weakest points of his theories.

This ideal posteriority of the organized system with respect to the concrete and psychological observation of the facts and processes of the mind, allows the reader great critical latitude and the possibility of partial acceptance. Croce's work (even limited to the area of pure theory, leaving aside his critical and historical works) is a collection of observations that it would be ridiculous to reject in their entirety simply because some data are disallowed. And this is precisely where its richness lies — not being constrained *a priori* by a necessary deduction that every detail has to conform to allows it to draw liberally on the multiple truths it suggests and sustains, with the option of excluding others or denying the final system in which they are organized. This system is reduced to a sometimes extrinsic attempt to unify the facts and mental attitudes that have been described.

It was quite natural that this method should be branded — as indeed it was — as empiricist and naturalist. But terms as vague as this should not be used to define such a particular and determined form of thought. And it is obvious that — even if the epistemological premises of Croceanism might perhaps be reduced to a form of idealist empiricism, with the English school of the 18th century, Locke,

Berkeley and Hume, as a starting point — one fundamental feature of naturalism is completely absent, and that is the transcendence of the object with respect to the subject. In fact, there is no guarantee that the historical, psychological data that Croce starts with are an external rather than mental reality, that the multiplicity at the base of his investigation is imposed from the outside and submitted to by the mind through a mysterious and unimaginable influx. Multiplicity does not necessarily mean naturalistic transcendence. "As for me," he says, "I confess that what has always aroused my interest is the moment of singularity. . . . I consider that the philosophical problems that have agitated people all come down to problems of transcendental psychology or philosophy of the mind. . . . There is no enigma but the infinite riddles of reality."[114] But does this psychological observation, this thought for the particular, really necessarily mean that the particular is detached from thought? Couldn't it be understood as being at one with it, a particular that is not really such except when it is known (i.e., universalized), an object that does not exist without the subject?

It is not true that to start from a single datum conjured in the mind — that is, from the presence in thought of a given content, is to imagine this content beyond thought. It only means that thought is not thought unless it is detected, and that it is inseparable from and at one with its content. Idealism does not begin and end in the position of a pure and separate self-consciousness. There is consciousness of the subject, or of thought, or of the ego, only insofar as it lives and acts — that is, is in complete unity with the object, the content, or the non-ego. And to make this non-ego emerge from the ego itself is to introduce it in an ideally posterior moment, thus supposing the primitive existence of the abstract subject.

In Croce, on the other hand, the subject is not seen in any way other than in its connection with the object. This does not take away its universality, but gives it that particularity which cannot be detached from it: "There is no doubt as to the necessity of the system:[115]

---

[114]*Conversazioni critiche* (Bari, 1918) p. 72–73.
[115]It goes without saying that here Croce is not alluding to the system in the extrinsic sense in which he spoke about it above, regarding the dialectic of distinct forms. System is for

to think is to systematize: even a very small, a very particular philosophical problem cannot be resolved if not in the totality, by systematizing. But what is the material that is systematized — that is thought
of, in other words? History. Every philosophical proposition (every
thought) is the answer to a historically determined question."[116]

Now, this history (like any object of thought) is not, except abstractly, "material" (and in our citation the term is used in a metaphorical sense), and indeed through its necessary union with the
universal, Croce would like to remove any character it may have as
a thing in itself. "The merely finite and particular do not exist other
than in abstraction. . . . There is no fact, however small it may be said
to be, that can be conceived (realized and qualified) in any other way
than as universal.[117] And concerning "those brute and disconnected
facts from which causal research claims to take its cue, . . . methodical
doubt suggests above all the thought that those facts are an *unproven
presupposition* . . . and putting them to the test will lead us, finally, to
the conclusion that *those facts, really, do not exist.*"[118]

In short, Croce's individualism is not necessarily in contrast
with his idealism. Indeed, it resolves the principle of self-awareness
— which is essential to idealism — into an awareness of thought in
the effectual of its thinking. It identifies the subjective starting point
with its necessary objective correlate, the universal with the particular. In this sense it is rather close to forms of contingentism and em-
pirio-criticism, and in this sense his keeping to the *data* and starting
from it is justifiable — since this data can only be understood as a
state of mind, an experience that must be lived intensely, and from
which from time to time the absolute must be drawn.

Thus philosophy proper can be identified with historiography or
awareness of the individual in the universal, and the science of the
mind can be expressed in the study of the forms, modes, and different aspects assumed by this activity. "Philosophy provides neither
the transcendent conception nor the ultimate truth. It is immanent

---

him synonymous here with universality.
[116]*Eternità e storicità della filosofia* (Rieti, 1930) p. 9.
[117]*Teoria e storia della storiografia* (Bari, 1920) p. 49.
[118]Ibid., p. 61.

experience and consists of investigations concerning the categories of experience, ideas or values, as we now like to call them, or in other words the mind in its forms and in the dialectical unity of its forms." "The categories are like the tools matter is made with, which get worn out from use. . . . And . . . just as tools are not real tools if not in the work they are made for and which wears them out, so philosophy is not real and concrete if not in experience and for experience, or, to use a broader term for it, in history."[119]

Art, philosophy, economics and morality are for him essential, eternal forms in which the mental — and therefore real — process can and does effectively unfold. They are forms experienced and recognized as autonomous in that exact same process, in life lived in a universal way — which represent a type, an eternal and irrepressible way of being of life, but which all have life itself and its universal individuality as their common ground. We will have occasion later to criticize some of the specifications of these forms, their connections, perhaps even their autonomous validity (and indeed the main part of our study will concern this). But once having recognized that their basis is the above-mentioned form of experience, it will be necessary either to deny this basis, or to accept it and presuppose it as a premise for criticism — to make use, that is, of the same universal experience — or individual judgment — to refute certain findings, demonstrate the partiality or lack of autonomy of certain concepts, etc.

That Croce reached an awareness of these necessary epistemological premises to his aesthetic, logical, political and moral theories is clear mainly in his latest writings, after the publication of the *Teoria e Storia della Storiografia* [*Theory and History of Historiography*]. In these he substantially modifies the concept of the individual that he had introduced in the first three volumes of the *Filosofia dello Spirito* [*Philosophy of Spirit*]: "The new universal is the actual relation between universal and individual, the concrete universal. In this regard, poetry is no longer theorized as the representation of the individual, in contrast to philosophy, which is the contemplation of the universal; because, given the concept of the concrete universal, poetry is not without the universal, nor is philosophy without the individu-

---

[119]"Punti di orientamento della filosofia moderna," *Critica* (1926): p. 922–29.

al — philosophy is always historically individualized. It is therefore theorized as the lack of distinction between individual and universal which thought in turn mediates — that is, distinguishes and unifies at the same time, converting the world of fantasy and poetry into the world of philosophy and history. Similarly, the spheres of the passions and of utility are no longer theorized as the sphere of individuality versus the moral sphere, which is that of universality, because universality is not absent in the former nor individuality in the latter. What is theorized rather is the sphere of practical naivety, in which the interests of the individual and those of the universal are indistinct, and into which moral necessity introduces its leaven, and, by means of its dialectic, by opposing the universal to the individual and filling the latter with the former, molds it into a new form."[120]

The difficulties that the dialectic of distinct forms finds itself in, given these new positions, is a problem that will be taken up later. Here it is worth noting only how in these latest formulations of Croce's (the passage cited is from 1928) there is a clear awareness of the absolute validity of the individualistic principle in every attitude of the mind. This will therefore have to be the point of view for examining all his work. But the fact that he arrived there so late, and that this has been virtually his most recent philosophical discovery brings disadvantages and imbalances for the doctrine as a whole, and mainly leads to the grafting of other conflicting directions of thought onto what was the instinctive Crocean methodology and to an insufficient demonstration of the very epistemological premises that should have been there to substantiate the method.

In Croce the primitive concept of the ideality of the real, which he arrived at at the beginning of his career as a thinker, and which would later permit his historicist and pluralist methodology to avoid the danger of falling into empiricism of a positivist brand, is at first closely linked with motives of absolute idealism. The recognition of the essential mental quality inherent in every known fact, and mainly the fight against the dominant naturalism that denied it, the consequent alliance with the Hegelian movement (to which his first philosophical ventures had been extraneous) —

---

[120]*Eternità*, cit., p. 68–69.

the cultural situation, in short, in which he found himself and in which the conquest of the ideality of reality was the first point to be promoted and spread, led him in that period to use, perhaps incautiously, formulas that only generically corresponded to his own philosophical orientation. The ambiguity of the word *idealism* (a term that is too comprehensive, able to include countless meanings) led him to include in his doctrine a preponderance of themes from the particular form of idealism that was still a firmly rooted tradition in Italy at the end of the century. And these themes were paramount for him in the most decisive years of his philosophical activity — it was only the controversy with Giovanni Gentile that pushed him to renounce them explicitly. This explains how so many elements of that mindset and culture found their way into his work and gave it their own generic flavor, and how many problems initially formulated in terms drawn from that context had such a hard time freeing themselves from it. And at the same time, if at first they seemed unsuitable and discordant in relation to that idealist form, eliminating it impoverished them and made them appear imprecise and tentative.

One might therefore say that a weak point of Croce's is the discrepancy between his spirit as a tireless experimenter and the need for *a priori* deduction that he inherited from absolute idealist philosophy. This meant that his attitude, which we consider at least tendentially post-idealist, had its wings clipped by the violence that idealism itself imposed on him. Possessing a system that was already well thought out and organized, idealism tends to attract into its orbit many movements that are related but distinct from it, and to reduce to absurdity the efforts of those trying to detach themselves. But such attempts, chaotic as they are, often represent a new need that should not be repressed.

Now, one of the points that can be most misleading regarding Croce's alleged idealism is precisely the identification of history with philosophy that he seems to have in common with the entire Hegelian school,[121] and which has contributed to his being crudely

---

[121]See also Croce, "Un cercle vicieux dans la critique de la philosophie hégelienne," *Revue de métaphysique et de morale* 38 (1931): p. 281–84.

judged as belonging to it. On the contrary, it is very clear that that identification, which in Croce is a reduction (so to speak) of philosophy to history, in Hegelianism is instead a reduction of history to philosophy. In this regard we might repeat what we have said about relations between the universal and the particular and about the original, non-deduced character the moment of particularity has for Croce, inherent in and inseparable from the universal. And this is nothing but the same problem expressed in another form. In both doctrines history has no meaning except when it is *thought of* — but while for Hegelism it is identified with the dialectical process of the mind, and like every mental movement, proceeds by thesis antithesis and synthesis and deducing the particular from this process, for Croce on the other hand, history is the utmost concreteness and particularity and — we would say — contingency. For Hegelian idealism, a universal first and a history that follows from it by necessary deduction. For Croce, a history that itself becomes universal time after time. The term *history* itself, in this sense, is nothing but a generic name for *what happens,* the actual *fact* which, as such, cannot help but be a fact of the mind.

But, we repeat, Croce didn't arrive at such an explicitly idealistic doctrine until the *Teoria e Storia della Storiografia* [*Theory and History of Historiography*], in 1915. And in all his previous development, from the first essay of 1893 on, there is an effort to make a place for history in the life of the mind. Reduced at first under the general concept of art, then identified, in the *Logica* [*Logic*], with philosophy, and returned afterwards to an unclear position involving both elements,[122] history in any case is at this stage a particular aspect of the mind identified with one of the terms of the dialectic of the distinct, and is not yet, as it would later appear (and particularly in the passage of 1928 quoted above), almost a generic substratum of every form of apprehension of reality, a participant — as the

---

[122]Cf. *Saggio sullo Hegel* (Bari, 1926) p. 88: "History, unlike art, presupposes philosophical thought as its condition; but, like art, it has the intuitive element as its material. Therefore history is always narration and never theory and system, although it has theory and system in its background." Cf. also *Filosofia della pratica* (Bari, 1923) p. 169: "History or historical narrative . . . unlike the abstract sciences, has a close kinship with art, for neither art nor history constructs class concepts, but both offer concrete and individualized representations."

union of universal and particular — in art as well as in philosophy.

The concept of history, in other words, which is fundamental in Crocean methodology, fits badly with the dialect of distinct forms and ends up dissolving it. We will not speak of this issue here, but will limit ourselves to some methodological considerations in dealing with the aesthetic problem. We will only note, as an example of the persistence of idealist schemata in Crocean thought, that the generic concept of the dialectic itself, taken from idealism, is not intrinsic — indeed it sometimes contrasts with the transcendental empiricism or historicism that underlies its philosophical procedures.

It is well known that Croce introduces, next to the Hegelian dialectic of opposites, a dialectic of distinct forms, unfolding through a mutual implication and sublation of those forms that he considers essential and eternal in the mental constitution of reality. But it is evident that while the dialectic of distinct forms has its own original elements, even its structure and the concepts of implication and sublation that act in it are analogous to and derived from the dialectic of opposites. Now such concepts correspond precisely to that form of idealism which has been seen to belong outwardly to Croce.

The Hegelian concept of the dialectic, or synthesis of opposites, is certainly closely connected with the process by which Fichte deduces an object from a primitive subject, and it is clear in any case that if the concept of the unity of opposites and the impossibility of isolating two terms of a relation is characteristic of Crocean individualism, it is not intrinsic to it to conceive of this unity as a process of the development of one contrary from the other. In Hegel the moment is essential when thought is torn "from that universality and from that satisfaction that it has found only in itself,"[123] and it is pushed *to develop by moving out of itself.* And Croce himself affirms that this is what happens in Hegel's dialectic: "The negative is the mainspring of the process: the opposition is the very soul of the real."[124] But just why, by what force or principle this mutual entailment of opposites should present itself almost as the generation of one by the other, is difficult to under-

[123]Hegel, *Enciclopedia,* § 12 (trans. Croce).
[124]*Saggio sullo Hegel,* p. 39.

stand. Why must we say that the Non-self, which is by its own definition inseparable from the Self, *flows, unfolds, originates* from it? That the particular *is born* from the universal?[125]

The particular (and this will be Croce's actual thesis) is implicit in the universal from the moment the universal is conceived — due to its very structure. And this does not at all mean that the universal *contradicts* itself or *particularizes* itself. The principle of the dialectic as unfolding and overcoming derives from needs of a completely different type from Croce's — that is, from the necessity of deducing the entire world in its empirical development from a single subjective principle. But in Croce — who denies that derivation and holds fast to the concrete, rejecting Hegel's concept of history as development over time of the Idea — one does not see how that concept is indispensable. And yet he welcomes it and involves it and bases numerous developments on it — more out of a generic spirit of consensus with its contents and with the mental tone it introduces than because of any real epistemological requirement of his thought. In Hegel it is the basis of everything, and without it his idealism itself as an *a priori* deduction of the world would not be conceivable. But in Croce the epistemological premises would hold up even without the dialectic, and the concept of knowledge as an individual or historical judgment does not imply a derivation of the particular from the universal.

The methodological principal behind the Crocean philosophical procedure is quite independent of the dialectic. The latter will constitute a further discovery, perhaps, one of the characterizations of mental reality that have been arrived at through that method — just like all the observations on the character of art, philosophy, economics, and morality. But it cannot figure as a necessary foundation of the concept itself of experience or knowledge. It could be imagined, in short, that Croce's method of psychological transcendental psychology might lead to a vision of the world that dialectics was extraneous to — and it would not for this reason lose its methodological character. For Fichte and Hegel, the first and only fact is Self-awareness, the Concept, which without a dialec-

---

[125]Cf. P. Martinetti, "Il metodo dialettico," *Rivista di Filosofia* (1931) p. 4.

tic that allows it to come out of itself, would remain abstract and dead. In Croce, the infinite variety of subjective and self-conscious data allows a varied and mobile vision of reality, even without that support. And in this way dialectics is reduced for him to a fact that proves itself effective in reality. Individual knowledge — history — supplies the data of reality, and these data present themselves, by their nature, as connected by the dialectical bond, in a never ending process of contradiction and sublation. Understood in this new way, however, the dialectic would require a justification quite different from Hegel's, and it would no longer be able to rest entirely on the principle of the necessary deduction of the object by the subject that lay at its base. The concept of the identity or reciprocal entailment of opposites — we repeat — is not enough to justify its progressive and developmental character.

The introduction of this concept taken from idealist philosophy thus creates difficulties and ambiguities for Croce and in this regard makes his doctrine imprecise. He sometimes reintroduces a notion similar to the Hegelian Absolute Mind, saying that "history . . . is . . . the work of that truly real individual which is the eternal mind individualizing itself," that "every adversary is at the same time its subject — that is to say, is one of the aspects of the dialecticism that constitutes its inner being," and that it seeks its explanatory principle "in the process itself, which is born of thought and returns to thought, and is intelligible through the auto-intelligibility of thought, which never needs to appeal to anything external to itself in order to understand itself."[126] Sometimes he instead reaffirms a form of pluralism and almost monadism, even in those cases where the dialectic would seem easier to introduce: "It is not true that men have concentrated upon one philosophical problem only, whose successive solutions, less and less inadequate, compose a single line of progress, the universal history of the human spirit, affording support and unification to all other histories. The opposite is the truth: the philosophical problems that

---

[126]*Teoria e St.d.Stor.*, p. 87. Cf. also *Eternità*, cit., p. 12–13: "The mind is, itself, all of reality, the only reality . . . it is a process of distinction-unification, and therefore of values, and, since distinction generates opposition, it is a process of values and non-values, of acts and facts, of being and non-being, of true and false, good and evil, and so on and so forth."

men have treated of and will treat of are infinite, and each one of them is always particularly and individually determined."[127] We do not mean to say that the two steps cited are contradictory, but certainly they represent two tendencies, two very distinct and contrasting mental tones, which sometimes intertwine and alternate in Croce, demonstrating that the concept of dialectics overlaps with and is not easily assimilated by his individualism. But given that he became aware of this individualism as a philosophical method, as we have seen, when the cycle of his philosophical experience had almost reached a conclusion, the contrast never seemed clear-cut to him, and the dialectic was able to impress itself on his doctrine and perhaps contribute to its construction as a harmonious and symmetrical organism — at the expense, however, of rigor and demonstrative completeness on some points. Thus it will be seen later, particularly with regard to aesthetics, how the distinctions between the essential forms of the mind that he succeeded in clarifying and configuring with a lucidity and acumen that was often conclusive, are organized according to a nexus of sublation of one by the other in a circle, whose demonstration is one of the least convincing aspects of his doctrine.

This observation of the foreignness of the concept of dialectics to the epistemological and methodological basis of Crocean philosophy will allow us to proceed more freely in analyzing his aesthetic doctrine. Having recognized the criterion of universal experience or transcendental psychology[128] not only as the basis of his philosophical conception, but as the active method of his investigative procedure, we can analyze his aesthetics in the light of and under the scrutiny of this method, confident that no dialectical connection and activity can be imposed *a priori* as necessarily linked to it, since the dialectic must in any case be shown to be present just like any other of the characteristics we will be examining. This meth-

---

[127]Ibid., App. II, p. 127. Cf. also *Estetica*, note to the 5th ed. Croce, on the other hand, refers once again to a conception of the history of philosophy as a unitary process in the article cit. *Un cercle vicieux*, p. 281: "The great idea of philosophy's identity with its own history . . . was only really established, put at the center and erected as a principle of interpretation by Hegel, when he represented the philosophies of the past as acts of a unique drama, which is also the very drama that is renewed in the mind of every thinker today."

[128]Cf. the term "absolute positivism" used by Calogero in *Studi crociani* by G. Calogero and D. Petrini (Rieti, 1930) p. 11.

od, favored by Croce, will make it possible to derive the maximum benefit from his work and, once the unacceptable elements have been eliminated, to gather all the aspects of truth and the motives of real life that it offers with such admirable richness.

II. Individual Knowledge, Expression, Language

The difference between the individualist method and the idealist system is shown in Crocean aesthetics through the reciprocal overlapping of two fundamental motives: the search for the essential characteristics of the work of art, and the problem of its function and position in relation to other forms of the mind; its intrinsic description, and the analysis of its meaning; the *semiotics* of the artistic fact and its *collocation*.

The moment one realizes the peculiar physiognomy of the act of aesthetic intuition, the question of its meaning also arises implicitly. The problem posed by aesthetics is not only "what does art look like?" but also "what does art mean? What place does it have in the world of the mind?" And it is clear, given the individualistic method discussed above, that this second problem should be dealt with last, following all the others.

Croce himself has recently declared that the science of art or Aesthetics is alive only in its infinite identifications, as the science not of one but of all "the infinite problems that have arisen and will arise" in the course of its history.[129] And each problem must offer an aspect, an essential side, a fundamental and eternal point of view about this totality that is art; and its function and meaning, its position, should flow from all the work of collection and should coincide with the conclusion of it. Isn't the description of the characteristics of an artistic fact necessary and sufficient to provide a complete picture and thereby distinguish it from the other forms of the mind? A clear awareness of what a work of art is, of how it manifests itself, of the consequences it gives rise to in the mental world of the individual is enough to determine its function at the same time. Its purpose is intrinsic to its characteristics — it is iden-

---

[129]*Aesthetica in nuce*, p. 13–14.

tical to the task assigned to it. Its collocation cannot therefore be determined except by its phenomenology as a whole.

In Croce, on the other hand, the concern to entrust art with a specific task in the life of the mind comes first in order of time and is already present in the pages that open the first *Aesthetics* as well as in his youthful essay "History Brought Under the General Concept of Art." It is safe to say that the definition of art as individual knowledge is the first decisive affirmation that we encounter in his philosophy, and it is precisely its positioning as previous to other characteristics that would be progressively discovered — this premature collocation — that would lend this definition weight in Crocean thought as it developed further, a framing that did not always correspond to the new elements discovered. It would be unconsciously modified in its makeup and meaning such that the difference would be increasingly evident between its descriptive value, so to speak, and the function it serves. For this reason, it will be necessary to attribute to this collocation — as to many other analogous affirmations of Croce — a purely descriptive and semiotic value, to consider it not so much as a definition of the function of art in the world of the mind, as an affirmation of what art is, a description of one of its characteristics.

To say that art is knowledge means first of all (and meant especially in the period when Croce was writing) attributing to it the status of an essential form of the mind, as against the positivism then dominant, and consequently hedonism and sensualism, or utilitarianism and aesthetic moralism. It meant the return to a more serious notion of art and the need to consider it an irrepressible phase of the mind. "Against all that [positivism and evolutionism] I . . . asserted and disseminated the idea that art is knowledge and not a hazy point and obscure vibration of pleasure and profit; it is an original and irreplaceable form of *knowledge,* individual knowledge that is in contrast and complement to conceptual knowledge."[130]

The identification "art — individual knowledge," in short, originally had a character that was much more generic than specific — and mainly pointed to the need for a more intrinsic consideration of the artistic fact and for the attribution of greater importance to it.

---

[130]*Primi saggi* (Bari, 1927)" Pref., p. X.

Just as, for example, the passionate nature of art and its sentimental and affective or perhaps sensual value as affirmed by *Sturm und Drang* and early Romanticism meant, in the face of abstractness and neoclassical precepts, the return of aesthetic values to the center of the individual and the human personality, and, in essence, a more autonomous consideration of them.

The essay "History Brought Under the General Concept of Art," with its attribution of a clearly cognitive position to the artistic fact and the identification of it with history, resolutely positions art as a true form of representation of reality, and is of interest not only for its position concerning aesthetics, but for the general philosophical position represented. Because by bringing art and history together, it indicates clearly how knowledge is conceived in early Croce — as immediate, specific, individual apprehension. This is intuitive and not apriorist knowledge.

In *Aesthetics* (1901), the definition of art as intuition or the first level of knowledge is closely linked to the firmly maintained identity of intuition with expression. That this is the fundamental thesis of the book is also signaled in the title, and there is no doubt that — whatever its origins and its derivations, from Vico or from Romanticism, from de Sanctis or from the European critical currents of the 19th century — it has been happily set and formulated in a decisive way by Croce, so that for us it now represents an indisputable point and an essential aspect of the identity of form and content. This is a fundamental conquest of idealism, and one which Italian thought, from de Sanctis to Croce, has demonstrated most clearly with regard to the artistic fact.

The fact that in art there is no difference between the experience of an emotion and the words — or the signs, notes, gestures or what have you — that express it; that the process of passing from an initial and unexpressed impulse to its concrete and developed manifestation is not mechanical and external, but is instead the actual development of the work of art in its formation and in its genesis as a complete entity; that what is said to be ineffable or inexpressible is not true intuition, but rather an initial stimulus towards it; that expression should not be understood as only verbal, nor restricted to what is represented by the traditional divisions of the arts, but includes all the infinite ways an artistic emotion can be manifested — each different from the others even if they belong to the same empirical category — which are an intrinsic aspect of the emotion itself, and inconceivable outside it; these are all concepts that, after Croce, we have a clear awareness of, a rigorous, exact and definitive formulation. It seems therefore incontestable that such identity is valid for art, which is completely invested in it.

But that it should be valid *only for art* and is a characteristic peculiar to it such as to distinguish it from other forms of the mind is a rather more arguable proposition. The affirmation of equivalence must be accepted only in a general sense, analogous to how we consider the Crocean definition of art as knowledge. It is an indication that it belongs to the essential forms of the mind, proof that it is an original activity, independent of others. Art is the unity of form and content (that is, individual and universal). It is identical with its expression — that is, not only does it not require that this comes to it from the outside, but including it gives art a value in itself that can support itself autonomously. It has no purpose outside itself and is not subservient to other activities. It is complete in itself, needing no assistance. Art therefore (or artistic expression, which is the same thing) belongs to the world of the mind as an original element — it is a *category*.

This does not yet demonstrate, however, that it has a place of its own in the mind, along with a function that separates it from the other forms. The specifications we spoke of earlier take away any possibility of its being ancillary to other activities or turned to their purposes, functioning indirectly, with conventional forms not its own. These determinations show that in art we immediately tap into a value of the mind. But in order to be sure that this value is well circumscribed and distinct, and that it does not resolve itself into any other of the essential modes in which the mind behaves, it would be necessary to show that these characteristics do not belong to any of these other modes. Otherwise the mental nature of art will indeed have been established, but not its autonomy. It is certain that it is not part of, or an instrument of other activities, but it is not certain that it cannot be identified with them.

Now, the autonomy of art is one of the points that Croce would never abandon throughout the course of his work, and it is surely the idea he would least like to give up in the field of aesthetics. But we can say that, having based it earlier on the characteristics we have seen, he would hold onto it thereafter even when these characteristics, having changed with further developments in thought, melted away in his hands and were shown to belong to other forms as well. And having thus lost its original support, it would need other justifications in order to remain valid. Now we propose to criticize the original Crocean justification for autonomy[131] and to show how the path followed and the recent conclusions Croce has reached lead to the disintegration of his bases. It may be possible in this way to put our hands on the origin of the difficulties and ambiguities that his doctrine, as a whole, gives rise to.

We have said that the primitive definition of art as expression is analogous to, and closely connected to that of individual knowledge, and we can add that this collocation relied on the as yet unclear notion that Croce had of the act of knowing and of the relations between the individual and the universal. We know that he would only arrive at that notion much later, following his meditations on the concept of history and its relationship to philosophy. Here the individual is understood as intrinsic to the universal and necessary to its apprehension and manifestation, but is not yet one with it and inseparable from its actual formation. The individual, in the first *Aesthetics,* is still, however you look at it, something that is added, grafted, applied to the universal, but is not an inseparable part of it. "If we have shown that the aesthetic form is altogether independent of the intellectual and suffices to itself without external support, we have not said that the intellectual can stand without the aesthetic. To describe the independence as *reciprocal* would not be true. . . . What is knowledge by concepts? It is knowledge of the relations of things, and things are intuitions. Concepts are not possible without intuitions, just as intuition is itself impossible without the matter of impressions."[132] Intuition is thus *a first de-*

---

[131] It should be understood that we do not wish to criticize the need itself for the autonomy of art, which we all feel is very strong, but only the formulation Croce has given it here.

[132] *Estetica,* 1ª ed. (Palermo: Sandron, 1902) p. 25.

gree of knowledge, through which we can pass to the concept. The concept, which gives us the Universal, Mind, or — as Croce very improperly says — the Noumeno, needs phenomenal perceptible intuition in order to actualize itself, express itself, be knowable.

But the reverse does not happen. Crocean intuition, unlike Kantian, has "excellent eyes of its own" and its own perfect independence and autonomy. But independence, in the world of the mind, implies — indeed, is synonymous with — universality. And even in this early Croce, intuition, art, is undoubtedly universal — for the eternal nature of its value, and the possibility of its being unanimously understood and welcomed and appreciated.

Now in what sense are we to understand this universality or mental nature or *form* that belongs to art, without which it would have no real value in the world of the mind? And how is it to be reconciled with the individuality that should be a part of intuition as the presupposition of logical knowledge? It is not possible to speak of pure individuality in connection with an activity that is in its essence *formal* — that is, which has been freed of every singular particularity by the universality of the Subject. And by individual, in the proper sense, we can only mean what is closely connected, indeed identical, with the universal. Just as the concept has its own aspect of individuality which is intrinsic to it and which it gets not from a different form but from its own essence, so intuition cannot function as a simple bearer of the individual element; this function would take away from it the independent and original value that it actually has, and would turn it into a part, an only abstractly separable instance of some other activity. If it is true that the universal aspect cannot do without an individual dimension (which no one wants to deny), what is the point of introducing a specific activity that has individuality as its distinctive character? This activity will either be individual in the worst sense of the word — that is, it will not contain anything that allows it to overcome its individuality and thus cannot even be called an activity since anything that is not *formed* and hasn't got within it the germ of universality is passive and not active. Or else it will contain this universality — and in that case what will distinguish it from the form that sublates it? What difference is there in substance between an activity that is universal but also individual and one that is individual but also universal? Nothing but a difference in tone; nothing that can be defined with precision.

This doctrine of Croce's undoubtedly has the great merit, in the field of epistemology and methodology, of affirming the concreteness of the concept, its inability to maintain itself in a sphere of abstract and inexpressible universality, and the need provide itself with a body. But it is arbitrary to suggest the individual aspect of the logical concept as a point of contact with art rather than as something intrinsic. Art cannot belong to it as an ingredient. It itself, like every form of the mind, is a synthesis or unity of the individual and the universal, in which neither of the two aspects can, without abstraction, be isolated. Indeed, because of this characteristic that it has, there is nothing about it that is different from conceptual knowledge, which is both sensory and mental. And if it were not for other differentiating criteria, there would be nothing left but to identify it with that form.

Similar to this exchange between the individual aspect, which art undoubtedly holds within itself, and an alleged *specifically* individual function, is the exchange between its identification with its own expression and its alleged resolution into a function *specifically* expressing the acts of the mind. "The first degree is the expression, the second is the concept: the first can stand without the second, but the second cannot stand without the first. There is poetry without prose, but not prose without poetry. Expression, indeed, is the first affirmation of human activity. Poetry is the mother tongue of the human race; the first men 'were by nature sublime poets.'"[133]

---

[133] *Est.*,[1] p. 29. Croce takes up this concept again writing very recently in *Critica* (1932) p. 78: "This *artistic side*, this beauty of exposition which distinguishes a fresh book on mathematics from a mechanical compilation, is not so much mathematics as it is fantasy and poetry, because the mathematician does not exist in concrete terms except as a whole person, and when he opens his mouth to speak, he speaks — this seems clear to me — as someone who speaks and not yet or not only as someone who mathematizes, and he puts into his speech the joy of invention, the rejoicing of the light that has shone into his soul, the love of his work — and his words and the rhythm of the words represent vividly what he feels." Here it should be noted that it is not at all true that "speaking" is excluded from pure "mathematizing" and belongs only to fantasy and poetry. And as for the description Croce gives here of the artistic emotion felt by the mathematician, it is notable that the words he uses, "joy, rejoicing, drama of research, love" represent feelings rather more passionate than the

Now, the fact that every activity, every mental form, needs to be expressed, that "thought cannot exist without words" is absolutely indisputable. What is disputed is that it uses artistic expression for this purpose, and that "every work of science *is* at the same time a work of art." It seems, in fact, that this identification with expression that Croce makes characteristic of a work of art — so that other forms would remain tied to it by this aspect — ought instead to be considered as belonging to the other forms in the same way as to art. Art is indeed expression, that is, but aesthetic expression, in the same way that philosophy is conceptual expression and action practical expression. This is the only way to eliminate the involvement and concomitance of art with every manifestation of the mind, which is so obscure and difficult to accept.

Even if we didn't have the example of daily experience to help us, which shows how artistic expression is completely distinct from logical expression and how the form of a line of reasoning is intrinsically — and not only because of its content — different from that of a poem or a novel, the sterility of this concomitance would be plain from the consideration that art, like logic, is a formal activity, in the sense that its process involves the sublation of any immediate data presupposed for it. If in that case one were to suppose that logical activity, devoid of expression on its own, for this reason avails itself of artistic activity, one would have to concede that art, at the moment when it expresses logical content, transfigures it and reduces it, inasmuch as it is logical, to matter — that is, to nothing. And then what we have before us is no longer logic, but art — and only as art can we enjoy and relive it.

We cannot relive the logical process underlying this artistic experience except by disregarding art and going back from here to the content that inspired it. But then, for what purpose is this content clothed in artistic form if to reach its true essence we must free it from that form and treat it as if it had not been applied to it?

Here again we see, therefore, that when art is considered as an independent and autonomous activity — as *form,* that is, it remains identical with expression, but this is not something that it

---

"serenity of contemplation" which he himself, a few pages later, attributes to art.

can lend or apply to other activities. Art is *artistic* expression, and cannot serve as expression for logic unless it takes away all its logical validity and transforms it totally into art. And even as logic it is identical to its expression. As in the case of individuality, expression is intrinsic to it and is not drawn from any other form.

Assuming that art differs from knowledge by the very conformation of its universality (and we do not want to go into this distinction now, since we are only offering a critique of Croce), it is evident that logical expression will differ substantially from artistic expression. And in fact could we not perhaps say that the framework itself of an argument (which is its truest expression) lives a life that is quite different from the phrases, the images, the metaphors that sometimes accompany it? That the central element of its expression is not so much the sentence or group of words, or the verbal arrangement, as a certain composition and organization and succession of developments such that its content can be clearly grasped?

Compared to the emotion and the permanent value of a work of art, some secondary elements, so to speak, of expression can be considered almost irrelevant — such as, for example, the mode of representation in the case of stage works, or the performance in musical works. These are elements that nevertheless are not to be excluded from art and that strictly speaking enter into the expression of the work. But common poetic sensibility easily isolates from them the essential emotion, regarding it as a separate and independent whole, and if anything offering them a separate artistic judgment.

In the same way, if less obviously, the basic expression of logical thought is extraneous to and can be isolated from the aesthetic expression that so often accompanies it. And aesthetic expression does not even mean verbal expression — even logical thought is fundamentally expressed in words. But many problems of arrangement, of relations, of emphasis in the words, which might interest art, are foreign and irrelevant to the emotion of logical knowledge. They accompany it, but are not intrinsic to it, and constitute a field in which it has no jurisdiction. It can be said that the poetic images that accompany *De Rerum Natura* are accessory to the speculative core of the work, just as the artistic value of the performance is accessory to a Molière play or a Beethoven symphony, even if they are performed by the author. The expression of logic has its own rhythm, its own play of relationships and connections and dispositions that is necessary and intrinsic to it and that constitutes its essential appeal and gives rise to its particular emotion, which is not *beauty* but *truth*. It is clear that the Platonic universal, for example, if not necessarily connected with the descriptions of environments or characters that accompany it in the dialogues and are admirable even to philosophical laymen, is nevertheless not extraneous to any of the connections of thought from which it arose, to any link, however minimal, in the philosophical development that led to it, or to any dialectical detail that colors and clarifies it. And this precise chain of developments, connections and relations — which perhaps come out of the particular expression of a particular work and relate it to other concepts and other discoveries — all this is the characteristic *expression* of logical thought. It too is expressed in words, just as it can be expressed in other forms, but what it is in the words that provides the aesthetic emotion is foreign to it.

Thus Croce's affirmation is unconvincing that what is well thought out is well written, and that "when we talk of books that are well thought out and badly written, we cannot mean anything but that in such books there are parts, pages, sentences or propositions that are well thought out and well written, and other parts (perhaps the least important) that are badly thought out and badly written — not really thought out and so not really expressed."[134]

Now it is obvious here that by "well written" Croce means "perfectly expressed," — done artistically, that is — and that his proposition is an affirmation that what is clearly seen as true is also beautiful. Whereas, if *expression* were understood not as a grafting of aesthetic activity onto logical thought, but as intrinsic to each logical thought in its own way — just as, indeed, it is inseparable from any aesthetic intuition — one could formulate the proposition in more coherent terms. One might say that a work that is well thought out cannot help but also be well written — if by writing we mean the clarity of the work, i.e. the clear, organic development of concepts and thoughts that make up the argument, the evidence of

---

[134]*Est.*[1] p. 27.

the passages, the fullness of its philosophical insight (which is not, we repeat, abstractly universal, nor for that very reason in itself inexpressible) — but that might be confusingly written or rather *not written* in the terms of the other activity, which might (but is not obliged to) take as its object, in the course of the same work, the very thought that is conceived and expressed therein, and again use it as material to make it universal in a new and different way.

This latter is the form (not necessary, but frequent) in which the thinker, at the moment of thinking about and knowing an object and deriving its consequences, suddenly sees it with new eyes and raises himself above it and makes himself a stranger to it (as to an object of thought) and loves it no longer so much for its dialectical significance and scope and the influences it may have in life, but in another way, for itself, as a great and eternal spectacle from which he asks nothing but the joy of being able to contemplate it. This is the art that arises from thought — not because thought needs it, but because often the person who thinks it does. It is the art that makes us cherish Plato or Schopenhauer for reasons other than their conceptual value. This is true of the work of Croce himself, with its clear and limpid pulse, with that broad epic tone which makes it a masterpiece of our contemporary prose.

It is clear that this separation between artistic expression and logical expression implies an effective separation between art and conceptual knowledge, a separation which we have presupposed, preferring for the moment to accept it as a fact of common awareness rather than enter into an analysis that would have distracted us from the subject at hand. Indeed, the present observations on expression may perhaps shed some light on the nature and basis of this difference. But whatever one may think of it, for our purposes today the arguments serve only to show that the autonomy of art can in no way be based on giving it the character of merely individual knowledge, or of pure expression. By showing that these two concepts are incapable of standing on their own and can only be arbitrarily and abstractly isolated from the universal experience (of whatever kind) that they must be part of, we wanted to emphasize the need for another criterion that justifies the autonomy of art, considering it — like any other mental form — as a unity or synthesis of form and content, of individual and universal, of expression and what is expressed, and which bases the difference on the intrinsic character, on the particular configuration this synthesis has with respect to the others, and on the particular and unique procedure by which it expresses its eternal function.

Croce himself would later modify these early positions, and as he gradually broke away from the formulas of idealism and reached his most original individualism, he succeeded in broadening his concept of art. In one of his most recent pieces, in fact, he notes that the unity of intuition and expression is valid "for all spheres of the mind," art included, giving it in the case of art, however, "an evidence and prominence that it perhaps lacks elsewhere."[135] But these new declarations constitute an element that is disruptive to his system and his doctrine on art. And we have lingered over them because they seem to be the basis not only of an interpretation of the artistic fact, but of the entire organism of Crocean thought and re-direction that he would later be forced to follow, regardless of new requirements in the study of relations among the various activities of the mind.

Deriving immediately from the concept of art as expression is the identification of it with language, which constitutes another of the fundamental theses of the first edition of *Aesthetics*. Here we can only repeat what was said about the previous two, which is that its validity is more general than specific, and that while it opens the way to a deeper and more psychological view of language, it does not succeed in identifying it with the specific mental form that is art. "It seems superfluous to demonstrate that language is expression,"[136] and it certainly is not this that we would refute. But, since it appears to us that expression is identical with every act of the mind, it must follow from that identity that language is one with the mental fact in its broadest sense, and not with any *particular* mental fact. "Language is perpetual creation" as is life itself, and the condemnation of any extrinsic and naturalistic consideration of language is fully acceptable, provided we do not wish to make it a new category in its

---

[135]*Aest. in nuce*, p. 16.
[136]*Est.*[1] p. 143.

own right, to be grafted now and again onto the others.

One of the reasons for the misunderstanding is the use of the term *imagination* which, along with others, is sometimes used as a synonym for art to indicate points of contact between the various forms of the mind — and there is a certain ambiguity in this use because it allows juxtapositions that the term *art,* which is more definite and univocal, would make difficult. We have seen that previously, concerning the expression of logical thought, Croce spoke of works as being "well or badly thought out" and "well or badly written," in which the term "well written," taken in isolation, fit in its verbal form with the interpretation we sought to give it, while in the Crocean context it could only be understood in the meaning of "expressed *artistically.*" Thus, "imagination" is a more generic term than art and, since it does not immediately suggest the idea of aesthetic catharsis, can also be applied without offending any sensibility to arguments that art has nothing to do with.

The presence of an element of imagination in logic should therefore not be the basis for arguing that it is also present in art, when a better definition of the term imagination puts it rather closer to the general meaning of *expression* or *language* than of art. The identification that seemed to exist between expression and whatever mental form it represents — that is, the expansion of the concept of expression to all spheres of the mind — makes us think that the imaginative dimension found in logic constitutes precisely its expressive aspect — it belongs to it as logic, and is not an addition of artistic elements. Logic, insofar as it expresses itself, is language, imagination. But just as there is an expression of logic and an expression of art, in the same way the imagination that belongs to logic has nothing in common with art, and the expression of it does not necessarily have to be in abstract and mathematical terms or in syllogistic form. And even if it were, aren't these also expressions of imagination? Art, we repeat, can graft itself onto logic and give it its form, but it does not do so necessarily, and if and when it does, it cancels logic completely and absorbs it into itself.

Language, imagination, expression, therefore, are identical things that represent the moment of manifestation of each act of the mind, and are indistinguishable from it — an aspect that cannot be isolated without abstraction, and is not autonomous. Indeed, it would be inconceivable if construed in isolation and separated from the vital whole it is connected to. It is therefore not possible that artistic expression is added to every form of the mind. Expression is intrinsic to it as something of its own. And it is not artistic expression, but expression that can be artistic, logical, or practical.

III. Lyricism and Representation

The various definitions of art thus far encountered (individual knowledge, expression, language) do not yet have the power, therefore, to establish its autonomy. They show its mental character, its universality, but they do not say whether and how it is different from other universal attitudes of the mind, whether and how it is distinguishable and recognizable among them. They do, however, serve admirably as premises for what we have called the semiotics of the artistic fact, given the affectionate engagement with his argument that Croce is able to constantly maintain. Indeed, we would say that in his account of the process of art, in characterizing and describing it, he rarely makes mistakes or proposes unacceptable formulas, but he is no longer so satisfying when he seeks to interpret those formulas with regard to the function of art and its meaning.

Its psychological character and inseparability from its own expression are true aspects of artistic emotion, but it is not true that they characterize it as art and determine its function in the world of the mind. Nevertheless, it is precisely this *collocation* that Croce is principally concerned with in the period of the construction of his system, and the desire for harmony and symmetrical development in the various spheres of the mind favors the parallelism that he postulates between practical and theoretical form, creating a correspondence between the dialectic of art and philosophy and the other dialectic of economics and ethics. We will not go into an analysis here of this new concept, which need not occupy us today. We will only note that the critique of the conception of an individual who is autonomous and self-contained even independently of the universal that validates him, applies here just as it did to the

aesthetic problem. With the difference that while in art it is necessary to recognize a universal, an autonomous and eternal form
of the mind, (and therefore the criticism ends up saying that the
characteristic of "individual" is not sufficient to determine it and
that new criteria will be sought to justify its autonomy) in economics on the other hand the universal side is more difficult to
find, and the individuality that distinguishes it is perhaps more an
index of its abstractness and inability to stand on its own.

In any case, it is evident that Croce, more or less unconsciously, felt the separation that remained between the individual and the
universal and the difficulties that this implied, and he tried to resolve the problem with his theory of *concomitance,* showing how
individual forms, although superseded by universal forms, do not
detach themselves from them, accompanying them always in the
form of *expression* in one case and *feelings* in the other. We have
already seen how expression, besides not necessarily resolving itself
into art, can never be considered an accompaniment of logic that is
detachable from it, but is rather — when it is logical expression —
an aspect of logic itself, quite unlike and unmistakable for aesthetic
expression. Concerning the economic mode as well, Croce wants to
make it a constant accompaniment of every practical activity and
— interestingly for the problem of art, and confirming our criticism
of the dialectic of distinct forms — makes it a generic concomitant
of every activity of the mind. The third edition of *Aesthetics,* from
1907, brings profound changes with respect to the first, in chapter
X. After identifying feeling with economic form, it continues: "But
if the activity of feeling in the sense here defined must not be substituted for all the other forms of activity of the mind, we have not
said that it cannot *accompany* them. Indeed, it accompanies them of
necessity, because they are all in close relation, both with one another and with the elementary volitional form. Therefore each of them
has for concomitants individual volitions and volitional pleasures
and pains which are known as feeling. But we must not confuse a
concomitant with the principal fact, and take the one for the other.
The discovery of the truth, or the satisfaction of a moral duty fulfilled, produces in us a joy which makes our whole being vibrate,
for, by attaining to those forms of mental activity, it attains at the

same time what it was *practically* tending toward, as its end, during the effort. Nevertheless, economic or hedonistic satisfaction, ethical satisfaction, aesthetic satisfaction, intellectual satisfaction, remain always distinct, even when in union" (p. 87).

In this doctrine of the economic accompaniment to aesthetic activity and in general to every activity of the mind, and in the problem — closely linked to it — of feeling, we may note many ambiguities and uncertainties from 1905 to 1907, crucial years for the formation of the Crocean system which saw the conception, with publication to follow shortly thereafter, of *Logic,* the *Essay on Hegel,* his talk on *Lyric Character,* the third (revised) edition of *Aesthetics,* and the *Philosophy of the Practical.* It is symptomatic that in these various writings the problem of feeling is not always solved in the same way, and above all that the reduction of it that we have noted to economic activity does not take place in the *Philosophy of the Practical,* where it is denied as an autonomous form and defined as the *provisional devising,* not yet well determined, of any attitude of the mind.

Limiting the question to the problem of art, here too we note that an intrinsic characteristic is combined and intertwined with a need for collocation. The need to close the circle of the dialectic of distinct forms comes to the fore now that this dialectic has been clarified in all four of its essential modes. And if from the beginning it was possible to place art as the first form of knowledge without worrying too much about the substrate it acted upon, and to speak of sensation, which "before the inferior boundary . . . is formless matter, which the mind can never apprehend in itself, in so far as it is mere matter . . . but of which it postulates the concept as, precisely, a limit,"[137] now this substrate is conceived as identical with the world of the will — with a clearly idealistic formulation: "Practical activity is reality itself in its immediacy and . . . no other reality (or we may say, other *nature*) is conceivable outside will-action"; "the will is the necessary precedent of knowledge,"[138] and, since the first form of knowledge is art, the will is the necessary precedent of art: "If there is not a desire, an aspiration, a nostalgia, there cannot be poetry;

---

[137]*Est.*[1] cit., p. 8.
[138]*Fil. d. pr.* (Bari, 1923) p. 189.

if there is not an impulse or a heroic deed, the epic cannot arise; if the sun does not illuminate a landscape, or a soul invoke a ray of sunlight upon the countryside, the picture of a luminous landscape cannot exist."[139]

This need for closure of the circle of the distinct converges and combines here with the other need to justify the sentimental and passionate side of art, the violence of joy and pain that plainly accompanies every production or reproduction of poetry. Hence the concept of art as *lyricism,* in which it seemed that a fundamental requirement of artistic progress was satisfied and the harmonious system of mental forms was completed at the same time: "The content of pure intuition can be neither an abstract concept nor a speculative concept or idea, nor a conceptualized or rather historicized representation. . . . But outside of logicality . . . no other psychic content remains except what is called appetition, tendency, feeling, will; facts which are essentially one and the same and constitute the practical form of the mind in its infinite gradations and in its dialectic (pleasure and pain). Pure intuition, not producing concepts, can only represent the will in its manifestations — that is, it can only represent *states of mind.* And the states of mind are the passion, the feeling, the personality that are found in all art and determine its lyrical character."[140]

Except that, is invoking the unity of the forms of the mind really sufficient to justify this concomitance of feeling with each of them? And why should it be the emotional or economic form — and not others — that has this accompanying function? If, then, the passionate and sentimental element were to be accentuated only in the artistic form, based on the fact that the practical element is the one that in the circle of the distinct immediately precedes it, would it not be possible to observe that precisely in that circle the economic phase has as its immediate sublator not the artistic, but the ethical phase, which it frees from passions, or at least transforms them into universal ones, and that therefore, if one wished to respect this order of precedence, should only the universal or ethical passion precede art?

---

[139]*Fil. d. pr.,* p. 190.
[140]"L'intuizione pura e il carattere lirico dell'arte," *Problemi d'estetica* (Bari, 1923) p. 23.

In the case of the economic form, in short, Croce creates a particular and ambiguous situation. It is organized and positioned in its place in the dialectic of the distinct, and yet, outside of it, it is linked and concomitant with every form of the mind, to a greater extent and differently than the forms themselves are with each other. And it is symptomatic also that in preference to the others, Croce has the economic form intrude unduly into processes which do not belong to it, making it the cause of error.

Now, the fact that there is a passionate element in art as in every form of the mind, that the poet and the thinker, the man of action and the saint should encounter in their work a passivity and resistance that it is a joy to overcome and painful to submit to — this is not what we want to deny. And even though the feelings are different for the different activities, and the artist's passion differs from the thinker's just as thought differs from art, nevertheless the essential character is always the same. The resistance offered, the effort it calls for, the turmoil involved is easily recognizable. Whatever one may think of the general problem of an autonomous and universal economic form, it is in any case certain that this indivisibility of sentiment from every spiritual form makes one think, rather than of a constant economic accompaniment, of an intrinsic aspect co-natural with the mind itself — of a passivity that is inseparable from activity. In this regard — although very imprecise and still imbued with naturalism and certainly less consistent with the system — we prefer the wording of the first edition of the *Aesthetics,* which in the third edition was replaced by the passage cited above: "The feeling of pleasure and pain is a simple organic fact. . . . But . . . there is nothing to say that it cannot be accompanied by activity of the mind. This, in fact, takes place nowhere else but in the organism: it is based on man's natural being. Not only does the psychic organ provide it with matter or content, which are the *impressions* without which it would be idle and restless in a vacuum; but the very development of the impressions can in turn only be a psychic fact — that is, other impressions. Considered *ab extra,* aesthetic activity itself is nothing but a succession of impressions" (p. 78).[141]

---

[141]Croce returned to the problem of the analogies between economics and aesthetics and

Another definition of feeling that gives rise to very interesting developments for aesthetics is contained in the *Philosophy of the Practical*, where passion or desire, is defined as a *possible volition*, not yet actualized (p. 140). This distinction is quite different from the one between economics and ethics, since the relationship between the individual and the universal does not enter into it at all; and it would be pointless here to mention it and examine its meaning and function if it were not linked to a definition of the relationship between art and knowledge that enables new views of the artistic fact: "It may be said that history always represents actions:... it is therefore perception and the memory of perception. And it would also be possible to say that art represents only desires, and is therefore all fancy and never perception, all possi-

---

their position in the world of the mind in a very recent work: "Le due scienze mondane: l'Estetica e l'Economica" ["The Two Worldly Sciences: Aesthetics and Economics"], *Critica* (1931) p. 401 ff. Here these two forms of the mind are theorized on the one hand as those that "intend to justify theoretically, that is to define and systematize what used to be called sense, giving it the dignity of a positive and creative form of the mind" (p. 404), and in the act itself they idealize it. While on the other hand they are seen as the representatives and bearers of what for the world of the mind that wants and knows is the object or matter or nature: Economics and Aesthetics in fact "prepare the data necessary to solve the problem, revealing the object as none other than that passionate life, the stimuli, the impulses, the pleasure and pain, the varied and multifaceted emotion that becomes the subject of intuition and imagination and, through it, of reflection and thought" (p. 409).

One proof of the difficulties encountered by Croce's attempt to place aesthetic and economic activity as objects of the other two, logic and ethics, lies in the scant evidence for these relationships. And in this same essay, in expounding on them, he never speaks, for example, of art as the object of logic; but he always attributes that function to economic activity, in the form of feeling. The object, as we have seen, is "nothing other than the life of the passions — which is what becomes the material of intuition and imagination and, thereby, of reflection and thought." Already here the presumed parallelism of aesthetics and economics collapses; but more explicitly it is later stated that "thought, even when it thinks and criticizes the thoughts of others and unfolds their history, does not think thought, but rather the practical life of thought" (p. 410). And even concerning the theory that sees evil and error as the primitive and inferior degree of the mind with respect to the superior degree that follows them, the exemplifications are always taken from the practical sphere: "Evil is . . . the agony of falling back without falling back from morality into mere and 'natural' utility" (p. 411).

Even here, therefore, the economic form sometimes usurps the place that the organization of the dialectic of distinct forms would assign to aesthetics. And if we observe that this always happens in cases in which it is supposed to have the role of content, of matter, of object, in short, of what in every mental form is to be considered substrate that is inconceivable if separated from the form itself, we can perhaps deduce arguments in favor of the universality and autonomy of art and to the detriment of the autonomy and universality of the economic form.

ble reality and never effectual reality. . . . It would be more correct to say
that art is located on this side of the possible and the real, it is pure of
these distinctions, and is therefore pure imagination or *pure intuition*. .
. . Likewise when art takes possession of historical material, it removes
from it just the historical character, the critical elements, it makes it the
instrument of its desire or its dream" (p. 171–72).

Some of the terms used here are the usual ones. But the analogy
and connection with the relationship that was noted in the practical
field, which is not a relation of individual to universal; the clear
distinction, on the other hand, from history understood as individual knowledge and just in this period definitively brought under
the concept of philosophy (and it must be noted that the progressive proximity of history to philosophy makes the position of art
as individual knowledge more and more difficult); moreover the
affirmed naivety of art and its being "on this side of the possible
and the real" — all of this leads us to entertain a momentary disregard for art as the first and fundamental theoretical form, and
to lean towards an intrinsic definition of it by means of its own
characteristics and not analogous to those of other mental forms, a
definition which, while perhaps destroying its position in the circle
of the mind, would nonetheless more firmly establish its autonomy.

Our criticism of Croce has so far been based on the observation that the characteristics he cites as specific to art actually belong to it in common with other spiritual forms and fail to demonstrate anything other than its analogy with these forms, without
however being able to distinguish it from them. Here instead we
have, perhaps for the first time, determinations intrinsic to art
that belong to it alone, to the exclusion of any other activity; and,
although still vague (dream, naivety) or only negative (indifference to reality and unreality) they allow us to begin to realize the
differences between the process and manifestation of art, and the
process and manifestation of knowledge. Even if, in the essay on
the lyrical character of art, Croce still adheres to the definition of
the artistic fact as the first and most ingenuous form of knowledge,
this accent placed on the lack of a truth criterion — on the pure
lack of discrimination between reality and unreality — gives this
first form of knowledge a different character from that of individ-

ual knowledge. And then, how is it any longer possible to call it knowledge if it doesn't discriminate between reality and unreality? In the first *Aesthetics* Croce had said that in art, at *first perception*, "everything is real and therefore nothing is real," moving it steadily closer to history, however, and making only an empirical distinction between historical and artistic intuition.[142] Here "art . . . grasps pulsating reality, but does not know it grasps it, and therefore does not truly grasp it . . . it does not fall into error but does not know it does not fall into it. . . . It is the dream (so to speak) of the cognitive life, and the completion of this is the awakening."[143]

Granted, the difference between the two definitions is not great — but while the first rested on cognitive character and on providing the data within which conceptual knowledge had to discriminate the real from the unreal, the universal from the empirical, here, on the contrary, the divergence from knowledge is accentuated, as is the disinterested vision extraneous to the reality of things by which art has its own universality, not cognitive and not even practical, but *artistic,* which provides an essential aspect of universal life, different from the one that gives us perception or concept or persuasion of a truth. An aspect that is itself reality but does not have reality as its object. As Croce puts it: "It may seem that in this way the field of art has been much restricted and the ingenuous representation of the real is excluded from it. But this ingenuous representation is just the representation of reality as dream. . . . The artist who represents it ingenuously, produces the lyric for this very reason. . . . The feeling that the true artist portrays is that of things, *lacrymae rerum.* . . . The characteristic that Schelling and Schopenhauer noted in music, of reproducing, not indeed the ideas, but the ideal rhythm of the universe, and of objectifying the will itself, belongs equally to all the other forms of art, because it is the essence itself of art, or of pure intuition."[144]

This universality attributed to art, the reality, if not of its object, of the thing itself, the character of its form, so different from cogni-

---

[142]*Est.*¹, p. 30–31.

[143]*Liricità*, p. 28–29.

[144]*Fil. d. pr.*, p. 173–74.

tive knowledge and indeed distinct from it in its fundamental characteristic, suggests that the term "individual knowledge" is retained
mostly out of a desire for coherence (and as we shall see, it would
later be abandoned permanently), and that art, through these characteristics, can assume an autonomous aspect, independent of all
theorizing. This position might perhaps be compared to the position on art taken by Kant, the first and perhaps only one who
succeeded in making it a mental form in its own right, alien to any
function that would subjugate it to the theoretical or the practical,
with its own self-contained function, identical with its phenomenology. The search for a position or task for art must not be separated (as it sometimes is in Croce[145]) from the search for its distinctive
features, and the features noted by Kant are decisive for its func-
tional autonomy. The absence of interest that he affirmed indicates
the detachment of art from any activity of a practical or cognitive
nature, which is analogous in Croce's formulation to its precedence
over the distinction between reality and unreality, between possibility and actuality. But Kant specifies with even greater precision
the characteristics of *taste,* which has its own particular physiognomy and needs a separate form to justify it. The first qualitative
definition that we encounter in *Critique of Judgment* attributes to
taste "a feeling of pleasure" that has nothing to do with the principle
of knowledge of the intellect or the practical principle of the will
and which, insofar as it can only be understood as attributable to
everyone, has an implicitly universal character. This is even clearer
when Kant distinguishes the judgment of taste from anything that
has any interest in either the good or the pleasant. There is a big
difference between *pleasure (Lust),* which is attributed to taste as a
characteristic of it, and the *pleasant (Angenehm),* which is distinct
from it. The latter is an empirical pleasure, in a specific subject —
usually called impulsive, sentimental. It is a form of the practical,
but the lower form of it, which sublates itself as nature, and it is
fully distinct from taste. But the practical understood as universal,

---

[145]See, for example, this symptomatic confession, in *Critica* of 1924 (p. 126): "If in the end
I defined poetry or art as the simplest theoretical form, it was because (to speak informally)
I found all the other places occupied. . . . Was I wrong? Perhaps. . . ."

the *good*, is distinct from it as well. Thus we arrive at a definition of taste as that which pleases (*gefällt*) "without any interest." Understood in this way, pleasure (*Lust*) takes on its own particular aspect. Kant himself determines it more precisely, calling it *contemplative.*

It might be said that this same patient and conscientious work done by Kant to distinguish art from any form of practical reason, whether empirical or universal, is done by Croce in a more hasty, obscure, and unconscious manner so as to eliminate all theoretical features from it. And in the final definition the two searches substantially coincide. Art comes out as a universal activity that "affords absolutely no (not even a confused) knowledge of the object" and is completely distinct from any practical interest, even the most universal, "contemplative and with no interest in the object," and in allegorical and more comprehensive terms, "purpose without the idea of a purpose (*Zweckmässigkeit ohne Vorstellung eines Zwecks*)."[146]

This accent placed on the contemplative and disinterested nature of art is thus more evident in the essay "Lyricism" and in the *Philosophy of the Practical,* two works in which the problem of collocation and the relationship to logic is not at the forefront. But certainly, after the new steps taken, the linearity and coherence of the doctrine is more difficult to maintain. Semiotics has by now begun to detach itself from collocation and to go its own way — so that when the two problems come into contact they do not always manage to coincide.

The *Breviario d'Estetica* [*Essence of Aesthetics*], which should organically conclude a whole period of speculative and critical experience, shows instead many ambiguities preparatory to new developments. Here the necessary precedence and concomitance of art with respect to logic is explicitly maintained, while art is increasingly stripped of its cognitive value. Of these two theses, the first derives directly from the primitive passage from individual to universal, and the second necessarily leads to the affirmation of a universality that belongs to art and is specific to it.

The individuality of art is again declared by Croce at the beginning of the book: "We do not here deny that the universal, as the

---

[146]Kant, *Crit.d. Giud.*, trans. Gargiulo (Bari, 1923) p. 70–79.

spirit of God, is everywhere and animates all things with itself, but we deny that in intuition as intuition the universal is rendered logically explicit and is thought through."[147] And although later this individuality would show itself to be such only with respect to the logical thought that sublates it, not in itself without its own universal character, it is nevertheless significant that such precedence is initially maintained only at this price. All the characteristics of art, in the *Breviario,* tend to make it an autonomous function, eternal and standing on its own. Indistinctness between reality and unreality, ideality (with respect to logic), dream, image, contemplation, representation, are all terms that in a vague way tend to differentiate its universality from the universality of logic. But what is most important is that this universality, this character it has as an *a priori* synthesis or "individuated universal" (p. 43) is stated explicitly and clearly as never before. Its autonomy is also affirmed with respect to the art of the individual, which belongs to logic, and, implicitly, so is the unnecessary concomitance of the artistic fact as the bearer of the individual or of expression: "The concept or idea always unites the intelligible to the perceptible, and not only in art, for the new concept of the concept . . . heals the breach between the perceptible and the intelligible worlds, conceives the concept as judgment, and the judgment as synthesis *a priori*, and the synthesis *a priori* as the word becoming flesh, as history. . . . To seek a perceptible element for the concept, beyond what it already contains in itself as concrete concept, and beyond the words in which it expresses itself, would be superfluous."[148] Now we are not sure what precise meaning to attribute to these words of Croce's, but it is certain that they decisively affirm not only the independence of logical fact from any injection of sensitivity or individuality that

---

[147]*Nuovi saggi di estetica* (Bari, 1920) p. 17.

[148]*Nuovi saggi*, p. 24. Cf. a similar affirmation in *Storiografia*, contemporary with the *Breviario*: "This sort of imagination, which is really quite indispensable to the historian, is the imagination that is inseparable from the historical synthesis, the imagination in and for thought, the concreteness of thought. . . . It is nevertheless to be radically distinguished from the free poetic imagination" (p. 30). Cf. also ibid. (p. 49): "The mere finite and particular do not exist other than in abstraction: in poetry and in art itself, which is the realm of the individual, there is no abstract finite, but the naive finite, which is the indistinct unity of infinite and finite."

might come from art — but along with it the autonomy of logic with respect to art, and implicitly the elimination of any question of art as an accompaniment to logic.

Art is therefore an *a priori* synthesis in its own right, with its own particular physiognomy, which needs investigating. Having established its negative features (what art *isn't*), we need to determine the positive ones: "What is the office of the pure image in the life of the spirit? or (which at bottom amounts to the same thing), How does the pure image come into existence?" (p. 23). And Croce's answer is that art is the synthesis of feeling and representation, "a powerful feeling that has become a razor-sharp representation," "an aspiration enclosed in the circle of a representation."

Except that this definition remains extremely vague precisely because of the imprecision of the term "feeling," which, as we have noted, has various meanings in Croce. If you want it to be already intimate with the aesthetic fact and no longer its content, i.e. "the universe viewed entirely *sub specie intuitionis*," it becomes synonymous with art itself and no new psychological characteristics are attributed to it. This reduces it at most to an affirmation of that sense of fullness and joy and having overcome passivity that is an integral part of the universal achieved not only artistically but also logically and morally. The only real possibility of giving an effective meaning to the word feeling, in the case of art, is to intend it as the passion that precedes and is surmounted by art, as a turmoil that it placates. Croce arrives at this position whenever he does not stop at a theoretical definition of the position of feeling with regard to art, but describes in concrete terms how it manifests itself and acts. In these cases it appears as a state of mind, aspiration, passion — a practical precedent that art transfigures and purifies and makes eternal. "They were all [Dante, Petrarch, Ariosto, Leopardi, D'Annunzio] deeply passionate souls, and their works of art are the eternal flower that burst from their passion." But in some way this feeling has to be intended as a presupposition to art and concomitant with it (a problem already mentioned). It is clear that, understood in this way, it does not yet characterize art in its particular conformation. It establishes what it acts upon (and we have seen that this object or correlate does not belong to it alone) but it does not establish the way in which it acts. And this way would be representation, image, imagination, contemplation — vague terms, indicating acts of the mind, whose inner conformation is not yet clear.

In any case, we have noted this attempt to describe the phenomenon of art as intrinsic and autonomous as the most notable part of the *Breviario di estetica,* which continues the references from the essay on lyricism. But Croce always resists departing from certain initial theses that are particularly dear to him, and which nevertheless seem to us closely connected with the ones he is about to abandon. And if in the first chapter, in the pure definition of art, he introduces the new elements that we have seen, in the others, where he wants to develop that concept and show it as if in action, he returns to his traditional formulations. Thus, with the identification of art with language, he reintroduces the concept of expression as an exclusively artistic form, and with this the concomitance and involvement of art in all the other forms of the mind. This way, the hint of an autonomous definition of the aesthetic universal clashes with the principle of the relationship between condition and conditioned, or of the circle of mental forms, which is maintained here and indeed explicitly theorized. But this circle arose as the repeated passage from the individual to the universal form, in the theoretical mind and the practical — and it implied a definition of art as individual knowledge, similar to the definition of economics as individual will. Now, with the new and more precise concept of art, it is more difficult to conceive of.

If earlier it was perhaps possible to admit that a supposed single and individual knowing (assuming for the moment that it is conceivable as such) would necessarily be sublated by a universal concept that applied the criterion of reality to it, how is it permissible now to think that the imaginary universal must necessarily precede the logical one, and the logical necessarily follow it? Couldn't the opposite happen, for example, with logic arising not from the artistic, but from another foundation entirely, with art — let's say — following it and transforming what had been established as true by reason into a beautiful fantasy and vision?

There is no truth in Croce's declaration that the artist "who has achieved the process of liberation from the sentimental tumult and

has objectified it in a lyrical image — that is, has attained to art"
does not find definitive satisfaction, that "a new demand declares
itself, a new process begins" and "the lyrical image changes, for him
and for us, into an autobiographical extract, or *perception.*" Transcendental psychology — to use a Crocean term — does not trust
any of this, or it trusts many other needs that appear, beyond the
cognitive one, in the realm of artistic intuition. It shows that, in
addition to and instead of the desire to know the reality or unreality
of what one has contemplated or represented or imagined, other
psychological needs may arise, and that desire for control and investigation may not be felt at all. Achieving an artistic intuition may
serve as the impulse to another work of art that unfolds upon it
and takes it as its object; or it may give rise to a desire — a drive to
act, or it may even give rise to no development whatsoever, and be
content with itself and blissful in the vision achieved and in the silence. And even considering that this silence eventually has to end
and give rise to a new activity, it is beyond doubt that, whatever this
may be, art — if it constitutes the starting point — will no longer
live in it as art, but as its object, the basis from which it started, the
content that it has given form to; something that, concretely, is at
one with the new activity and, considered abstractly, is passion (in
the etymological sense) or — to use the idealist term — *nature.* We
know that art, like any fact of the mind, indeed like anything at
all, can be taken as an object and transformed into *nature.* But this
does not necessarily happen because of logical knowledge; and every mental, logical, artistic, practical form can have art as its object,
and therefore take art as its starting point.

The knowledge to which art would be prior is taken by Croce
in two senses: either as a new way of forming and making universal
the same content, perception of it supervening on its image; or as
a judgment of the artistic activity itself and on its value and meaning — criticism or philosophy of art that acts and discriminates
on art itself. Now, this second kind of sublation cannot be taken
as actual proof of the necessary precedence of art over knowledge,
because the criticism is not meant here as knowledge *in general,*
but only as knowledge *of art,* which naturally, as such, follows —
just as the practical act and the cognitive act itself can be followed

by self-knowledge as such, not because of the laws of the dialectic of distinct forms, but because in the mind or in man, who participates in every mental form, each form it can act by taking another as its object. And, as for the first mode of sublation, we repeat that does not seem to us to exist at all, and we do not see why the imaginary picture of an object should precede its historical knowledge, and not vice versa; nor why the one cannot exist without the other.

The dialectic and circle of distinct forms thus appears as a concept that Croce introduces from outside in order to unify and connect the data and mental forms that his continuing exploration of his universal experience made progressively clearer to him. The more such forms take on a clear, distinct and autonomous shape, the less they fit this dialectic, this relation of condition to conditioned that he had taken up, in a more abstract way, from Hegelian philosophy.[149] In that dialectic we observed at greatest length the passage between art and logical knowledge, which was important to our argument. But the other passages are also forced and, if art is a living and self-contained synthesis of its own particular universality of representation — just as it is not clear how "without art, philosophy would be lost to itself, because it would lack the very thing that determines its problems" — in the same way it is not at all obvious "that practice is not practice when it is not driven and enlivened by aspirations, and, as they say, by 'ideals', by the 'sweet imagining' that is then art" (where it would have to be demonstrated that the ideals and the sweet imagining that follow the practice have the characteristics of *a priori* imaginary syntheses). Nor can we accept the affirmation that "art without morality — the art that usurps from the decadent the title of 'pure beauty' . . . — is degraded as art by the lack of morality in the life it arises from and which surrounds it, and becomes caprice, lust, charlatanism,"[150] when it seems clear to us that artistic futility and dissolution is not conditioned by moral breakdown, and that a vivid representation of an experience of moral disintegration cannot be ruled out. It is only permissible to say, in a generic and approximate way, that, in the

---

[149]Cf. *Nuovi saggi*, p. 54–56.

[150]*Nuovi saggi*, p. 67.

individual life and mental health of each person, a deep and heart-felt moral coherence sometimes (but not always) favors the unity and purity and composure of art.

IV. TOTALITY AND REPRESENTATION

The further development of Crocean thought is closely related to the influence it has exerted on the Italian cultural environment. It is no longer a polemic against external adversaries unaware or incapable of understanding the doctrine, but a discussion internal to the doctrine itself and originating from its own developments — continual answers to questions and objections, clarifications of controversial points, solutions to difficulties, the defeat of arbitrary interpretations.

Among the basic accusations brought against Croceanism, we would like to mention here as one of the most repeated and fertile, that of *fragmentism*. The essay on the lyrical character and the affirmed emotional nature of the artistic fact seemed at first to justify conceptions of art as an immediate release of subjective passion, and the poetics of the cry, the scream and the words uttered in absolute freedom that began raging in the immediate prewar period. But more than from Croceanism, such poetics derived from misunderstood experiences of Bergsonism, and Croce himself had already struck back against a fragmentism in some ways similar (although very different in others) in his essay on Pascoli. In any case, it is clear that he cannot be blamed for that confusion to anyone who observes (as we have done) that for Croce, passion and feeling are always a presupposition, a content, a precedent of artistic intuition, necessary but not sufficient for it, and that he emphasizes what sublates feeling — that is, the universal that is intrinsic to art.

To call Croce a fragmentist in this sense would therefore be an error. But often this accusation has been linked and confused with another sort of fragmentism that Croce is said to be guilty of, in the sense most specific and intrinsic to art. This is the fragmentism of those who isolate poetry from the overall human world of artwork or the artist in order to grasp it and enjoy it separately in all the multiple places where it appears, almost through a process of distillation. Against this danger, stemming from the desire to prove the affirmed autonomy of art in its concrete manifestations and implementations, there was an insurrection in the name of the unity of the mind and the overall, all-inclusive, human importance of the artist as such. There was a complete denial of the value of this division of elements, which caused many works to lose their character and sense of unity. And the dissatisfaction with the practical and critical results led to a more or less conscious denial of the theoretical principles which they were derived from.

Now, undoubtedly the distrust of some was justified towards a system that could lead to the kind of disruptive consequences, for example, that marked the essay on *La poesia di Dante* [*Dante's poetry*], and that could achieve a unitary and overall vision only for certain poets such as Ariosto, who fits particularly and we would say almost exclusively into its premises. But it would have been preferable in this case to attribute the defect to a scarcity of penetration on the part of the critic than to an error of the theorist — to his scant ability to engage with the unitary and comprehensive poetic tones prevalent in a work, and especially to his desire to undertake operations that, while not illegitimate in themselves, bring out only certain elements which, in the human sweep of the work, are important but not decisive.

But considerations of the acuity of critical observations aside, the theoretical inappropriateness of the essay on Dante lies in the limited nature of the task the critic sets himself in it, and (in addition to having limited his art more than he had to) in not having clarified sufficiently that not all of Dante is there. The error (which then becomes an inadequacy) is in having conceived the variety of mental forms contained in the *Divina Commedia* [*Divine Comedy*] as a mixture, rather than as a synthesis, and in not having noted that, given the autonomy of each form and its possibility to stand on its own, even in isolation, what joins them all in a unitary complex can itself be form and mind, and is not necessarily an arbitrary and empirical aggregation. Nor is it noted that, if in a work one finds artistic intuitions together with processes of thought involving impulses of personal or moral passion, and if each of these elements can be isolated and has its own eternal value even if separated from the context, it may be (as in Dante's case) that that very mental act that unites them — by which they were conceived together and almost as a function of each other — that act itself has a universal and eternal value that deserves to be understood and analyzed. Leibniz would say, in his own way, that the monad is indeed the only reality and the aggregate is material — but what keeps the components of the aggregate united, that *vinculum substantiale* by which they came together and mingled, can be itself a monad, have its own eternity, and represent an aspect of the world. Croce's error lies in not having sufficiently highlighted this mental character of the connection between the various units, which constitutes the absolute and unmistakable unitary nature of the *Divine Comedy*. This error, we repeat, is rather one of omission, because no one would want to deny the possibility of considering Francesca or Farinata or Belacqua or Sordello as autonomous works of art capable of lives of their own. But everyone (including Croce, we believe) agrees that since the comments on them have been separate, not all there is to say has as yet been said about them.

This is the sense of Croce's fragmentism and the criticism of it. But perhaps not without reason this fragmentism has at times been confused with the other kind — subjective disordered passion. Because probably this neglect of the connecting tones, the search for the unity of inspiration only in the single composition and in the punctual arrival of the lyrical and representative outburst, betray the idea — never clearly formulated anyway — that artistic intuition is something very brief and instantaneous that takes place in the course of a single mental pulse. Whereas it is well known and evident that art — like every act permitting reflected consciousness — is often matured and elaborated at length and, I would say, held back, and that inspiration is not an initially complete illumination later mechanically reproduced by means of recollection, but rather something whose formation is (or rather, can be) long and laborious, whose progress can be lovingly fostered and cared for. Art, as we know, is not knowledge, and taken on its own, there is nothing about it that is thought out, intentional or controlled. But this does not prevent the artist who has discerned more or less clearly within himself the still unformed seed of inspiration, from using all his powers of knowledge and will to create the right conditions for its completion, development and definitive formation. Sketches and notes are only means to this end, the various drafts of a work represent nothing more than a single artistic process that is gradually being perfected, purified of dross and passivity — a single inspiration in its genetic development. This is the only way to explain, holding firm to the identity of intuition and expression, the length and laboriousness with which many works of art, perfectly unitary and linear, come to light. And only in this way can unity of inspiration be explained, even in the immense variety of the world brought back to life and (how should I put it?) the secondary inspirations contained in a work such as the *Divine Comedy*.

But it is in any case worth noting that some of Croce's critical essays were written I would almost say as propaganda, with a view of demonstrating in the artistic fact itself the autonomy he claims for art. It is thus natural that he should tend toward an isolated consideration of poetry, fragmentary though it is, and toward favoring its placement at the foundation of the solution. At the same time it is important to note that there is no part in Croce's critical essays for the form of connection of art with the other forms of the mind, which we had felt ought to be rejected, but which Croce had theorized and which in this case might have been useful to him — the dialect of distincts and the sublation of the artistic phase by that of knowledge. This absence is another proof of the lack of precision in the concept and shows its ineffectiveness in solving the concrete problems of art.

The isolated and fragmentary character that art seems to assume in the complexity of life was then linked to the primordial, *auroral and naive* position attributed to it by Croce with respect to logical knowledge. This was a position that had largely lost the meaning of individual knowledge, but when seen from that point of view it could still seem, and perhaps to a greater extent, indicative of incompleteness, impermanence and almost inferiority. These reasons, together with others such as the distaste for conceiving a history of art that did not present continuity between successive artistic movements, and more than anything a generic need for unity and completeness of the mental fact that had made itself felt through the influence of actualism — helped to accentuate the human value in art, overall, pushing Croce himself to evolve in the direction of *totality*. What was then sought in the artist was above all the *person*, and in the work of art a cosmic character that involved all the values of the mind. There was a repudiation of art as something separate, almost inferior, a pre-knowledge activity extraneous to morality, and an affirmation of the dignity of the artist as a prophet, discoverer of eternal truths and upholder of irrevocable duties. The problem thus reappeared of the relations between art and morality that had seemed to have been definitively buried. It was no longer a question of art having to serve the purposes of morality or that the artist's task was to teach by entertaining. It was rather that the artist, as such, contained the highest morality — that intrinsic to artistic activity was an affiliation with that superior world of purposes to which only human life can be elevated.

The impossibility of reserving for art an exclusively initial position in the process of the mind and a sporadic place in the composition of immortal works called into question the definitions and descriptions that Croce had given it and of its processes, and instead of seeking the possibility of cosmic and universal values in these same definitions, the choice was to modify the very concept of art in the direction of those values, adding new characteristics to it, enlarging its function to the point of identifying it completely with the act of the mind in its most generic sense, and transforming it into universal knowledge and will. The necessity of seeing the person above all in the artist led to the identification of the concept of art with the overall concept of humanity, a position that has its own function of prevention against the dangers of fragmentism and reaffirms for humanity the universal and essential value of the artistic act. At the same time, however, it once again raises the problem of distinguishing that act from others that are also universal and essential to humanity and in which characteristics different from art must nevertheless be recognized.

Such a distinction is very difficult for those who have positioned themselves on this basis of a generic and comprehensive mind. Indeed, in the combination of art and universal knowledge, art loses its distinctive characteristics and is reduced to the semiotics of self-awareness, or else knowledge is itself modified, assuming all the characteristics of art.

It is clear, for example, that the definition of art as feeling offered by Gentile does not make this distinction. We do not wish to deal here even briefly with this doctrine, which deserves a more thorough examination. But we would only point out, for our present purposes, that feeling intended as an initial phase, immediate, subjective and anterior to mediation (but inconceivable unless this follows it and makes it real) cannot be valid except in the mediation itself — that is, when it emerges from this pure subjectivity and immediacy that characterizes it as art. In Croce, we have seen how the autonomy of art is hindered by its concomitance with logic and by the position it takes in accompanying reflective thought. Here it is not only presupposed by reflected thought, it presupposes it, and it is not valid except as an intrinsic — and only abstractly isolatable — phase of it. The need for art to be total, cosmic and infinite here supersedes the search for its distinctiveness and the possibility of an independent life. And it is denied even the autonomy, however "unilateral," that Croce consistently affirms.

It already emerges from its pure subjectivity to reach what is most closely related to it: expression. And this, we believe, is not because expression is not intrinsic to it, but because this exit from itself and this passage to mediation is intrinsic to it. "When feeling is expressed, its actual expression is no longer feeling, but thought. . . . Our world in the depths of its subjectivity is one; distinction arises within it through expression, which is thought, and which fixes subject and object as distinct, alienating the subject from its original unity."[151] Art, therefore, as soon as it is expressed, ceases to be itself as subjectivity — indeed, only in this exiting from itself can it acquire the multiple determinations of different works of art. In all its unfolding, in its manifestations, in the joy it gives and the anguish it imposes, what is essential is that it be resolved and realized in what completes and supersedes it: "Since the synthesis in which art is actualized is also the synthesis that sublates art and gives us the concrete totality of the mind and therefore of the world, the pain that art frees us from is not only that pain that devel-

---

[151]G. Gentile, *Filosofia dell'Arte* (Milano, 1931) p. 202.

ops and matures through the single work of art."[152]

In these citations, taken at random, we can already see the different angle, with respect to our problem, taken by Gentile, whose theory, however, has its origin in many other motives besides this and is derived mainly from methodological premises and philosophical foundations completely different from those of Croce, and which would need to be clarified before its specific aspects could be appropriately assessed. But we are interested in this reference just to indicate one direction the need for totality has developed in, arising as a reaction to some of Croce's formulations; and although Gentile has only recently expounded his doctrine on the subject at length, treatises on the problem can also be found in his earlier writings, which have also contributed to moving some currents of criticism and taste in that direction.

The desire to grant a human value to the work of poetry thus resolves art into thought, and attributes to it the dialectical forms that are considered proper to the theoretic process.

The desire to recognize the human value in a work of poetry thus establishes art in thought and attributes to it the dialectical forms that are considered proper to the theoretic process. But for someone with strong artistic sensibility who has experienced the inner unfolding of intuition and its concrete manifestation it will not do to give up some characteristics particular to art. And the given need for totality is satisfied by reducing knowledge itself to the semiotics of art and making this the sole or highest representative of reality. But in this way reality is modified by the very faculty that perceives or represents it, and ends up acquiring characteristics which, although perfectly consonant with that faculty, are in themselves questionable and difficult to justify epistemologically. Thus Borgese, for example — who has a very clear psychological awareness of what art is — out of a need to attribute to it not only a real, universal and eternal value in itself, but also the function *of* representing reality in its most absolute form (a function that is essentially cognitive), has arrived at a determination of this reality as a form that transcends the senses, as a superworld of which art

---

[152]Ibid., p. 297.

would provide only fixed, immobile, ecstatic visions. This solution is interesting as a way of grasping some characteristics of art (and we do not want to deal with it in depth here either), but it is not demonstrable, like all solutions involving transcendence.

It is also significant that the attribution of the highest cognitive function to art generally leads to conclusions of transcendence and mysticism. Art, in fact, when it is made into an instrument of knowledge, transforms the reality it knows into something eternal, fixed, and immutable, through a process of self-delusion that makes the intellectualist poet in aesthetics a partisan of transcendence and a mystic in philosophy. In the following passage from the *Critica del Giudizio* [*Critique of Judgment*] by Kant, aesthetic judgment is conceived as the bearer of knowledge: "We have only to do with nature as phenomenon, and this itself must be regarded as the mere presentation of a nature-in-itself (which exists in the idea of reason). But this idea of the supersensible, which we can no further determine, — so that we cannot know but only think nature as its presentation, — is awakened in us by means of an object, whose aesthetic appreciation strains the imagination to its utmost. . . . And this judgment is based upon a feeling of the mind's destination (i.e., upon moral feeling) which altogether transcends the realm of the imagination" (p 117).

Now it is this precise passage that can help us find new determinations of art that more clearly distinguish it from other activities. What is it that is in fact known through mystic ecstasy if not what is immutable and settled, rather than dynamic and progressive? And what is transcendence, hypostasis, if not an attempt to go beyond the mobility and mutability of experience — to which one does not wish to attribute universality or view as fixed and immutable and *given* — to what instead, insofar as it is always newly "known" and "acted out," can reconcile universality with movement? If immanent universal knowledge is inseparable from action, and is essentially a prolonging activity producing consequences and developments, the immobility of mysticism cannot be part of it. And one might think not so much that since the object to be known was foreign and transcendent one sought an activity that could fix it in an eternal vision, but rather that, in order at all costs to provide this activity with a cognitive value, its known object had to be moved into an abstract and uncontrollable world, outside that of knowledge. And the difficulties every mystical conception runs into in the field of testable and demonstrable epistemology show that, in that field and on those bases, it is not possible to attribute a real cognitive value to art.

But they also show that such immovable fixity and eternity is a characteristic of art which better defines it as a cathartic activity, free of any practical tendency or impulse towards application, and which almost crystallizes its content in an eternity of contemplation.

Having closed this brief parenthesis on the motive of truth and on the dangers of the objections leveled against fragmentism and affirmations of totality, we observe that Croce, for his part, also felt this need and tried to satisfy it in his doctrine. And no doubt possibilities of this kind were not lacking among his definitions of art. But the new emphasis that would on one hand contribute to making the concept more precise and autonomous would at the same time increase the ambiguity of its collocation.

We have seen up to now how the primitive and uncertain autonomy of art, initially defined as an individual form of knowledge, is accentuated and better determined through the discovery of new features — mainly the lack of distinction between reality and unreality, in which we thought we could see a detachment from knowledge — unfolding and expressed as "contemplation," "representation," "dream," "naivety," "image," etc. And we have seen how these further definitions became conjoined with an ever clearer awareness of the artistic act as universal, and of its character as an *a priori* synthesis, a sign and indicator of every autonomous form of the mind. Totality and autonomy thus find themselves naturally connected, making it possible to attribute to art a value that is properly cosmic and constitutive of reality, without confusing it with other forms or attributing functions to it that are not its own. But the difficulty of morally justifying a purely artistic value (that is, one that does not have morality and knowledge as a peculiar characteristic of its function), the apparent impossibility of a universal that is not theoretical or practical (derived perhaps from an inexact notion of the term 'universal') and, on the other hand, the absolute dialectical necessity of connections, of the passage from one form to another and of reciprocal sublation — all these reasons, in part Croce's own, in part imposed on him by the suggestions of other doctrines and cultural movements, nevertheless kept him close to the cognitive function of art and to the struggle against anyone who denied it "in its theoretical character and in the serious role that it fulfills as the first consciousness that the mind acquires of itself and of reality as a whole."[153] This appears to be in clear contrast with the position illustrated earlier of autonomy as the lack of distinction between reality and unreality — but which also, in its way, could have resolved the question of the dignity of the artist, whom it seemed to lead back to a vital interest in the essential values of the mind.

Croce oscillates continually between these two ways of understanding the fundamental and cosmic meaning of art, following the contrasting needs of his thinking and the various directions it follows. And he emphasizes first one position and then the other according to the specific problem that he finds himself tackling — thus showing how the new definition that he has come up with and that he would now like to substitute for the other one, can no longer stand up with all its characteristics if not by continually resorting to the latter. Just recently[154] he has recognized that the definition of art as individual knowledge "proved not to be fully adequate and therefore he corrected it," affirming at the same time "the philosophical principle that matter *per se* does not exist, but that the previous form serves as the material of the next in the circle of the mind. Just how this passage takes place in the case of art, and what the exact meaning might be with respect to theoretic activity of the term "auroral form of knowing," which in this regard has now been substituted for the other, is difficult to understand. This word "aurora" seems to be a generic metaphor rather than the definition of a precise and determined cognitive function. What this function might be — once individual knowledge, shown to be unacceptable, has been excluded — is not easy to see. And

---

[153]*Nuovi Saggi*, cit., p. 290.
[154]*Critica* (July, 1931) p. 300–01.

we have already seen how art is not at all necessarily previous to knowledge. Even the passage from one form to another, in these latest writings, has an embarrassing definition: "Concerning the 'passage' that one would like me to assign of art to philosophy, it is clear that if by this request, one intends the critical passage from one to another position of thought, I, who deny the conceptual, judgmental and rational character of art and do not want, as others do, to lower it to a *philosophia inferior,* cannot but reject the request as illegitimate or empty of sense. With a passage of this sort, goodbye to the autonomy of art! If, on the other hand, one intends simply to ask what the relationship is of one to the other, that relationship is determined by the definitions of the one and the other, which put them in a living relation. Those famous "passages," "transcendental deductions," and other such operations, are rather provincial remnants, sometimes thanks to their expository clothes, sometimes to the undue pretensions that belonged to the philosophy of more than a century ago."

From here one could easily draw disruptive consequences for the whole system of distinct forms, a place where Croce never explicitly arrives, continuing on the one hand to clarify and deepen the phenomenology of the artistic fact, and on the other to speculate on its position and its relationship with knowledge.

In the meantime it is worth noting that the need for totality gives Croce the opportunity to achieve increasing precision in the description and determination of the artistic fact. The essay entitled *Carattere di totalità della espressione artistica* [*Totality as a Characteristic of Artistic Expression*] is among his best for its adherence to the concrete nature of art. And the assumption — devoid of other systematic concerns — by which a universal character is attributed to that activity, allows him to color this universal with shades that are his own.

Its position here with respect to other universals remains ambiguous. The terms "auroral," "individual," "elementary and primitive forms," alternate and rotate. But what is important is the fact that they are never disjointed from the cosmic and total character that is in itself perfect and has no need of sublations. And an aspect is attributed to this universal that is only metaphorically individual and auroral, and is effectively *artistic* — that is, living on its own characteristics. "In it [art] the individual pulsates with the life of everything and everything in the life of the individual, and every genuine artistic representation is itself and the universe, the universe in that individual form, and that individual form as the universe."[155] But this universe is not the universe of knowledge or that of morality. It has its cathartic nature, a melting away of all practical concern, and a fundamental affinity with the concept of the "classical," in which true artists "are all classical in the best sense of the word, which is . . . a particular fusion of the primitive and the cultivated, of the inspiration and the school."[156] In brief, what is emphasized here is the character of freedom in art, its detachment from its own object, the way it sublates its own content — not the primitive and immediate form, but the mediation and point of arrival.

And the content selected, the object to be sublated, is of course feeling — which is however, as we have seen, a function that for Croce always oscillates between a category of the mind and the mind itself insofar as it is passivity, and we also found this last determination acceptable. Now if feeling is not an essential form, but a way of being, let's say, of each form at the moment when it is sublated and becomes nature, these same definitions of Croce's can be used to conceive what is no longer a generic universality that sublates a specific feeling (since in this way it would always be this feeling that gave art its decisive character), but rather a specific universality which, like every universality has or abstractly places beneath itself a generic feeling. And now, if we keep in mind a characteristic of the cognitive universal, always and inevitably tending towards actualization, capable of development, linking itself into a logical, discursive, demonstrable process, we can perhaps understand this catharsis not so much as a generic liberation from passion (which can take any universal form) but rather as a characteristic specific to artistic liberation — which takes place in a contemplative way, not developing into actualizations and consequences, static and not dynamic.[157]

---

[155]*Nuovi Saggi*, p. 126.

[156]*Nuovi Saggi*, p. 136.

[157]It is interesting that in the notes following the essay "Totality" there is also a clearer

And yet still universal — and in Croce an absolutely autonomous determination of it would have required greater independence from system requirements of an absolute idealist type, from which he has never been able to free himself completely.

This universal character, held for a moment in its own equilibrium, soon lapses in Croce, however, into analogies and identifications that do not belong to it. In emphasizing the creative quality belonging to artistic activity, for example, he also emphasizes its similarity with doing theory: "Whatever is life and feeling must become, through artistic expression, truth — and truth means overcoming the immediacy of life through the mediation of imagination, the creation of a fantasy that is that feeling set within its relations, that particular life placed in universal life and thus raised to a new life, no longer passionate but theoretical, no longer finite but infinite." A totality, then, that might (and in some cases does) more decisively establish the independence of art, but that more often than not makes it lapse into forms of knowledge.

Moralism is another risk inherent in accentuating the totality of art without a decisive awareness of the character of its autonomy. And this is the case not only because knowledge is inseparable from morality, and there is no theoretical act that is not extended inevitably into practice (so that art, made the bearer of knowledge, cannot but be the bearer of morality as well), but also because in Croce, in addition to the identifications necessitated by the rigor of logical transitions, recent years have seen the emergence, perhaps even for polemical reasons, of a broad feeling for totality, the need for art-as-life, the artist-human, complete, not foreign to any attitude of the mind — indeed, encompassing in his activity as an artist every possible attitude. In *Aesthetica in nuce* [*Aesthetics in a Nutshell*] we read that: "The artist . . . must have that involvement in the world of thought and action that allows him to experience . . . the full human

---

distinction between the expressions of the various forms of the mind — that is, "expression that is pure feeling or pure intuition (poetry) and expression that is the instrument of affective emotions or actions (oratory). A fundamental distinction for anyone dealing with art" (p. 140). And later: "It might also be worth noting that philosophers ought to know how to write about philosophy, with what attitudes and pathos, accents and emphases, inflections and refinements" (p. 150).

drama. . . . He must keep alive, in one form or another, the feeling of purity and impurity, of righteousness and sin, of good and evil. . . . Many artistic aspirations arise not from what the artist is practically as a man, but rather from what he is not and feels that one must be."[158]

One must always exercise caution in drawing conspicuous conclusions from the words of a thinker, and the aim of these is to affirm, more than the morality of art, the necessity of previous moral experience with respect to artistic elaboration. This is also shown in the immediately preceding passage in which, having placed feeling as the content to be superseded in art, Croce continues: "And this state of mind that we have called feeling, what else is it if not the entire mind that has thought, desired, acted? . . . Therefore the basis of all poetry is the human personality, and since the human personality is fulfilled in morality, the basis of all poetry is the moral conscience" (p. 11). In short, the point of attack by the central core of the Crocean system is here as well and consists of justifying the overall morality and humanity of art with its position in the circle of the mind. But we have already noted the difficulty of this idea of feeling with respect to the dialectic of distinct forms — belonging to and identical with the economic form, and at the same time accompanying each sphere of the mind to a greater degree than the other spheres do with each other.

This ambiguity of function makes it easy for Croce to frame in the body of his concepts all the various characteristics of art that his researcher's acumen and his interpreter's sensitivity progressively provide him with and which he then wants to highlight. In this way, feeling, as a passionate, impulsive, economic form, served him in the past to explain the lyrical character of art. Now, as a participant in the life of the whole mind, it is the introductory element of totality.

But it is precisely this part of his doctrine that seems the most tenuous. Certainly this justification of totality based on the precedence of feeling turns up almost out of nowhere to maintain the unity of the system and frame within it what is new. This require-

---

[158]*Aesthetica in nuce*, cit., p. 12. *L'Aesthetica in nuce* is the Italian edition of the article "Aesthetics," written for the 14th edition of the *Encyclopaedia Britannica* and published in Naples in 1929 as a non-commercial limited edition.

ment derives from other motives to which we have alluded, and the evaluation of it and of the various aspects it takes on in Croce can do without this justification.

Aesthetics in a Nutshell is the most extreme point Croce has reached so far in the sense of the overall totality of art and its identity with the entire life of the mind, and it has great significance in showing us the consequences of emphasizing a totality that attributes to art, more or less consciously, functions that properly belong to the other forms. The citations above are significant on this point and fail to persuade us of the necessary precedence of a moral experience for an artistic fact, because Croce himself convinced us of the independence of art (as of every fact of the mind) from its content taken on its own. But further on art is understood as morality and supreme knowledge, not only in its actual content, but in the very form of its own operation — assuming an almost pantheistic aspect.

The first definition given in the article is similar to the one we already know: "the contemplation of feeling," "lyrical intuition" this side of the distinction between unreality and reality. Indeed, the autonomous characteristics are accentuated. But later these characteristics are given functions that are not their own and which call this autonomy into question. One thing emphasized, for example, is the necessary presence of art in thought (and thus in action) that had seemed to us so difficult to grasp: "Without the poetic imagination that . . . becomes representation and word . . . logical thought would not arise — thought which is not language, but is never without language, and uses the language that poetry has itself created. And . . . without thought, action would be impossible, and along with it good action, moral conscience, duty" (p. 12). So not only is good action presupposed as necessary for art but art is presupposed as necessary for good action — which is even more obscure and incomprehensible.

But it is significant that this presence of art (as language — i.e., expression) in all the forms of the mind should be so much emphasized here, where the thesis is affirmed (explicitly for the first time — I believe — by Croce) that identification with expression holds not only for art, but for all the spheres of the mind. From this statement, instead of deducing the invalidity of that characteristic in distinguishing the artistic act and the need to base its autonomy on other aspects, he derives instead the artistic nature of the other facts of the mind as well: "This identity, which is to be affirmed for all spheres of the spirit, has an evidence and a prominence in art that it perhaps lacks elsewhere. In the creation of a work of poetry one looks on as if at the mystery of the creation of the world; hence the effectiveness that aesthetic science exercises on philosophy as a whole, because of the conception of the One-All" (p. 16).

We were not used to these sorts of comparisons from Croce. The sort that might almost make us think of that reaction we spoke of, exercised by art — when an apprehension of reality is attributed to it — on reality itself. But in any case it is clear that the precise characteristics that in the first years were set as distinctive to art — and seemed poorly suited to that role because they belonged to all forms of the mind — now serve to lend an aspect to art that is generic to the mind, so that it will come into the functions of the other forms — showing, if nothing else, the soundness of our criticism. But this introduction of them now takes on a very different tone. While at the time it meant at least the affirmation of art as a mental fact against those who did not even recognize this quality, now it only serves to confuse it with other facts of the mind. And indeed to justify its totality — but at the price of its autonomy and that of the other forms.

Now the totality of art, that is, its universality and human dignity, its eternal value, does not necessarily mean that it participates in all other forms of universality, much less that the latter are present in it as presuppositions. If the concept of the universal is strictly connected (as it is in Croce) to that of the individual, universality has to be understood as the recognition or attribution to a given individual of an eternal, mental value, indeed constitutive of the mind — the value of an essential and indispensable point of view toward the world. But this point of view does not exclude others, and if on one hand it can be said that it is *the whole world,* then it must be added that it is the whole world *in this determined way,* and that it admits the possibility of other modes and aspects that the world as mind can assume. Just as it cannot be said that a work of art includes in itself or presupposes all others (and yet all true works of art are universal), it cannot at the same time be said that the artistic universal includes in itself and presupposes the other universals, each of which has its own characteristic way of being such and of transfiguring content into an eternal form.

Art is an essential way of being that justifies itself, like thinking, wanting, acting. But this does not mean that the necessary presupposition of art and its constitutive aspect is the mind that thought, wanted, acted. Presupposition and content, as we have seen, can be anything at all; and in relation to art, when they are expressly detached from it, they are still matter or nature — and also feeling, not because they have to be these things before art frees and transfigures them, but because art makes them such in the very moment in which it acts.

This way of conceiving totality as the involvement of art in all the other forms of the mind, however, is an extreme conclusion which we do not believe Croce will linger over, and which in any case is not essential to the development of his work. To us it is important as an indicator of the consequences that result from moving without caution in a determined direction. But in Croce, more than a doctrinal significance, it has a polemical motive which, as such, is perfectly justified.

We have seen how critical fragmentism is the unjustified consequence of the autonomy of art. Now from this principle another form of fragmentism could be just as erroneously derived, this time not in the evaluation of the work of art, but in its actual production. This the position that an awareness of the specific nature of the artistic universal will give rise to a program of "pure" and distilled art, reduced to its quintessential state and intolerant of any other form. Now this program, not illegitimate in theory, has in fact shown itself to be harmful at times for art itself, given the exclusions it easily leads to, the impoverishment of content, and the fallacious incompatibilities that it leads to. And art comes out of it rarefied, incorporeal, and both intentional and laborious. Against such poetics, the pedagogical precept of being first of all *human* is fully valid — that is, of being concerned with reaching the universal in whatever way is granted to us, rather than aiming *a priori* for a determined and exclusive *way* of reaching it. And it is also worth remembering that a breadth of intellectual, social and moral life, and a generically human experience also promotes the depth and scope of that specific form of humanity that is artistic inspiration.

But above all, against these fears of contamination by other mental forms there is the valid objection that these forms are not in fact impurities or imperfections — they too are universals. If a work of art includes a mixture of artistic intuitions, insights of thought and impulses of moral will, the work will not be less pure, but instead admirable in more ways. And if within it a unitary mind should stir (be it artistic or logical), a universal above the universals that connects these disparate elements with a single overall tone, the emotion reached can only be richer and more diverse. Universals do not exclude each other when they are conceived as diverse aspects of the world, and the true critic, in distinguishing them and recognizing in each its own particular characteristic, will have to savor them all and exclude none from the overall description of the work.

It is only in this preceptive aspect that the concept of totality fulfills its true function as the "perpetual resolution of poetic struggles in a cosmic vision . . . the perpetual return from partial human determinations to pure, complete and indivisible humanity."[159] Arising from a polemical need in the field of art and in militant criticism, it is there that the concept fulfills its most vital task. But the true theoretical value of totality, as we have seen, is something else — it is in the strong consciousness of the universality of the artistic fact and of its eternal nature as a constitutive element of the mind, a consciousness that can only lead to a search for the specific character of this universality, which grounds its autonomy in itself.

V. COROLLARIES

The problem of criticism and the history of literature and art is symptomatic; Croce's various oscillations on it both follow and indicate the oscillations of his thought in general. Just recently, the question has come up again and again regarding the co-presence, necessary in the critic, of artistic qualities and logical qualities, and regarding the continuity between one work of art and another,

---

[159]*Critica* (1928) p. 230.

progress in the world's artistic consciousness, and the relationship between the poet's human personality and work of poetry.

It was natural that, once the criticism was understood as logical knowledge applied to the artistic fact, and therefore as recognition of this fact as such (a legitimate definition in itself), the problem of the relationship between these two phases and of the predominance of one or the other would arise differently depending on the greater or lesser independence of art with respect to logic. The critic's need for a strong intuitive capacity appears fundamental and Croce has never denied it. But once thought was understood as a faculty subsequent (if not superior) to intuition and able in itself to resolve and comprehend in synthesis both imaginative and cognitive forms, it was natural that criticism should no longer be understood as knowledge of artistic intuition, but as knowledge *tout court,* which by its very conformation cannot help but contain within itself an artistic fact. This leads to the concept of literary criticism as philosophy, which affirms not only the "indispensability of the philosophical premise," but also the "philosophical nature of the whole of the work that is called judgment or criticism or literary history" because "in judgment, concept and intuition constitute synthesis or unity, so that they cannot be treated as two things that are separate from one another" and "there can be no serious thinking about art, without the conjoined ability to understand the single work of art."[160]

This assertion does not give rise to absurdity, formulated in this way, but it actually becomes untenable when we consider that since for Croce concept and intuition constitute synthesis and unity in any judgment, not only artistic, then given that premise, every judgment, whatever its object and conformation, should be an artistic judgment. It is also untenable when the inversion of terms in the relation "literary criticism=philosophy" leads to the deduction "philosophy=literary criticism." To save the situation from this absurdity Croce at this point introduces the concept of history, as bearer of the individual, alongside art, splitting that identity into the two others of "philosophy and history, theory of art and art

---

[160]*Nuovi Saggi,* p, 216–17.

criticism" (p. 217). Doing this, however, once again raises the issue of the relations between the two individuals, artistic and historical, the first capable of standing alone, in the "understanding and appreciation of the work, critically mute," and the second incapable of this autonomy in the face of the logical universal, and therefore, unlike the other, intrinsic to that universal.

All this shows that bringing the two activities, artistic and logical, into contact with one another leads to unsustainable conclusions when this contact is intended as the unfolding of a single process, indeed as a unique and indivisible act of the mind. It is more than possible, however, to define criticism as the grafting of a cognitive process onto an artistic emotion, as long as this grafting is not a necessary development intrinsic to that emotion that unfolds by an inescapable order of precedence. It is rather a deliberately willed act whereby artistic intuition is assumed to be the content of thought, just as any other act of the mind could be assumed to be, so that artistic intuition unfolds in knowledge, just as it could unfold in some other activity, in new art for example.

In Croce himself this composite nature of critical activity makes itself felt, albeit not consciously, in the continuous oscillation between the emphasis given one moment to the artistic phase of it and the next to the logical phase. Thus he often insists on the "necessary and pre-critical" reproduction of the work of art as such, a reproduction that, as an artistic act, has autonomous and independent validity, and which sometimes, in a more or less clear way, is identified by him with criticism itself. The definition of criticism as philosophy — i.e. a logical and discriminating act, is precisely to understand it as a pure and exclusive judgment of the value given by the work of art, or the discrimination of poetry from non-poetry and the eventual recognition of the different positivity to be attributed to what is not art. The insistence on the artistic aspect of the critical activity is, instead, a consequence of the descriptive procedure that Croce sometimes mentions without ever arriving at a precise concept.

It is in fact clear that in addition to establishing the artistic value of a determined mental phenomenon (its place, that is, in the category of intuition) the critique has the task of illustrating this by reconstructing the formative process, explaining what it consists of, and describing and recounting the kind of artistic emotion this phenomenon gives rise to. Not only must it establish that it is art, but also how it is and what particular expressive tone in it has assumed an imperishable form. This task can of course be carried out (as it usually is) in logical terms, but recourse to fresh contemplation and artistic representations is in no way ruled out. Has it not been said that the essential and indispensable moment for criticism is the reproduction of the work of art? And since this is essentially an artistic activity, will it not be inseparable from expression? And won't this new expression, in addition to having value in itself, also serve to facilitate understanding, to bring states of mind "into focus" concerning the work of art that provoked it?

If the response to this is that the expression of an artistic emotion felt in front of a work of art is a new work of art and not criticism, we are not about to argue over a question of terms that would be all about the scope and meaning of the term "criticism." It simply seems that once we have ruled out viewing criticism as a passage to knowledge, necessary and intrinsic to the nature of art and knowledge itself — which would, as we have seen, resolve all of philosophy into a sort of literary criticism — once we have eliminated, that is, the illusion of a cognitive phase supervening out of necessity and almost inherent in the power of the artistic moment, the best course is to consider criticism generically as one activity taking place on top of another — a form of mind that is still reducible (like all of them) to one of the essential categories (art, philosophy), but distinctive for the function that it proposes. And this function is to facilitate by its action the understanding and judgment of another mental manifestation — an artistic act, for example, through a new expression of art or through the analytical and logical determination of its emergence; or an act of thought, through a new cognitive procedure; or even (and this often happens in so-called emotional interpretations of philosophical procedures, or rather in the vast panoramas of culture of which the great artist that was de Sanctis has given admirable examples) an act of thought through its own artistic intuition.

Criticism is always art or knowledge, and the critic is an artist or a philosopher or both together. But one who is distinguished from other artists or philosophers in that he recognizes in the object of his intuition or philosophizing, which can only abstractly be isolated and which takes the name *matter* or *nature,* a dignity and value independent of the form in which he presently receives it. A stimulus can be recognized in every fact of the mind, a starting point that generally has no meaning except in view of and in unity with that fact itself, and which taken on its own has a life that is abstract, inconceivable, and not autonomous. Now in critical activity as well, insofar as it leads to a form of knowledge and art that can only be universal, the stimulus or content is, in relation to that knowledge or art, abstract and non-isolable (an essay by de Sanctis, for example, is an artistic or thought unit complete in itself and not divisible into elements). But the essential notion is that this stimulus is content elevated by it to new life, and was itself a universal — that is, the elevation of yet another content.

We do not at this point want to go into an examination of the concept of matter or nature with respect to the act of the mind, and the problem of its greater or lesser positivity. But it is clear that in every mental act, taken in its individual universality, the pure object, the content, the stimulus considered in isolation, is an abstraction and thus negativity and non-being.[161] Now in criticism the previous universality of the abstract content is essential and conscious, and the inevitable duality of experience which results from this characteristic justifies the definition of criticism as a *composite* activity. Which does not invalidate the universal and eternal value of its action, but implies the necessity of another universal action before it.

This explains the need for a duality of attitudes on the part of the critic, who is actually defined by this — by his keeping alive what might be called the vitality of the object, by the apparent incomplete re-absorption of it into himself, by allowing it to have a

---

[161]Cf. *Critica* (1931) p. 408: "What else is . . . the object, the object per se, as something other than the subject, if not the returning phantom of that unconscious, of that non-mental, of that matter, of that nature, not dissected in criticism, or imperfectly dissected or dissected for an instant, and immediately then recomposed by the tenacious imagination, and which therefore reappears in a new attitude?"

life of its own, referring to it almost externally. Compared with the emotion (artistic or logical) that gives rise to criticism, every other emotion considers its object, whatever it may be, as nature that resolves itself into mind. The critic, on the other hand, is always conscious of the dignity of his object and keeps a little distance from it. Even feeling and being moved and acting in a certain way, a certain modesty leads him to reflect this emotion back on what stimulated it. Essentially, the critic also makes his object *nature*. But he lacks the nonchalance that characterizes so-called pure art. Thus, for example, the description or representation of a natural spectacle makes us want to see the places that have evoked it much less intensely than a commentary on a work of art (however valuable in itself and constituent of a complete unity of mind) makes us run with our thoughts and desires to the work of art itself.

This characteristic distinguishes the critic from the artist and the thinker. It is worth repeating that it is a characteristic that does not imply a fundamental difference in mental attitude. The categories and the great phases of the mind are still the same: art, knowledge — the difference is only in the tone and mode.

We might even define the difference by saying that the art critic considers the object of his emotion as artistic beauty, while the artist considers it to be natural beauty. And we know that Croce, both in the early *Aesthetics,* and in the *Essence,* as well as in his recent formulations, never makes a real intrinsic distinction between the two concepts. They are both stimulants for artistic emotion, devoid of any meaning if emotion is not present, and therefore considered only in view of it. The difference between them is only one of degree: "Artificial beauty, fashioned by man, is a far more ductile, firm, effective aid."[162] But the essence is the same, and the function with regard to art is identical. "It is evident that beyond the instruments made for the reproduction of images, already existing objects may be found, whether man-made or not, that fulfill that function — that is, that are more or less adequate for fixing a memory of our intuitions, and these things take the name of natural beauty."[163]

---

[162]*Estetica*[1], p. 99.
[163]*Nuovi Saggi*, p. 41.

Now, once an artistic emotion has occurred it is always possible to consider its object and the physical or psychic or natural facts that gave rise to it as adequate for provoking it and fixing a memory. In a certain sense, the content of an artistic intuition can always be considered natural beauty. The feature that distinguishes pure artistic emotion from that of the critic thus lies in the fact that the critic considers the beauty underlying his emotion as artistic beauty — as something produced with the precise purpose of making his emotion an object and awakening it. And this is where the flavor of his action lies — here, and in the pretension to arrive, by means of this natural object that is the work of art (the painting, the statue, the book, the musical score), at the exact and identical reproduction, in all its intimacy, of the primitive emotion.

But achieving this absolutely is something the critic can never be sure of. The problem of communication, which Croce tries to solve using objects produced for mnemonic purposes, can never be rigorously solved on this basis. This is because, since these objects are mnemonic, they become *natural* for the reproducing artist, and a hiatus is introduced that is sufficient to remove the authenticity of the passage. To bridge this hiatus, Croce speaks of the "mental nature of the real,"[164] and of the "idealist conception of the world, which is all life and mind."[165] Imprecise words, ambiguous in meaning. Indeed, how is it possible to speak of the mental nature of objects that, being mnemonic, were explicitly placed by the mind outside itself, as nature? Reality is not mental except when it is assailed by the mind. And the mnemonic object will certainly be mental insofar as it is learned and relived, but in being relived it will cease to be mnemonic, thus preventing the persistence in itself of the mind that created it, once it has become estranged from it. This establishment of a mind outside ourselves that we can enter into contact with, comes down to a form of panpsychism.

Croce himself implicitly recognizes this difficulty, saying that in the same way that it is difficult to penetrate the mind of an artist distant from us, it will be even more difficult to penetrate the

---

[164]*Critica* (1928) p. 121.
[165]*Aesthetìca in nuce*, p. 20.

mind of a cat or a plant.[166] But he leaves room for the doubts we have voiced when he states that "the process of poetic communication, just as it takes place with artificially produced objects, can also take place with naturally given objects. . . . True it is that these formations are labile. . . . And, unlike artistic works, they do not allow for authentic interpretations."[167]

Now, keeping to these formulations there is no way to judge the possibility and authenticity of works of art, and in this way the problem of communication cannot be said to have been solved. The critic, in the activity he carries out, can (indeed, must) reach the universal — but it is not possible to know if this universal is identical to that of the artist being criticized. We know only that he refers to the latter as his agent, and this is the essential characteristic of the critic.

Croce's conception of criticism as the application of logical knowledge to the artistic act is only partial and does not exhaust the concept, which can also take in other modes of description and can also be extended to the consideration (logical and artistic) of the fact of thought. But this would only be a difference in terminology if it didn't also entail the negation of a fundamental assumption of Croce's derived from his concept of the dialectic of distinct forms — that is, that the passage from art to logic is natural and necessary in the development of the mind; that thought, on the one hand, needs artistic form to express itself, and that art, on the other, can only develop into knowledge. These affirmations should both be rejected.

In any case, given Crocean theory, it is natural that there is a correspondence between greater independence of the artistic phase and an emphasis on the qualifying or descriptive character of criticism — the aspect of it, that is, that stops before a work of art not only to evaluate and judge it, but first and foremost to tell about it and relive the emotion of it. Except that the impossibility of conceiving this descriptive function as an artistic rather than logical activity blocks Croce from reaching an intrinsic determi-

---

[166]*Critica* (1928) p. 121.
[167]*Aesthetica in nuce*, p. 20–21.

nation of it and obliges him to limit it to the surroundings and background of the true work of art. Thus he speaks of criticism in which the beauty of a work is determined by "describing its inspirational motivation with the help of empirical or approximate concepts" all directed at the "infinitely varied material on which poetry arises, and the kinds of moods that are elevated to purity of expression," all the while maintaining, however, that "strictly speaking there is nothing but poetry, without adjectives,"[168] and that to recapture the character of the work of art, "one must do no more than recite the poem."[169] And he still accepts and theorizes this qualifying function of criticism only to the extent that it facilitates understanding intuition by clarifying what is presupposed for it, and almost never what is intrinsic to it.

In Croce's view de Sanctis, faced with the canto of Francesca, proceeds "by process of elimination," "calling attention to what makes up the poetry of the canto and to the particular feeling that Dante expresses," and as for the art itself and that feeling itself, liberated in imagination, "de Sanctis was unable (except by reporting Dante's verses) to reproduce its own individual character — its own individual physiognomy and accent."[170]

Now if by this requirement of reproduction he means the identical repetition of a mental fact or emotion with all its characteristics (and thus with its own the unique expression), this obviously cannot happen except through the material repetition of the fact itself (when possible) without the slightest addition. And in this way it is reduced to a superfluous act both in the case of art and of any other state of mind — even, that is, of all the precedents and presuppositions of art. But if qualifying criticism refers to a mental act taking place based on another act — an artistic or cognitive emotion felt in the face of another emotion — it is hard to see why this work of elaboration or clarification, narration or representation, should take place only as applied to the precedents of art and not to art itself. And it is hard to see why it is not possible to delve with

---

[168]*Critica* (1923) p. 112.
[169]*Critica* (1924) p. 127.
[170]*Nuovi Saggi*, p. 227–28.

one's thought into the meanders of an artistic emotion, to study its emergence, unfolding and coming to maturation, to determine and describe its particular tone and unmistakable individual essence — what is its own even in its universality, and to recite or express artistically the emotion that it stirs — on the understanding that each of these acts, cognitive or artistic in itself (and always universal) is still criticism, thanks to that reference to previous artistic emotion as a presupposition and agent and producer.

The imperfect awareness of the autonomy of art, which Croce nevertheless managed partly to characterize, and the need always to explain its connection with knowledge, thus leads him to conceive some characteristics that might belong to the artistic universal itself independent of the logical universal, as grafts of logical form. This gets him into the sort of difficulties we have seen an example of in the awkwardness that his concept of criticism falls into.[171] The problem of the history of art — which is whether or not any continuity is possible, either between works or generally in the artistic consciousness of the world, reflects this ambiguity, along with the uncertainty it finds itself in when faced with the idealist frameworks still not abandoned, and the epistemological individualism that Croce has now arrived at.

In the first *Aesthetics,* he states: "We can represent the entire history of science on a single line of progress and regress. Science is universal, and its problems are connected, subordinated, coordinated and unified in a single vast system and overall problem. But art is intuition, and intuition is individuality, and individuality does not repeat itself" (p. 136–37). But now that even the history of science is seen by Croce as the resolution of many single problems, no longer linear and unitary but rather multiple, the distinction disappears between it and the history of poetry and art: "The procedure is in fact neither more nor less than that of the history of art and poetry. . . . Nor must we say that every philosophic problem is linked to all the others and is always a problem of the whole of philosophy, making it different from the cases of poetry and art, for there is no diversity here either, and the whole of history and

---

171   G.A. Borgese, "Il metodo nella storia dell'arte," *Conciliatore* (1914): p. 16–38.

the entire universe are immanent in every single work of art."[172]

The individualism that is more and more explicitly introduced, through history, into the concept of knowledge, thus leads in some manifestations to a greater similarity between the cognitive and the artistic individual. On the other hand, this precise new concept, monadistic and devoid of dialectical developments, can also include art. In a recent article, "The present state of historiography in Italy," Croce contests the idea that the concept of art as individual must lead us to deduce the impossibility of a history of art or poetry. This inference negates — he says — only "an improper form of history." The true history of poetry is "the history of each true poem that finds its material in its own time as well as in the past and in presentiments of the future and its form in the original form that the poet has given it, and which represents a new fact without equivalents, the historical event in the aesthetic sphere.... This is the reality of every historical work, which is always particular and universal in the particular."[173] The commitment to bringing art into the mainstream of human activity and preventing its being detached from history is thus favored here by the altered concept of history, which itself becomes similar to art inasmuch as it is imprinted with a universal pluralism.

But regarding the other *history* as well, the idealist, Hegelian, dialectic type — from which Croce has never managed to free himself completely — he feels the need to include art. Art has been increasingly losing individuality as a distinctive characteristic of its own, and in its new and specific universality it no longer has the monadist aspect that made it impossible to organize it into a continuous line of development. Thus we note the various and increasingly pronounced attempts to justify progress and the passage from one work to another — an increasing desire to establish connections. There is the statement from 1922 that "art also progresses in a certain sense — i.e., it becomes more mentally complex, charged with new history; not from critic to critic, but rather from poet to poet (say from

---

[172]*Teoria e st. della Storiografia*, p. 128–29.
[173]*Critica* (1929) p. 86 and seg.

Homer to Goethe)."[174] And from 1925 the affirmation that "every true artist binds himself to those that came before . . . but in binding himself to them he breaks free and asserts his status as himself."[175] And again, recently, Croce has affirmed the "importance of tradition in the history of poetry, the impossibility of disrupting it and skipping over it, the necessity of preserving it while always innovating. Poetry, and with it the whole life of the mind, is like a chorus that continues down through the centuries, and a new voice cannot resonate as new unless it listens to and accepts into itself those that preceded it, and responds to them, resuming the song and continuing it in its own way and theirs at the same time."[176]

A desire, in short, for history no longer in the individualistic and monadistic sense of the past, but in the dialectical sense of the ideal passage from one intuition to another, of the progressive absorption of all the artistic experiences of one period into the next, and of the grounding of each on what went before as if on conditions. This uncertain and insecure desire is never explicitly recognized, but it is certainly present in Croce's inner consciousness, and implicit also in the need he has to continually correct his primitive concept of the work of art as specific and isolated, and to enrich and adorn its history with contours and relationships and connections.

We have seen such connections between works of art in the history of literature as well as in the single personalities of each artist. It may be said that this desire — arising in Croce from the need to give more dignity and universality to the artistic act, and from his defense against the accusation of fragmentism — becomes more than anything a generic need, taking different forms according to the occasions in which it appears. One notices in him the widest variety of attempts to bring art and art criticism closer to history — the word which, in the world of his emotional preferences, comes closest to the overall meaning of "humanity." And since the concept itself of history undergoes various oscillations, this analogy and connection with art takes on a variety of designations.

---

[174]*Critica* (1922) p. 59.
[175]*Critica* (1925) p. 379.
[176]Preface to De Lollis, *Saggi sulla forma poetica dell'Ottocento* (Bari, 1929).

So that in addition to a distaste for the isolation of each work of art from the others, he shows a notable desire to justify its unity with the human complexity of the artist, with the artist's personality. The sort of *essay* or *monograph* that Croce proposes as the true and proper form of literary and artistic historiography, as a way of reaching "the character of the single artist and his personality or work, which converge into one,"[177] appearing to be the definitive theorizing of an individualist conception, gives rise to connections and passages that in the light of Crocean theories themselves, are very significant.

That character is, he says, "genetic and historical, and is realized as the delineation of the personality and artworks in their development . . . reflecting the internal dialectic" (p. 175). But what is this concept of personality? Does it have an autonomous and irreducible meaning, or does it not instead resolve itself into a criterion of connection that can be valid in some cases and not in others? Has Croce himself not said elsewhere that the individual is an institution? And in this same collection of essays does he not say that "there may be . . . extreme cases where the same personality is divided among several biographical individuals and two or more different artistic personalities follow each other and alternate in the same biographical individual" (p. 233)? In such a case the character of the personality could in principle extend itself to the artistic unity of several individuals or to an entire *school,* and such connections would no longer be grounded only in the emotional or moral or social substrate — in the material of the work of art — but in the autonomous and intrinsic value of art itself.

But the truth is that these relations — and any other relation between one work of art and another, between a work of art and a work of thought, between human personality (biographical, social, moral or what have you) and artistic personality — these relations are there when they are there. And when they are there they have to be discovered first of all by the critic, who must study, illustrate and *report* on them. But they are not an indispensable necessity of a work of art, which in itself can be grounded in any material. They cannot be shown to be implicit in the concept of it. They are with-

---

[177]*Nuovi Saggi,* p. 174.

out doubt always *possible* and do not contradict any of its basic characteristics. We have seen, in the case of Dante, how it was necessary to consider as a fact of the mind, universal and eternal, even the connecting tissue of his work and life, and that spirit that pervades all and makes individual artistic intuitions inseparable from the mental whole from which they arose and in which they took place. That connection, we have said, is not *aggregate* but *monad* itself. Now the case can be generalized. We can say that always, in a work of art, connections with what preceded and followed, with the other forms of mind etc. may or may not be intrinsic. They can be monad or aggregate, an integrating part of the work itself or a related accessory, a mental fact or a random accompaniment.

And this is true not only as concerns the material and content of a work, but the work itself in its artistic value. It can happen that a tone, a poetic emotion unfolds as the elaboration, consequence or prolonging of other tones or emotions, or that it springs spontaneously from the material, oblivious to similarities or perhaps aware but independent of them. It can happen that at the core itself of an artistic emotion there is an intrinsic continuous reference to a moral or intellectual experience, not as its own content, but as a factor that modifies and determines and identifies that same emotion. Or this may not happen. If such a connection or dialectic is present it cannot be neglected by criticism, and the transition from one artistic tone to another, or the relationship between an intellectual experience and an artistic tone, will constitute one of the fundamental fields of investigation. Indeed, the critic's main task will be to search out which of these relationships and dialectics are alive and idealized in the work, which should be emphasized and which neglected.

Croce has a propensity, in the general direction of his work (and the contrary passages cited are a significant exception), to interpret every common element that brings an intuition close to another as belonging to a preceding substrate of a work of art rather than to the work itself. "In order to situate works of art within their developmental frameworks ... it is necessary ... to compare them with each other and to extract certain general characteristics. . . . No general abstract features can be extracted from a series of artworks except those concerning their subject matter, which are thus not artistic but intellectual and poetic."[178] Here again, in short, as in the case of qualifying criticism, he invokes elements that do not belong to art.

But we know that Croce feels the need for such connections, more or less explicitly, since he has a clear concept of the universality and totality of the artistic fact. Now the reasons for them, if they truly exist, cannot be extrinsic to them but rather belong to their true essential form. We have seen that qualifying criticism addresses not only the content, or the emotional and impassioned material that gave rise to the art, but to the way the art freed this material from its partial nature — that is, it addresses the art itself. And it determines what essential form or mode of art the work in question belongs to, what other similar emotions it can be compared with, and what others it could have, or actually has, given rise to.

Every work of art, if it truly is one, gives us something absolutely new and everlasting — a new form, a new visual tone that, once it is expressed, constitutes an eternal acquisition for the human mind. Qualifying criticism can analyze and explain this tone, dissect its originality, study its relations and similarities, if there are any, with other tones and works of art, and its connections with cognitive forms and morals. Frame it, in other words, bring it into focus. And once framed and described in this way, will a work not find itself part of a development process? Cannot its originality, that singular contribution that it has made to the world, have its basis in a past continuity and lay the foundations for a future continuity?

This continuity, of course, will concern not only the content of the work of poetry, but rather its very way of being art — and it will clarify, or rather, it will make it possible to witness, the birth and development of that particular accent, that particular way of singing and seeing and contemplating the world. Because art, which is one of the *forms* through which the single and partial can become universal and eternal, has life only in the infinite processes in which this passage takes place — that is, in the infinite (in theory, very few in fact) works of art, each of which represents an eternal and original way in which that passage was able to take place.

---

[178]*Nuovi Saggi*, p. 168–70.

VI. Conclusion

We have tried to capture the riches and the deficiencies of Crocean aesthetics by analyzing the successive positions that the problem of art has taken during its development. Each of these positions has shown its vitality, and its motivating truth, its deep theoretical significance, or else its polemical function in eliminating prejudices, proposing a more intrinsic view of the artistic act and opposing dubious or dangerous attitudes. And the difficulties arose principally in the incorrect interpretation of observations and discoveries, and in extending their function beyond its limits.

The need for collocation — closely linked with the idealist and dialectic premises that were left out of Croce's true philosophical core — exerts its influence at times on observations that ought to have a simple *descriptive* validity with regard to the artistic process in its emergence and manifestation, independently of what *function* has been served. The circle of distinct forms, which in its way represents the need for apriorist and deductive justification, imposes itself on transcendental empiricism, distorting the data at times and rendering it unacceptable. And yet it is precisely in this empiricism that the riches of Croce lie — his ability to stick to his guns about art, at times drawing from it universal determinations. So that when we disregard the necessities presupposed for the passage from one form to another, the pre-established order of precedence, and if the various definitions of art are to be understood in their own right, each one as the highlighting of an essential and constitutive aspect of a mental event, then Crocean aesthetics represents an ever-growing patrimony of statements that enrich and clarify the concept of art. And if these were at first generic and intended simply to bring the form under the general notion of the mind and to demonstrate its leading character, its non-subservience to any other activity, later they increasingly came close to a more intrinsic account of the artistic fact, and to determinations that more closely grasped its distinctive universality. In this way the nexus of the distinct forms, though unflaggingly affirmed, crumbles — and the observations concerning the *location* of art almost always have to be transformed and interpreted as notes on its *semiotics*, replacing forced compactness and coherence with a new coherence in research, consisting of going deeper and deeper into the problem, clarifying an ever-increasing number of its aspects.

Thus, the primitive definition of intuition as individual knowledge, was (as Croce explicitly admitted) meant to establish, against some European schools of thought at the time, the mental value of art, giving it an essential theoretical function. And later, all doubts about its validity dispelled, and a concept of theoretic activity established such that all of it (and not only the artistic phase) should be thought of as individual knowledge, the definition of art as individual knowledge ceases to be valid and is suppressed, nevertheless retaining the theoretic character that makes its rigorous distinction from knowledge problematic.

Here the concept of the identification of intuition with expression was very useful and crucial for breaking down the prejudices of formalist and content-oriented criticism. But if in the case of art it was more urgent to establish it, this did not mean that it was therefore the exclusive property of art — indeed, identity of something with its own expression belongs to all the spheres of the mind, and making art its lone carrier forces the involvement and concomitance of art (in the form of language) with all other activities, which is difficult to demonstrate.

These determinations, in short, do belong to art, but they are not characteristic of it. And that illusion — that they were — led to a series of errors on the relationship between art and the other forms of the mind.

Not even the so-called lyrical character — that is, the element of feeling — seemed to be a determination able to serve as a decisive distinguishing criterion for art, one it could found its autonomy on. Not, that is, if it is true that feeling must be understood as a generic substratum of every mental form, an element of impulse and struggle that is part of its processes, rather than an autonomous and therefore universal attitude of the mind. And this also helped us refute the required precedence of the practical phase over the aesthetic phase that Croce had used the precedence of feeling to establish.

None of the characteristics used to justify and theoretically ground the dialectic of distinct forms and the collocation of art in the circle of the mind appeared specific to art, belonging instead to the general idea of an act of the mind. And we believed we recognized the most intrinsic determinations, those that most closely grasp the precise and particular tone of artistic activity, in concepts of pure representation, lack of distinction between real and unreal, and catharsis (liberation, that is, from any impulse toward application or the production of consequences), that theorize, albeit implicitly, its detachment from any cognitive form.

When the requirement of totality arose forcefully in Croce along with this most intimate study of the artistic act, it seemed to be a fact of great meaning and importance, indicating that the better and better delineated autonomy and specificity of the artistic act coincided with its universality — indeed it was its constitutive form — and that its autonomous nature did not put it second to any form of the mind, but rather made it an inalienable way of being. But an imperfect awareness of this, and the permanent need for connections with the practical and theoretical forms, led Croce to then conceive of the human dignity of the artist not as *artistic* humanity, intrinsic to the nature of the artist's activity, but as a requirement of involvement in other activities. No one would deny that such a requirement is fundamental to the mental and artistic health of any individual, but it does not represent the greatness and eternity of the *function of the artist*. And at the same time, when one wants to attribute humanity in this sense to art itself, and not to its surroundings, it requires that art be rendered such that its makeup involves participation in the functions of the other activities, and that it be relegated under the concept of them, thus destroying the autonomous character of its universality.

Set out and interpreted in this way, free from the framing of his dialect of distinct forms, Croce's aesthetic system looks like a collection of information and universal observations that can be called complete (if anything is complete in this field) for the acuity of its research and the variety of aspects considered and needs met. We may say that none of Croce's observations is without motivating truth, or indeed without deep, useful and topical lessons. We have sought to free them all from the interpretation that Croce himself gave in attempting to adapt them to his presupposed organizational framework, and we have tried to reset them, one might say, so as to be able to discern in them their true system, not imposed in advance, but deriving from and identical with the actual data itself.

We shall certainly not set out a program for this system — beyond what has implicitly emerged. We would only note the new concept of the universal-individual, which Croce only arrived at in his *Historiography,* a conception freer than its forerunners of any dialectic connection, the unitary and linear development of a single mental process that thus opens the possibility of a history (philosophy, that is) consisting of multiple developments, a solution to the infinite variety of problems that life incessantly presents. We would point out that this new concept could also serve to introduce a new consideration of the relations between the various ways the universal can position itself — that is, between the various forms of the mind. The dialectical relationship between condition and conditioned that Croce speaks of has shown itself to be unsuitable for solving various problems, and Croce himself, rather than uncovering and proving it, had deduced it by the exclusion of others. "Considering the matter in general, it seems that there is no other way of thinking of the joint independence and dependence of the various mental activities than to conceive of them in the relationship of condition to conditioned."[179] Once the conformation of each activity of the mind has been established, along with its similarities and differences with respect to the others, is it really necessary that there be a relationship between them in the sense of a passage from one to the other according to a fixed order? We do not seek to resolve the issue here, but rather to affirm that we cannot resolve it until we have fully described these various mental activities and seen, based on their characteristics what relations are necessary.

So this task of description is the first order of business. And for art — once we have accepted (with Croce) its primary mental character, its validity as an essential, irreducible form of the mind — we must seek its distinctive nature, delving to the root of its universality to see how it is set apart from the other forms and studying its conformation, phenomenology and effects.

---

[179]*Nuovi Saggi,* p. 55.

Some of Croce's observations may be of great value for this. We have already seen that his concepts of representation and contemplation, along with the lack of distinction between reality and unreality may point in very interesting directions. And some of the definitions we have criticized from the standpoint of collocation may serve as cues for description. The term "individual," for example, and the specific nature (affirmed in the early years) of an art incapable of continuity and history may indicate not so much its role and position in the world of the mind, but rather an essential characteristic — a certain stasis, that is, of the aesthetic universal, and its non-production of consequences or developments (unlike what happens in the case of knowledge), a contentment with its own vision without a need for corollaries and deductions, along with the ability to be the stimulus for a new activity when enlisted as such, without being active in itself or tending toward actual application. And its identification with expression (which we have seen is inherent in any activity) — could this not have been eminently recognized in art, as an activity entirely directed towards representation, image, and spectacle, which any kind of content transfigures not into a logical organism and an impulse to act, but into vision and calm narrative?

This way individuality would not belong to art as a constituent element of knowledge, of which it and only it was the bearer. Instead, recognizing the individual essence of every universal, this metaphorical "individuality" would indicate a specific trait of the artistic individual-universal. Thus, granted that each mental form is identical with its own expression, the metaphorical character of *expression* would accentuate a particular way of being of artistic intuition-expression.

These are only examples, and may even turn out to be inaccurate and false. In any event, there is much work to be done, moving in this or in other directions, to clarify the conformation and essential characteristics of the artistic universal — and it is mainly in this sense that the great work of Croce should be utilized and continued.

II: Young Eugenio

"Review of *Critical Essays,* by G. Debenedetti" (Florence: Solaria, 1929; *Leonardo* 2 (1930): 92–93.

These essays by Giacomo Debenedetti may be read more for their own sake than for their significance as comments and evaluations of works of art, and are of interest mainly as examples of a type, a style of criticism.

The focus of Debenedetti's central critical problem could be said to oscillate between two poles, art and biography. Once the stark Crocean scheme of "poetry or not poetry" has been rejected, the dilemma moves between the fragmentary capture and re–enactment of the artistic moment, and the psychological narration of the work's process of formation. As between the Child and the Man, it might be said that Debenedetti has chosen the latter, at least in his intentions. His book, he says, is "entirely aimed at demoting the carefree figurine of the artist who opens his mouth and sings, in favor of the example of the fully conscious man who stands on his own feet and expresses, albeit with difficulty, his own moral interest."

Debenedetti has had the good sense not to stick too closely to this rigid position, and the form of criticism that has emerged we would say strikes a perfect balance between the two extremes. Take, for example the long essay on the poetry of Saba. It is styled as a continuous sentimental biography of the poet, dealing, as a Crocean would say, with the "content." But the discourse is conducted in such a way that the passionate or psychological element is captured at the moment closest to when it is released in artistic expression, so that the narration itself is already a commentary and, the point having been reached when biography has ceased and art begun, words are almost no longer necessary. This is not because, as Croce says, before a work of art one can only admire in silence, but because the commentary was already implicit in the previous narrative, whose object was indeed an emotional impulse, but one already intended as a candidate for artistic expression.

Debenedetti's great merit is in this power to uncover psychological mechanisms with a delicacy that does not obscure their poetic flame, which allows him to avoid fragmentism without at the same time reducing the author's unity to a mere unity of structure.

It must be noted, however, that the authors Debenedetti has chosen are those most readily suited to such a strategy. The emotional and psychological content of the lives of Saba and Proust, lived entirely for art, has almost no other purpose than to become poetry. Even what is most deeply theoretical in Proust, for example, the mechanisms of the "intermittences du coeur" or the search for Lost Time, are almost inconceivable except in the light of the artistry of their presentation. Indeed, for these men art is the unifying element of their scattered psychological experiences — poor men, if in the eternity of contemplation they did not find their own dignity and composure.

But there are others for whom art emerges like a sporadic and fortuitous flower from a strong and steady logical and moral life. Or still others in whom it gathers and presents an immense patchwork of life experiences, each of which has its own richness of meaning — great souls whom humanity salutes not only as its storytellers, but as its fathers. How will the critic deal with them?

Already in his essays on Croce's style and on Michelstaedter, Debenedetti implicitly asserts a strict distinction between logical content and art, clearly delimiting and isolating in the works of the two thinkers the elements of lyricism, which he quotes separately and with the satisfaction of a gourmet. But even here he has an easy time of it, dealing with authors nobody considers to be artists, and whose art can be reduced to a few fragments. But what would his approach be towards artistic personalities like Goethe or Dostoyevsky?

Our view is that he would have to change his method — which does not invalidate the one he used here for these authors, just as the considerations on the biographical method do not invalidate the warmth of some beautiful pages of pure criticism (for example in the first essay on Proust), in which the tone of the poet, the character and manner of his releasing his individual and sentimental experience into eternal vision, is described in terms that can only be defined as artistic.

This said, we would have wished for greater streamlining in the exposition and a brevity more terse. We regret somewhat his lingering over the image, the need to show the object in all its aspects. We cannot believe that this derives from the desire to "say it all." Proust did the same, but in him the stubborn slowness melts into the whole work as its "tone," that element which, beyond the single sentence or the page, constitutes the pervasive epic quality of his poetry.

"Review of *Shaftesbury (Ethics and Religion — The Morality of Feeling)*, by L. Bandini" (Bari: Laterza, 1930); *Leonardo* 4 (1930): 241–42.

Bandini gives a clear and accurate profile of this author, little known in Italy, and does not neglect appropriate historical references — a sober framework that is enough to give us a fairly complete picture of Shaftesbury. In this intention to inform, Bandini may be said to have fully succeeded. On the other hand, since most of the work focuses, as the author himself acknowledges, on the exposition of doctrine, "maintaining as far as possible its literal expression," would it not have been preferable to provide a good translation of some of Shaftesbury's essays (if not of the entire *Characteristics,* not a very large work) preceded by an ample historical–critical introduction?

Nevertheless, the Italian audience is given a fairly clear idea of who Shaftesbury was and the place of his philosophy in the history of thought. As to its value, Bandini tries to uncover all the elements of modernity in it, and is satisfied with the thesis that positions Shaftesbury almost as a precursor of Kantian and post–Kantian formulations.

At the same time, one would do well to be very wary of such anticipations of doctrine. The misunderstanding in which Locke was made an *ante litteram* Kant is well known (and Bandini, on p. 30, perhaps falls into it), and care must be taken not to make the same mistake with regard to Shaftesbury. There are undoubtedly elements of modernity in him, but perhaps more in the state of urgency and implied necessity than as expressed formulations. All thinkers, and especially these limpid and naive Englishmen, frequently offer us grounds for bold inferences; but it would be contrary to the truth to attribute to them all the "arrière pensées" that we have when we read them.

Bandini showcases the anti–religious character of Shaftesbury's moral position and the validity of his opposition to Hobbes using the latter's own weapons — indeed, this last observation struck us as one of the sharpest and most notable in the book. But, if it is true that the "Hobbesian methodological presupposition is fully accepted by Shaftesbury," who "resumes the research with a new spirit and arrives at a result that, by correcting Hobbes's, in reality completes it" (pg. 92), then it is precisely on the basis of this methodology that Shaftesbury's work should be judged, and not based the morally dogmatic conclusions that it arrived at.

There is no guarantee that one moral doctrine is superior to another simply because it preaches more elevated virtues, and it seems to us that Shaftesbury's morality does not depart from the empiricism that was typical of his times. Conceiving of ethical activity as *affection*, feeling and impulse is to give it the same character of passion and egotism that he reproaches Hobbes for. And just because Shaftesbury's *affections* are more elevated than Hobbes's instinct, this is not a reason to believe that they belong to a different mental physiognomy. In this regard it does not matter what the contents of the passion are — *homo economicus* is what he is, for example, whether his instinct is expressed in the form of hate or of love.

The difficulty of basing an independent morality on feeling is demonstrated by the problem that Shaftesbury encounters in determining the specific content of his morality. Bandini notes very clearly all the different determinations that his author is led to attribute to moral affection in order to distinguish it from other affections — how one moment he must resort to "pantheistic elements joined by clear motives of a personalized transcendentalism" (p. 81), the next to a concept of sociality, and finally to analogies with the artistic fact (whence the serious and elevated conception of art that Croce highlighted so clearly in his own essay on Shaftesbury). But these determinations remain extrinsic to the moral fact — they are still addressed only to its content. While we now know that in a truly autonomous attitude of the mind form and content are identical, and that in our case it is not possible to speak of an *instinctive* affection that then has as its object a social, or aesthetic, or other reality.

Bandini is well aware of these intrusions of intellectualist or

metaphysical — that is, extra–empirical — elements into Shaftesbury's empirical conception. And he tries to eliminate the contradiction. But in our view he is forced to stretch the author's thinking
somewhat. We know that the contradiction cannot be remedied except by attributing a transcendental quality to moral affection — by
making it truly participate, that is, in the totality of the mind, which
is both theoretic and practical. This is what Bandini does, and what
leads him to deduce the modernity of his author. But these formulations belong more to Bandini than to Shaftesbury, in whom the
presence of dissension does not yet imply its resolution or even that
its terms are consciously set. Shaftesbury stops at the empirical, and
evidence of this is his loathing for any theoretical basis for morality
and any dependence of it on religion. This principle constitutes its
strength as well as its weakness — because, if in this way, as Bandini notes, he contributed to bringing morality from heaven to earth,
against the abstractness of the Cambridge school, he was on the other hand unable to give to it that aspect of "form" in the Kantian sense
that is inherent in the modern conception, and he could not reach
a theoretical formulation that was epistemologically detached from
that of Hobbes.

But if Bandini perhaps exaggerates the more properly philosophical meaning of the author, he instead succeeds perfectly
in identifying the human character, so to speak, of his work —
a living and agile organism, in which the desire for concreteness
and immanence joins with the tendency to a morality that reflects
the universal. It is true that these two needs are not reconciled in
Shaftesbury. But their aspirational value remains, and this characterizes the figure of the thinker. And to us moderns, regardless of
the results achieved, it brings out our sympathy for those who have
attempted the same path as us.

"Review of *Justice, Essay on the Philosophy of Law,* by Max Ascoli"
(Padova: Cedam, 1930); *Civiltà moderna* 6 (1930): 1223–27.

The great virtue of this book is the open honesty of its relations with contemporary philosophy in Italy. In an age in which

philosophical battles and polemics are so fierce and violent, when it seems imperative for a young person to immediately join in and belong to a "school," Ascoli manages to avoid these affinities, which weigh, to a greater or lesser degree, on independence of thought. Even while recognizing the great impetus that Italian Neo–idealism has given to his philosophy, he is free of any commitment to one or the other of the doctrines that lead back to it. His thinking thus exists in the context of the problems marked by this philosophical tradition — but in complete independence. And rather than limiting himself, as many others have, either to accepting or partially correcting a particular idea, he freely takes up some of the fundamental data and absorbs and assimilates it in his own autonomous attempt at a system. An attempt that in its very ambition points to the pitfalls that await. And nevertheless it seems that only this reckless spirit can move us closer to a clearer understanding of the problems that traditional doctrines have left unsolved.

Ascoli's system starts with a denial of the Crocean definition of economics (i.e. as individual volition) and the reduction of the philosophy of law to the philosophy of economics. He attempts to graft law and normativity onto everything that is commonly understood as practical life, making it an essential and indispensable element, an eternal aspect of the mind.

This brings him face to face with a problem that is highly topical at the moment, following the idealist and contingency–based negation of all abstract schemata, all aggregates or, as Croce would put it, all pseudo–concepts. Because whether one denies the schema (as idealism does) by reducing it to nature and error, or attributes to nature and error (as contingentism does) all the characteristics of the schema, the negative emphasis on the latter is evident. And while it could be said that all the dominant doctrines of today are fighting and disagreeing over the value and conformation of knowledge, over its presentation and object, they nevertheless agree on one point — that all the essential determinations of the mind must be sought in data that is primitive and simple, not constructed and complex. Schemata, norms and generalities are conceived as successive formations, not original, constructions whose value lies entirely in the material they are built with. And the functionality by which these buildings are constructed, this faculty of aggregating, of schematizing, of pinning down the immobile aspects of the mutability of life, has been understood as a faculty that is essential and indispensable to the life of the mind, but which inevitably, fatally, through a necessary but legitimate process, leads to error.

Thanks to this indispensability of its origin, however, the error comes to assume an important function, its aspect as an essential element in the dialectic that makes up the life of the mind. Hence the identification of *error with nature,* which simultaneously serves to place a negative accent on nature and to attribute to the error a legitimacy of its own.

The schema, in short, set against the original and essential fact of life, is understood by these philosophies as an error. But this error, when we come to analyze and justify it in terms of its foundation, reveals itself as a necessary function of truth, and its formative process appears inseparable from every act of the mind. So, why persist with the negative tone about it? Why deny the essential value of fixed and schematic complexes, while at the same time recognizing the essential and irrepressible nature of the process that causes them to arise? If this process is arbitrary, why not eliminate it from mental life altogether? And since it instead turns out to be necessary (including as the position of an aggregate) it will have to be accepted among the legitimate and essential forms of the mind.

This is what Ascoli does when he positions the abstract norm no longer as an inferior aspect of mental activity, but as the primordial and essential form in which it manifests itself: "The first initial moment of the life of the mind, the first of the two poles between which it takes place, is in fact the norm, as the first fundamental and necessary form of knowledge of reality and of ourselves and of our action in relation to reality. In the beginning was the norm" (p. 29). This attempt to look at the process behind the abstract schema philosophically, and to recognize its essential value therefore strikes us as fully justified and rich in developmental potential. Ascoli, starting with an idealistic diagnosis of its emergence, nevertheless reverses the assessment, and from its irrepressible formation he deduces the essential nature of its function.

Whatever results may emerge from this study and closer consideration of the abstract schema, it is undeniable that they will respond to a felt need and fill a notable gap in modern philosophical methodology.

Ascoli's book comes across more as a rapid system design than as an in–depth examination of certain problems. It is almost a research program, for which it will be necessary come back to each point to give it a more rigorous treatment, a panoramic summary of what will be the definitive work when each individual part is brought to completion. It is thus understood that what must be judged in it are mainly the directions it indicates — and this one, the norm intended as an essential form of the mind, seems highly productive and original.

Less convincing, on the other hand, is the use Ascoli makes of this concept and the structure he attempts to build on it. This normativity, this defining in generic and abstract forms is attributed by him exclusively to practical activity. Indeed, it is made so closely a part of it that it constitutes almost its only fundamental characteristic. It could be said that practice is defined as normativity itself, and comes to be identified with it.

But set against it is another activity which surpasses and purifies it, and, although it needs to be explicated in the form of normativity, the universality of its physiognomy differs from it. This is theoretic activity, which includes knowledge in the strict sense of the word (philosophy) and ethics — that is, both of the forms that have universality as their essential characteristic. These can only manifest themselves in the form of normativity, and on the other hand they represent the necessary overcoming of normativity, the catharsis. Thus a dialectic is established between these two forms, a mutual conversion of one into the other. We cannot help but observe, however, that with this formulation Ascoli falls back into that dialectic of distinct forms that he appeared at the beginning to want to free himself from.

Any dialectic of distinct forms inevitably bumps up against the difficulty of maintaining the validity of the sublated datum in the face of the datum that has accomplished the sublation. Because if, in fact, the one cannot exist without the other, then they are no longer distinct data, but simply aspects of a single unitary datum —

aspects that it is not possible to consider abstractly nor characterize as autonomous functions. And if, on the other hand, this autonomy is possible, how is it possible to justify the necessity of being sublated or of being realized in the other, which is part each datum?

The impossibility of an autonomous permanence of the individual with respect to the universal, which must necessarily overcome it, has already been noted in Croce's philosophy (and it seems to us that Ascoli makes this objection his own). Now Ascoli denies the dialectic of individual and universal, but replaces it with a new dialectic of, in his words, the practical and the theoretical, but which ends up taking place between the abstract norm and the universal principle. He too, however, in describing the process of passing from one term to the other, is compelled to show the defect of each of them taken on its own. And concerning the normativity specific to the juridical world, he is forced to attribute to it a nature inferior to ethical normativity.

This autonomous and primordial form, in short, like all those analogous to it (art and economics in Croce, for example) is forced to resolve itself into those that follow it (and therefore to lose its own autonomy) or to eliminate its relations with all the other forms — demonstrating that in any dialectic it is impossible to consider one of its terms as autonomous, and that the autonomy of a function can only be found outside the dialectic, where the function can live its own life closed in itself, with its own inner dialectic perhaps, but without the need to be sublated by some other function that transcends it.

What naturally follows from this criticism of Ascoli's distinction between theory and practice and the reciprocal conversion of one into the other is the impossibility of any third element that might serve as mediation between the one and the other and that might bring about a passage from the universality of ethics to the normativity of the law. For Ascoli this element is Justice, but since we cannot conceive a clear detachment between the two forms, this third form meant to seal their union is plainly superfluous. The union and mediation presuppose a detachment between the terms to be united and mediated. And to those of us who cannot justify the autonomous validity of each of these terms, any development that has this detachment and mutual autonomy as a pre-requisite is inconceivable.

Ascoli, we repeat, is right on target when he wants to re-evaluate the schematizing and normative function of the mind. But perhaps he is mistaken in giving this reassessment the traditional form, and in wanting to create a special faculty to guarantee the autonomy of the function he wants to highlight. With this autonomy he doesn't save the function, he dooms it — because, not being able to conceive of it in isolation, he is obliged, willy-nilly, to place it as inferior to others that sublate it.

But the vitality of the attempt remains. And if, in the future, he concerns himself not so much with the "collocation" of the function's normativity, but with its inner characterization as an inseparable aspect and essential manifestation of any and all forms of the mind, we believe that his words will be important, and destined to be not without consequences in the development of contemporary thought.

"Review of *Aesthetics,* by Adriano Tilgher" (Roma: Scienze e Lettere, 1931); *Il Convegno* 7.1–2 (1931): 85–88.

It goes without saying that this book, like everything on aesthetics published in Italy for the last quarter century, takes its cue from Croce, showing that even today we still cannot do without his organic system, his formulation, his terminology — whatever judgment we may wish to make — if only as a starting point. But, if it is true that Tilgher sometimes misunderstands and argues idly with Crocean thought, it is also true that he is trying to solve problems that are still open and alive and urgent in our intellectual and cultural climate.

Completely saving the autonomy of art against its more or less obscure reductions to other activities (individual or auroral or naive knowledge, active and practical feeling, intuition or presentiment of a superior reality), avoiding aestheticism and fragmentism and not giving up on the vital function and human dignity of the artist — this is a very real problem for everyone, and the solution Tilgher offers in defining art as "life that loves itself" or *amor vitae* is well worth discussing.

Like all definitions, this one acquires importance only from its relationships and interactions and from the results it gives rise to. And it strikes us as important, first of all, that it arises from the problem of the relationship between art and cognitive and practical activity. It is clear, in fact, that the definitions known to us, when not reducing the artistic function to a form — inferior or superior, primordial or absolute — of knowledge, determine it with characteristics that are not specific to art, but to generic activity of the mind, belonging, that is, not to art alone, but also to any other manifestation or aspect of the mind. What else is it to say that art is *form* or *expression* except to give it characteristics that it certainly has, but which do not distinguish it from knowledge or practice? And these, if they are mental activities, must necessarily be form — and they cannot in any way be separated from their own expression, on pain of reducing this form to abstract materiality.

It is necessary first of all to study art in its particular conformation, and to find those elements which really distinguish it from other activities of the mind. Among these elements, one of the most important is disinterestedness, not striving for a goal and not organizing itself into practical consequences — this much seems certain and evident. And if, as we believe, *amor vitae* is to mean precisely this independence of art and its being contained in itself without turning to anything else, it is a determination capable of pointing us towards an aspect of art that we ought to highlight to a greater extent. This is love, Tilgher says, to explain the sense of emotional and enthusiastic joy that always accompanies a work of art. But love that loves itself, in that it has no object outside itself to strive for, nor does it place outside itself (as knowledge does) an object to grasp. Concerning this definition, and especially the concepts of knowledge and will, and what Tilgher calls the "individuality of the work of art," there would be much to discuss. But here we only want to note that the distinction based on disinterestedness and lack of ends or extensions or consequences is, if not clearly defined, aptly sketched out.

Another interesting element is the denial of any dialectic between art and real life, which might risk compromising the autonomy of art: "One never passes from lived life to art, just as one never passes from one straight line to another parallel to it even traveling forever, except by an abrupt jump. They are two planes, two totally different dimensions of the mind. They can have a homologous correspondence, but there is no continuity from one to the other." This does not invalidate the fact that in taking place each has its own overall totality, and that "the whole of the mind is present in the artistic experience." We would almost prefer to say that the two forms are two different, parallel, incommunicable ways of living life.

From this observation, given the premises, Tilgher easily could have, and should have, deduced the dignity of the artist and the human significance of his work. Instead, to demonstrate this assumption that means so much to him, he chooses to resort once again to the relations with real life that he had previously denied. To say that art is extraneous to the categories of reality and unreality doesn't mean that it has gone beyond them, and to affirm that it does means once again introducing the dialectic that he wanted to eliminate. But Tilgher has no hesitation in affirming that "art assumes the realm of reality and the knowledge that reality is already established" and that it is "distinct from life and superior to it." Why? Perhaps to be able to better determine the human dignity of the artist and the level of its elevation as a function of the greater or lesser universality of the life that is the object of his love: "The more life is actualized as universal, the more it is able to offer itself completely to the breath of love." But didn't we say that love is itself universal in itself, and has no outside object? And indeed that "the work of art does not express, signify or mean anything other than itself, and does not evoke anything beyond itself"?

Constructing a hierarchy of works based on the fullness of life they can offer to the breath of art means posing as a criterion for artistic evaluation an element that does not belong to it and that actually precedes it. And this is in contradiction with what was stated earlier — that there is no precedent to a work of art.

This re–entry of contenutism, in contrast to the basic line of Tilgherian thought, shows us the difficulties that any sort of aesthetics experiences in addressing all problems and meeting all needs. But this is not to say that it reduces to absurdity the other affirmations that we have tried to highlight above. The error is perhaps incidental to the doctrine as a whole and can be eliminated.

"Review of *Words in My Ear*" (Lanciano: Carabba, 1929) and "Review of *Let's Talk about Italy*" (Firenze: Vallecchi, 1931), by Vincenzo Cardarelli, *Il Convegno* 12.3 (1931): 125–29.

It is not necessarily the case that a doctrine of art must always be united with the precepts that follow from it, and that a poetics is necessarily connected to every aesthetic. Someone who studies in a universal sense what the artistic phenomenon is and the particular attitude of the mind that produces a work of poetry is not for this reason required to preach the application of their discoveries to individual artists. Indeed, it would be better not to, so as not to risk misunderstanding oneself and mistaking such discoveries for concrete methodological lessons. This is the case, we presume, for the principle that if art is an irrational form of the mind then all art must be concerned with irrational subjects.

Certainly, aesthetics can — indeed, must — have an influence on active and militant art, furnishing artists with the self–knowledge that allows them to know and delimit their own field of action, to live with and judge their own work. But this influence is all the more upright and fruitful when it is indirect and makes use of the channels of criticism and culture. The pure artist, placed in front of a pure theory, is always drawn to consider it not so much a definition of the artistic function in itself, but rather a collection of recommendations given to those who want to produce art — and in this transition to precepts it risks the distortion of the theory itself. The latter would therefore do better to explicate and apply itself in more generic and less delimited fields than direct artistic production — where it will eventually arrive richer, by this route, in developments, and connections, and be more accessible. And in such a way it avoids transforming itself, through contact that is too raw and direct, from morality into etiquette.

But anyone who wants to start with etiquette and place their own affirmations in the form of precepts and programs obviously has to refer, more or less explicitly, to a theoretical arrangement — and every article of an artistic code fatally rests on an axiom of aesthetics. For this reason, we believe that in the collection of aphorisms and "moralities" that makes up these two slim volumes of Cardarelli's, the doctrinal motive that more or less consciously inspired them should not be overlooked. And that, if it is true that they can be considered as the justification for, and almost the autobiographical comment on certain attempts at art, it is also true that they have in them the programmatic ambition of someone who wants to point the way to the new literature and is considered the theorist of a school. A school that has had the virtue, in Italy, of stemming currents whose irrationality was reducing literature to the chaotic expression of passionate and fragmentary feelings, but which runs the risk of falling into a similar fragmentism precisely because of the defect we were talking about — that of transforming what should be pure and generic statements about the essence of art into actual recipes for its construction.

It seems to us, in short, that Cardarelli's propositions on the value of the "technical and instrumental questions of art," on "formal perfection," on style, and on language, are more than anything important in the field of pure aesthetics — as a correction, or rather an addition of some positive observations to the artistic fact. Their aim is basically no more than to highlight the importance of research, study, and development that belongs to artistic emotion just as it does to any other function of the mind. In the doctrine of art as intuition this feature was somewhat obscured, and if we grasp the gist of what Cardarelli is saying and try to harmonize what is true about it with the rest of what we know (or believe) to be true, these statements are the result: Artistic intuition (or whatever name you give it) is neither a gratuitous possession nor an immediate gift, but rather a continuous and laborious conquest that must be earned through hard work and protected through vigilant care. It is not a complete and perfect initial impulse, but a goal to be reached a step at a time through the constant refinement of our tools. And you can still call it intuition — but it is an initiative that is fully achieved only after a long, hard effort. The technique is nothing other than this labor of continual approximation — the struggle to free the material from its obtuseness. And art is not just the end of the task, it is the task itself — if it is true that the goal is at one with the means used to achieve it. In this way art is defined and identified with technique.

This, in terms of pure theory, seems to represent the core of Cardarelli's precepts, the meaning of his insistence on the study of language and the importance he gives to style. Which might also be used to accentuate the autonomous nature of art, the function of the artist as such, in his specific role as a pure representer. These are all important concepts, worthy of discussion and, if not new, opportunely introduced at a moment when they tended to be overlooked. But we still say that these affirmations would be truer, richer and more fruitful in the realm of pure theory than in the form of concrete precepts imposed on artists. Not that theory, we repeat, has to remain as it is and shy away from application. But the present application reflects it only in a literal way and falsifies its spirit.

It is right, then, to press the point that the poet, in refining his powers of expression, also refines his own sensitivity. But it would be wrong to forget that this is no more than an example of something that generically happens for every so-called means of expression. And nothing says that linguistic expression is always fundamental, even in the arts based on language — in which a thousand other elements (of disposition, succession, dramatic contrast, temporal or visual distance) can serve the expressive function that Cardarelli attributes only to language. He is right, in other words, to promote the standing of the "profession," but there are so many professions, even in just the literary arts (as many as there are artists, we would say) that it is impossible to judge all works by the standards of one of them alone.

This explains the lack of satisfaction that comes from the critical insights in these books which, even though they are barely sketched out, are meant to be interpreted, it appears, as programs. They often limit their focus to partial or incidental features of a personality (as in the case of Dante or Pascoli), or we are required to stretch excessively the criterion of linguistic perfection on which they are conducted or to abandon it altogether. Significant in this regard is the naivety of a passage that speaks of "our great poets whose value, *given their poetic gift*, is precisely in the specific use that their intelligence has been able to make of the linguistic element." But isn't this "poetic gift" already all the art there is? And if this is the premise, what room is left for language?

The principle of stylistic and formal perfection might be valuable, we repeat, as justification of a specific type of art, in defense of a personal poetic tone. But set up as an absolute precept it excludes many aspects that are intrinsic to art. It risks leading to the Parnassian cult of the fragment, and to the constant reduction of the surface to be polished so as to make it as shiny as possible. But this kind of shine sometimes dazzles in a way that is less than genuine. And even when it is authentic, who is to say that the beauty doesn't lie elsewhere?

Cardarelli misses many elements of art that do not fall within his restricted definition. And faced with Goethe and Shakespeare, for example, he almost regrets their avoidance of pure verbal lyricism in order to reach broader conclusions. "Certain forms of expression, immediately linked to the reality of feelings and impressions that I call lyrical and primitive, are smoothed out into others that are more adult, even if (why not say it?) more ambiguous and impure." So for him even the drama is perhaps outside of art.

But we all know that art is something more and other than lyricism and the linguistically polished fragment. And if language, as a technique, is also an essential aspect of it, it is not at all the case that it is exhausted and resolved in it. Criticism cannot be limited in this way if its scope is to embrace in its entirety the figure of the artist. And we would even say that at times it has to go even beyond the boundaries of art. Boundaries that we would be the last to deny, since they seem to us essential to the autonomy of art and its distinction from other mental forms. But there are personalities that escape and will not be reduced to one aspect, albeit fundamental, of the mind — that seem not to be content to give us reality in a single form, but want to present it in all its aspects. In cases like theirs the scruples fade that distinguish art from knowledge and morality, because in trying to keep these considerations separate, we risk losing an essential reason for their work.

"Review of *The Flesh, Death and the Devil in Romantic Literature*, by Mario Praz" (Milano–Roma: "La Cultura," 1930); *Il Convegno* 12.5 (1931): 275–80.

This book is an example of the kind of research that ought to be extended and developed.

The position of modern criticism regarding erudite investigation and analysis of sources, in limiting its significance and conceding only its partial usefulness, has ended up stopping its development and renewal, if not its life. Once it was established that only the artistic criterion is to be used for art, the field was left free to anyone who wanted to work and experiment in other ways with works of imagination, as long as no claim was made of a final judgment, that being reserved for aesthetic considerations.

In this way, behind a facade of tolerance and recognition there was an absence of any interest that was not anecdotal or simply curious, almost sporting.

But no one ever thought that, beyond a generic and limited free pass, it might be advisable to give more precise tasks to those activities — that it might even be possible to put their tools to use in clarifying new problems of psychological interpretation and cultural analysis, and sharpening the focus of aesthetic judgment. Every critical methodology inclines towards a certain group of assumptions and precedents for art that it prefers to linger over. It has its own way of coloring these substrates in preparation for the catharsis they will reach. And to be topical, the work of studying and researching them can and must follow such preferences.

Praz's book is one of the few (that I know of) that fulfills this renewed and current function of data research, and for this reason it may be an indicator of a possible way forward. The task it sets itself is to isolate and document the part played by erotic sensibility in the development of Romantic literature. The topic is obviously partial and unable to stand on its own, and this is explicitly recognized by the author, whose method of study is deliberately extraneous to aesthetic criticism. But this precise awareness of the limitations of his assumption enables him to keep perfectly within its terms, and greatly increases the effectiveness of his study. Aesthetic criticism is never achieved, but always implicitly posited as the ultimate purpose the work must serve. Facts and documents are chosen precisely in the light of the work that will have to be done on them, by a method that can no doubt be imitated.

It would therefore be absurd to reproach Praz, citing as defects what are actually only the limits that he himself has imposed, repeating that eroticism is not the only aspect of romanticism and that it is only a psychological premise for certain artistic achievements. The book seeks only to document this aspect and premise just as it is — and its value lies precisely in the awareness that circulates in it of the possibility of going beyond it.

While recognizing the legitimacy and great usefulness of this purpose, we would have preferred that the overall evaluation, the general framework — whose importance is always recognized and implied in the book — had been expressed a bit more explicitly. A bit more information on the ideological premises and on the social, moral and cultural foundations that gave rise to this unwholesome product, a hint (more than in the introduction) as to its meaning and its importance for the achievement of individual expressions of art, a sketch showing the positive and lasting results it has led to — would not have harmed the informative intent of the work and would have served to guide readers in the work of interpretation that they will inevitably begin on their own. We would have preferred it, in short, if Praz, without crossing any lines, had lingered a bit at the margins of his work and, having explored one stretch of the path in detail, had provided some information on the preceding one and some indications about what was to follow. Instead, he almost seems pleased with this reticence, and while by no means lacking in opinions and ideas on the subject, he has decided at all costs not to compromise himself. He throws into the reader's arms his entire collection of reports, comparisons, and analyses and then he withdraws, somewhere between discreet and malicious: "I have prepared your fare; now feed yourself."

◆◆◆

He does take a position, in fact, in the introduction, and it is full of incisive and interesting ideas. But it is more a generic thesis than a specific interpretation of the data contained in the book. It considers the romantic concept, more than an eternal moment of the mind, as a particular orientation of taste that emerged and developed in a determined historical period through deliberate artistic processes. One fundamental characteristic of this new taste is meant to be the erotic sensibility, the subject of the book. And romanticism, in this sense, (and eroticism along with it) would be a full fledged discovery, an area of sensibility newly brought to light. But the quantity and variety of documentation of this sentimental tone that the book offers makes us curious to know the degree to which it directly determined authentic artistic achievements. The relationship between taste (that is, a basic set of emotional inclinations, sympathies, and preferences) and art is today still too uncertain and controversial for the widespread and general presence of some particular taste to imply a communion of artistic styles among the authors who share it, much less the introduction of a new way of feeling *like an artist*. Praz never affirms this thesis quite so categorically. But it is this that most easily insinuates itself into the mind of the reader, and the author's silence on the subject is perhaps more dangerous than useful. The same intelligence and agility Praz shows in dealing with this material can lead him into error and to mistake for the specific emotion of art what he presents as generic emotion, a sentimental (which does not mean artistic) tone that recurs in numerous authors of the same period. On the further problem of the aesthetic value of that emotion he modestly refrains from declaring himself. But readers must beware of inadvertently making such a dangerous crossing on their own.

It is also worth noting that some of the authors Praz cites as the most fully steeped in such taste are not really great artists. And in the case of Baudelaire (also Swinburne) he notes that some critics see the highest artistic achievements precisely where the influences he is talking about are least apparent. But even where they do operate, is it so clear that they are the main source of the artistic style? And could we not say that in Baudelaire what is appreciated as art is entirely formal, beyond feeling, and consists in a majesty of expression and contemplation, in certain bursts and movements, in certain visual detachments and in the broad progression of his verse that makes this author almost a classic? In moments of true inspiration, taste, fashion, sensual and sentimental tone are sometimes pushed into the background. And it is symptomatic that in the case of Flaubert the work he cites least is *Madame Bovary*.

Once again, the intention here is not to refute Praz, who takes no clear position on the issue, but merely to warn against the danger of interpreting generic tendencies in taste and temperament as an author's artistic style. Indeed, it often happens that an authentic work of art requires a grounding that does not perfectly coincide with the personal tastes of its creator, that makes him uncomfortable and requires him to control himself and rein in his instincts. Flaubert, while he was composing his masterpiece, wrote to Louise Colet: "The books that I most aspire to write are precisely those for which I am least suited. Bovary, in this sense, will have been an unheard of tour de force that only I will ever be aware of — subject, character, effects, etc., it is all out of my hands. . . . Art has nothing to do with the artist" (*Correspondance* 3, p. 3–4).

♦♦♦

In Praz's work, in short, eroticism is an integral part of a taste, a system of emotional preferences — not yet an artistic tone.

But how do we explain the violent emergence of these sensual developments and their elevation to conscious prominence precisely in that period? Taste (like every form of collective sensibility) has in it much that is reflective and intellectual. The movements of thought that justify the extraordinary importance assumed in those years by various forms of eroticism, are barely mentioned by the author, who notes the similarities with the Promethean representation of Satan in Milton, along with derivations from the Enlightenment concept of the return to nature. These and other cultural and intellectual elements are said to have flowed into the theory of moral and physiological perversion represented in the work of the Marquis de Sade. And speaking generally and without exploring the question, it could be said that this tendency is closely connected with the general character of all of romanticism as a

movement of the mind — which is, briefly stated, a violent con-
veyance of the world to the center of the individual and the substitution of the laws of personality for the abstract laws of reason.
Within this great movement, however, eroticism is only one of the
more equivocal and unilateral aspects. Interesting, yes, but hardly
universal and comprehensive in content, and with a tendency to
develop in one sense only, by insisting to the point of hallucination
on a partial affirmation, in a way similar to what might be done in
a more strictly intellectual field by solipsism.

Praz notes with great acuity its evolution and development
along its own paths; and he gives us a glimpse, in a way that could
have been more explicit, of how in the end, through a process of
sublimation, it was able to arrive at formulas for an abstract and
symbolic art that were equivocally referred to as neoclassical.

But Praz's book offers inspiration for many other questions.
And this is the best proof of the interest it arouses and the vitality
of its treatment of the subject.

Answer to "Inquiry on Radio," *Il Convegno* 12.7–8 (1931): 395–98.

For a person whose background on the subject of radio is limited to the last essay by Enzo Ferrieri,[1] it is very difficult to judge
the value and feasibility of the suggestions and concrete proposals
contained in the essay itself. I will say, however, as a pure outsider,
that the essay struck me as typically representative of a phenomenon that today is widespread, I would call it universal — the assault by art on the new forms of technology by which civilization
is gradually enriching itself.

This is the way art is, tending inevitably to reach out towards
everything, to take possession even of things that arose for other
purposes. At a certain point in the development of an invention
and the process of its influencing everyday life, we see its initial
economic utility, its popularizing and instructive purpose, re-

---

[1]Founder of the cultural circle "Il Convegno" led by Giuseppe Antonio Borgese and by
other intellectuals. Cf. Gerbi 1999, p. 39 (editor's note).

placed or supplemented by the disinterested emotion of art. We can leave our familiar Vico aside — this is what has happened and is happening with the press and with reinforced concrete, with cinematography and with the radio.

Now, without doubt this is not only possible but desirable, and of course new technological discoveries can serve art as means of expression. But it is interesting to see how this happens and to what extent.

In this regard, it is dangerous to lend the name of art to any coherent or totally effective development these new techniques produce. It is perhaps too common a habit today to consider what they produce all the more artistic, the more they stick close to their nature, and achieve their purpose in the way that is most contemporary and immediately derived from the tools they use. A "beautiful machine," that is, a perfect, coherent and agile organism suited to its function in every part, arouses pleasure in the observer, satisfaction in the user, and perhaps, due to certain sensibilities developed thereby, emotion as well. But this pleasure and satisfaction and emotion are not necessarily artistic as such.

Here, as in all fields, it is right to champion the perfect adjustment and connection of ends and means which, when achieved, will lead to perfection. But this perfection can be artistic, or it can be economic, or practical, or pedagogical, or popular, or whatever else one might wish. And it is essential not to mistake the joy that comes from the harmony and coherence of the forces in action for artistic joy.

This is how it is for Radio — and Ferrieri did well to talk of a creative force, rather than artistic. It is always creative, meant in the complete sense that he intended, because in this way it will always create values (whatever kind they may be) that are original, independent, and autonomous. And artistic only when it is artistic — that is, when it directs the line of its action to that particular thread of emotion, of creation, of contemplation (and we will not pause here to define it) that is called by the name of art.

In brief, then, Ferrieri's essay has taught us this — that Radio is a form of expression that requires, for whatever purpose it is used, directness and linearity of method, and that has no true meaning except when it expresses things that can be represented only or primarily through it. Now whether this expression is artistic or not, whether it carries out tasks of instruction or information or propaganda rather than the pure tasks of art is something that cannot be decided a priori. All these functions are possible, and when one of them is completed appropriately and with originality it may be said, if you like, that it is beautiful — but "beautiful" here means "perfect, coherent, autonomous."

There is something else that Ferrieri's essay tells us. If Radio is a new mode of expression added to those we already know, and a new possibility for acting artistically, the artistic manifestations it represents (and that can only be represented by it) will be able to provide something new, bring to light a new tone for art and mental activity in general. It will react in a certain way with human sensibility, favoring the emergence of those emotions that find their proper expression in it.

Naturalism? Materialism? Not at all. This does not negate that art is a fact of the mind, that it emerges in the mind. It only means that by giving man a new sense, it becomes a fact of the mind in his hands, and allows him to open new doors in his sensibility that have until now been ignored.

Now Radio is in a certain way a new sense, added to the others that man–the–artist has available. And without saying that a type of art corresponds to each sense, it cannot be denied that the concrete and material form of expression is of some importance in research and descriptions concerning the particular tone of an artistic emotion. Don't we talk about (meaning something not theoretically distinct, but nevertheless generically placeable in the topography of the various artistic intuitions) tones that are pictorial or musical, inner and outer, etc? So that we will be able to speak of a "radiophonic" style — which will indicate, approximately, a certain artistic intonation for which Radio is best suited as a means of expression.

Ferrieri has begun to indicate what this style might be, speaking of rapidity, release and surprise and, conversely, of an inclination towards indeterminacy, hinting at analogies with some of the tones of futurism, the function of silence, and so on. And most likely it will be possible to be more specific as the radio, in concrete action, manifests with increasing clarity its possibilities as a form of artistic expression.

Berlin, November 1931

"Review of *Crocean Studies,* by G. Calogero and G. Petrini" (Rieti: Bibliotheca Editrice, 1930); *Il Convegno* 12.11–12 (1931): 620–24.

The unity of these four essays by two authors, very different in cultural background and inclination of thought but very serious, precise and competent in their fields, lies in the emphasis they give to what is even now the most widely discussed problem in Crocean thought, and which still remains unsolved. This is the problem of distinct forms. Dealing with aesthetics and economics (as Calogero and Petrini mostly do) means studying their relationship with the activities that Croce says immediately follow them and sublate them (logic and ethics) and, basically, reviving the problem of the legitimacy of these distinctions.

This problem is posed explicitly and systematically by Calogero, who comes from the actualist school, and is indeed perhaps the most independent and original of the young students of Gentile. It is implicitly posed by Petrini, who mostly deals with the consequences and the practical and human value that theoretical principles acquire when applied in the world of active and militant art, criticism, and public and moral life.

On the other hand, dealing with these problems means taking decisive positions in the field of general philosophy. And this is what Calogero does in his first essay, "The Character of Crocean Philosophy." In this attempt to summarize the meaning and the scope of that body of thought, the definition of it as "absolute positivism," — that is, "considering what happens in the world as a total effect of history, as pure doing," is very precise and perfectly adequate. But what does not appear equally justified is Calogero's reduction of Crocean thought to actualism.

There is a certain obscurity in the attention given to the concept of "doing" — which can be understood either simply as the indispensability of a subject for conceiving of any object (in other words the principle of subjectivity or rather of the ideality of the real) or as an actual affirmation of the priority of practical reason over theoretical, which is always introduced into idealism to justify its positioning of an object and its concept of nature. The first is Croce's meaning; the second Gentile's. And Croce's "doing," as Calogero understands it — that is, as "absolute positivism," cannot be reduced to Gentile's.

If Gentile were to stop at that first concept, he would be (as, in the end, Croce is reduced to being) a pluralist, a conception he utterly rejects. To avoid it he has resorted to the formulations that have given him the unity of his philosophy, but sometimes at the price of the most rigorous immanence. That actualism has been "not infrequently adapted to summarize, in new formulations, the same aspects and attitudes and terms as the ancient epistemology" is also affirmed by Calogero. But he should perhaps have seen in this, rather than a marginal error, a characteristic and highly significant difficulty of this philosophy.

In any case it is useful and safe to stop in this way at the point of contact between Croce and Gentile — at this subjectivity of the real, or as Calogero puts it, knowing as doing. Which, while it may be a concept that is still very generic and imprecise, seems to us a positive and genuinely acquired fact that these philosophies have had the merit, if not of discovering, of vigorously affirming and disseminating among us.

When the unity of the mind as both individual and universal is seen in this way, it is clear that an explanation is needed that is different from Croce's for art and economics — for those forms, that is, that Croce had defined as individual moments of knowledge and practice.

In his second essay, starting by affirming the identification of knowledge with the will, and the requirement that every cognitive affirmation be the positioning of an end, a program to be implemented, Calogero defines art as a contemplation of reality from which the concern for implementation is extraneous, a rejoicing "in the program as a program, without the need to rejoice in its transformation into reality."

Whatever reservations we might have about this identity between knowledge and will, and the idealist–absolute or actualist premises that it springs from, we cannot deny that the conclusions are fully satisfactory, and that Calogero's collocation of art with respect to knowledge–will is justified and especially convincing. Even someone who attempts to begin with non–actualist premises and views the individualist principle in Crocean philosophy as irreconcilable with actualism (unless actualism itself is reduced to a form of individualism) will arrive at conclusions concerning the relationship between knowledge and morality, especially where art is concerned, that are perfectly analogous to Calogero's. And the observation that they were reached by very different pathways will only add to the trustworthiness of the conclusions themselves.

The second part of the essay, on relations between economics and ethics, is much less satisfying. Calogero's reduction of morality to economics boils down to a reduction of idealism to mere subjectivism — a subjectivism of the empirical self, which (as he himself basically admits) can only resolve itself into a solipsism. Seen in this way, a practical act cannot of course be anything but economic — that is, carried out by a subject isolated amid a world of objects. And morality arises, according to Calogero, on the basis of economics, as a supposed and arbitrary "will" to consider objects as subjects, i.e. as one's own kind.

But what justification and foundation does this will of an individual have in the face of facts that are material because they are external to him? And with what authority can the dignity of a subject be attributed to a material fact?

This formulation of Calogero's is not satisfactory and seems to fall into an empiricism from which individualism or "absolute positivism" should be excluded. But what is important is the attempt to break free of the most explicitly metaphysical and, I would almost say, ontological bases of actualism, and hold on to a concreteness which, even if it still has the defect of falling into particularity and naturalism, has the great merit of showing a way forward.

◆◆◆

The late Petrini, (whose untimely loss we mourn) dwells mainly on the importance of Croceanism in the world of culture in general.

In the field of aesthetics he believes he sees in it an affirmation of classicism — that is, artistic totality and catharsis in the face of the fragmentism and passion of the romantics. This is a principle that should be emphasized, as long as care is taken to distinguish the totality and cosmic value of art from the cosmic value of philosophy and morality. When Petrini says "that there is no great art without great morality," he means, we believe, that the breadth of moral experience is often a precondition for art to have its own breadth and consistency of development, but not that artistic totality is identified with morality — which would cause him to fall back into confusing art with intellectual form, and into the return to artistic moralism that contemporary criticism always risks falling into.

That Petrini keeps away from such conceptions is confirmed by his splendid pages on criticism, in which the function of the artistic "form," whereby "from the inner life of the artist's feelings, one rises to grasp the formation of the work in its lines of poetic creation" is vigorously affirmed. Speaking of a problem with stylistic tradition, he alludes precisely to what is particular to art as opposed to the other forms of mental life — that is, re-establishing its autonomy. And then even its total and cosmic nature, previously affirmed, assumes a very special and vital aspect.

Also interesting, if once again not always convincing, are Petrini's observations on Croce as a historiographer, which are too extensive to discuss here. It is worth repeating, as a conclusion, that the problems stirred up in this book are lively, the points of departure for new developments are of great interest and, while not entirely convincing, are undoubted signs of a vigorous soundness of thought.

"Review of *The School of Dance*, by Arturo Loria" (Firenze: Solaria, 1932); *Il Convegno* 8.7–8 (1932): 332–37.

A first reading leaves the reader feeling that Loria's themes have lost color but grown in depth. The violent effects of bright hot lights are muted, as are the somewhat stagy dramatic turns and sudden shifts in action that in *The Blind Man and the Beauty*, and already less so in *Fannias Ventosca,* represented the essential style of the narrator — a look in the eyes between astonishment and complacency, following the story to enjoy the spectacle in a mean, coarse and pompous world full of the sort of feelings and passions that bring out the exception in the midst of mediocrity. In the light of this third book of novellas, the passage between the first two proved to be an organic process that culminates in this one, and you might say that for that earlier world that he had loved with the gusto of the spectator for its flashy exterior action, the author now feels more of a human interest and an intimate involvement — that his feeling of curiosity has been transformed into compassion and understanding. This also explains the constant fidelity to a single subject, otherwise strange in an author as non–autobiographical as Loria.

The characters in this new group of stories are not actually very different from each other or from the ones in the previous collections. Fat, lewd little bourgeois mutually aware of their obscene lusts, wretches and losers intent on discovering in their neighbor's eye that same brutish gleam of desire that warms them in their loneliness; women who give themselves out of laziness and without conviction just for lack of a conviction to the contrary — a world tortured by perennial relapse into banality and filth, in which every attempt to rise from it is doomed to the melancholy end of those who are already prepared for failure. This world, which served in the stories of the first two books mostly as background and as material for the colorful developments that were then the essential thing, has now become the protagonist, and the stories have become static and devoid of movement and twists — more like sketches than stories. Not that action has ever been a value in itself in Loria — it has always served him more as a pretext to get to the picturesque side of the situation. But whereas the picturesque situation used to be the first point of arrival, prepared and justified by the complicated and clever plot, which was also an inherent part of the show, in these new stories (except perhaps the last one, "The School of Dance," which marks a more apparent than real return to the old style) the basic scene is the actual body of the story, which the author works on in depth. There is no flashy sudden final catastrophe that brings down the curtain, but rather, I would almost say, a motionless living picture in which the development is the result of the scrutiny of the eye that discovers in it new sources of interest.

Loria's abiding concern for visual and plastic evidence is demonstrated by his attachment not only to the characters, but also, as mentioned, to the colorful and exotic environments of his earlier stories, the only remaining aspect of his early style of writing. The trappings of his scenes always feature the fabulous and the grotesque: the masquerade of old, petty bourgeois men with a woman in the basement of a suburban cafe decorated in the oriental style; a scene of wild gluttony among the old men of a nursing home; the meeting in a greenhouse on a snowy winter's night between an elderly countess reduced to misery and a gardener; the frenzied dance of two married couples in a mountain meadow under the malignant and ambiguous guidance of an itinerant dancer; a brothel; the heavy and treacherous atmosphere of a dancing school.

The settings are meant to impress themselves on the memory, but they are themselves imprinted with the poetic tone and the melancholy typical of this new side of Loria, which goes hand in hand with his detached and violently candid way of looking at things — a removal of veils and metaphors, calling a spade a spade not as a courageous pose or out of some heroic love of truth, but matter-of-factly, without enthusiasm, because eyes have to see; and a painful shaking of the head over what has been seen, and over the tears for things that one cannot and would no longer want to ignore.

One of the most frequent themes in these novels is lust, which becomes evident as a common destiny from one man to the next, creating a hot and bestial atmosphere one moment ("The Arabian Cafe," "The Repainted House") and a situation quivering with embarrassment and anxious connivance the next ("The Hour by the Sea," "The Dance in the Meadow"), and in one case a tragedy (in "Little Brother," the most painful and human of these stories). "The Tired Bricklayer," which tells of the horror of a father and son enjoying the same lewd vision together, finishes thus: "The boy's frightened eyes no longer resembled those that had targeted the beautiful female; but when he stood up to face his father and said: 'The swans, Dad, the swans! I think I killed one of them with a stone' — the latter found himself resigned to listening to the shameful lie of another man like himself." And these words might be taken as a definition of a central feature of Loria's art.

This feature has the great merit of unconscious moralism — that is, of proposing neither morality nor art as a well-defined goal to be obtained through certain processes, but of achieving art through the native gift of inspiration, in which things and judgments on things are mixed in a fluid tone of narration that does not assert but sees, and can now weep without the bitterness of something suffered or the fire of a mission to be accomplished. This is what brings humanity to Loria's art, this morality that in him is art in the making. He can stop concerning himself with it or worrying that it will be overpowering and mutate into oratory, because in him it is no more than a spirit that allows him detachment from the things he is narrating, and which is as natural to him as breathing. It would be out of place here to look for labels and speak of the Twilight School or something else. The tone is particular to Loria and is unmistakable, and finding it to be so explicit in these stories gives us the joy of observing that he has now freed himself from the commitment to the fantasy and ostentation that somewhat disturbed the spontaneity of his first works, and has found, with an honest effort and at the price of giving up easy results, his own full and genuine tone.

There is, however, in addition to this, a commitment to beautiful writing and to achieving effects through style that Loria perhaps gets from environmental influences and, while (naturally) not illegitimate in itself, seems to us superimposed on the genuine character of his art. It is evident that Loria wants to give his scenes a tone of enchanted fatalism and ecstatic certainty, which is a somewhat primitive way of understanding classicism. To do this, especially in the first novellas, he relies on scenes of embarrassment and sudden chills to which, in a somewhat banal move, he tries to impart tones that when forced become almost primitive. The detachment, the reflection is too deliberate here, and the artifice is too obvious: "By now the four had become seven, but seven who were knowing and taciturn, seven who ordered their drinks in a flat voice, without familiarity, and in that altered air the friendly waiter had turned shy and served silently, moving with cautious steps. . . . Someone else came in — the one they were waiting for." And elsewhere: "With a slow gesture the coffee man combed his beard, patted his silk-wrapped body. The intermittent flashes of the neon signs on the avenue broke the stagnant indirect light like cries in the empty and echoing hall and each flash marked a step towards an image buried in the memory like a white rock in the blue of the sea. The coffee man immersed himself in this wave with the distress of suffocation and the trepidation of touching a bottom he would rise from with the torment of now–ancient pain and regret." These machinations, whose literary origin is all too evident, these efforts to exaggerate and make something mysterious and solemn that needed a light touch can only be defined in Loria as naivety — and what also seems naive and tainted with the same defect is his sometimes overly explicit claim to be a "prose writer" and his taste, so foreign to the normal rhythm of his prose, for the typical incisive and trenchant sentence. The phrases that flow from his pen are thus needlessly contorted and incomprehensible, or so deliberately dense and full of conceits that they become grotesque. Two examples, from "The Repainted House": "Anna, intent on mutating her love for him into an almost maternal love — too demanding and needy, even though, thus purified, it could not admit any intermittency." The thought here, correct and normal, becomes heavy and awkward thanks to the excess of abstraction. And a bit later: "Lucretius had felt irritated disappointment and then the emptiness of someone who cannot imagine the hopeful commitment and company of a lengthy new project."

We have deliberately referred to these defects of Loria's as naive to show that they belong to the baggage of preconceptions that all young authors struggle to get rid of in order to find their innermost sincerity.

Loria is well along on this road of clarification and liberation, and his efforts at honesty and clarity are highly admirable. He has succeeded in this book, and will succeed more and more in the future, to speak his message in a full, clear and convincing voice.

III: Adult Eugenio

Eugenio Colorni, Involuntary Critic:
A Brief Collection of Literary Judgments
from His Letters — 1938–40

Trieste, 21 Sep. 1938

My Dearest,

I'm reading *Faust,* one page per day, and to me the two pro-
logues are better than Faust's famous monologue. What strikes me
about Goethe is his—how can I put it?—his doubtfulness before he
gives an opinion or makes a value judgment. Take the "Prologue
for the Theater." Are you really sure he agrees with the poet rather
than the theater director or the actor? OK, he agrees. But he seems
to want to say: "I am capable of understanding the others' points of
view as well. The way the others see things also 'exists'". It's almost
tragic when the actor tells him: you have your eye on posterity, but
what about the living? Who's looking out for them? It's the same,
basically, in the scene between God and Mephistofeles. In Goethe,
as in Dante, Hell is more alive, more human than Heaven. (See de
Sanctis's review). But Faust's famous monologue, reading it again,
was a bit disappointing: it's a bit pompous and started to get tire-
some, that "living with all the senses" and "identifying with nature"
etc. It's true that it was Goethe who invented it, but by now, for us,
it's become commonplace. Schiller's byword is "judge," Goethe's is
"understand." In this sense Goethe is more humble than Schiller. If
all of this seems like nonsense, please tell me; and don't try to spare
me just because I'm in prison!

your Eugenio

◆◆◆

Trieste, 4 Oct.1938

My Dearest

I try to take my mind off things reading the books from the prison library — I read a couple of the great historical novels from the last
century (Tommaso Grossi, Sienkiewicz), which I hadn't read before,
and I was quite disappointed — flat, banal, lacking the most elementa-

ry psychology, coarse in every way. Kipling's *Kim,* on the other hand, I liked a lot more. I think he is able to give the story a color and tone that you don't easily forget. I also read Chesterton's *The Man Who Was Thursday*; it's one of those novels that you find so often today, like Kafka, all hinging on a gimmick, a transposition of terms between ironic and hallucinatory. I've now managed to get hold of two of Shakespeare's tragedies from the prison library, and I've promised myself to read them very slowly, savoring them word by word — so they'll last longer. But I really miss my books and my work.

Your Eugenio

♦ ♦ ♦

Trieste, 8 Oct. 1938

My Ursula,

I'm reading some of Shakespeare's magnificent tragedies. The characters — all monumental, and in so few words! I'm beginning to think that all the greats (Dante, Shakespeare, Goethe) stand out for the few words they use to express themselves — their work is epigraphic and sculptural, and in Goethe it becomes succinct, like a proverb.

Eugenio

♦ ♦ ♦

Trieste, 12 Oct. 1938

My Ursula,

I think what you write about Kipling is absolutely right: just as you say — a world without beginning or end. People who don't know what it means to hurry. And hurrying always includes the sense of finishing, the sense that there is a beginning and an end. I found the same feeling a bit in the short stories of Turgenev I'm reading, collected in *Sketches from a Hunter's Album.* The eastern world has no fear of dying. It stands still, waiting. Time has no value.

I'm also reading *Il mio Carso* by Slataper. I like it quite a lot and I think you would too, because there's a physical, almost sensual feeling for the landscape here around Trieste.

Your Eugenio

♦ ♦ ♦

Trieste, 15 Oct. 1938

My Ursula,

My reading during the last three days has been: *Il mio Carso* by Slataper, and Ibsen's *Hedda Gabler.* The first of these interested me a lot: a man. A being who is passionate about sincerity, someone you would like to have as a friend. He is a born writer — a poet even when he confesses in the most personal and almost immodest way. *Hedda Gabler* impressed me as well. She is one of those female literary figures of the last century, like "Anna Karenina," "Madam Bovary" etc., who would be the perfect part for Greta Garbo (or maybe she has already played her?).

Your Eugenio

♦♦♦

Trieste, 17 Oct. 1938

My Ursula,

My regular and monotonous everyday life here goes on. I read, from the prison library, Schiller's *Don Carlos* and Shakespeare's *The Tempest.* I liked *Don Carlos* much more than I thought I would. It's a complex tragedy, human and without stereotypes. It's the best thing of Schiller's that I've read (although I've read very little). And *The Tempest* is a delight. It pairs up well with *A Midsummer Night's Dream,* but is perhaps even more beautiful. It's strange how Shakespeare is able to make you feel and breathe an atmosphere and landscape almost without describing it at all. There are almost no descriptions in *The Tempest* — but still the reader experiences the landscape of that island in every minute detail. As you see, I am acquiring literary culture and practicing my critical skills.

As there is nothing else . . .

Your Eugenio

♦♦♦

Trieste, 25 Oct. 1938

My Ursula,

I have read Shakespeare's *The Tempest.* It's one of those plays in

which genius borders on madness — it's so strange and bewilder-
ing, fragrant and mysterious at the same time, burlesque and tragic!

I'm also reading Massimo D'Azeglio's memoirs — one of those
books I should have read as a child, but which interests me now
because of the environment it describes.

Your Eugenio

◆◆◆

Varese, 16 Dec. 1938

My dear good Ursula,

I'm getting on with my studies and reading. I would like to read
Haas's book on material waves and quantum mechanics in German. But for now I still have a long way to go to finish studying the
physics in Perucca's book. I've finally finished *Don Quixote*. It's a
fairly entertaining book, but it didn't impress me as the great masterpiece everyone talks about. I think it loses a lot in translation
and in Spanish the style must be wonderfully fluid and familiar, like
Voltaire and Diderot. The second volume (written ten years after
the first) is the best, and it is touching to see how the author's affection for his characters grows and he makes them more and more
human and almost melancholy, and less and less clownish.

Your Eugenio

◆◆◆

Trieste, 22 Dec. 1938

My dearest Ursula,

As I said, I would like you to pack a suitcase for me with physics
and mathematics books, some things by Goethe and by Nietzsche
and Scheler, and some good novels, mainly the famous ones I haven't read, and also mainly ones that you have read recently. I ap-
point you director of my literary education, authorized to make me
read whatever you want — and above all if it would help you with
your thesis. Of the famous books I haven't read, the ones that come
to mind are: Tolstoy, anything except *Anna Karenina* (I've read
War and Peace, but I would happily read it again), by Dostoevsky

I've only read *Crime and Punishment* and the *Brothers Karamazov*. Stendhal: I've only read *The Red and the Black* and the *Charterhouse of Parma*. Flaubert: I would only willingly reread *Madame Bovary*, I've read nothing by Merimée, and I haven't read *Les Liaisons Dangereuses*. Proust: I've read barely half of *Swann's Way*, and I know almost nothing of Montaigne and Pascal, nor of Saint Augustine. Balzac: only *Father Goriot*. By Zola I know nothing (!!!) Maupassant: I only know *Bel Ami*, *Une Vie*, and *Boule de Suif*. Dickens: I know nothing, and the same for Swift. Huxley, I only know *Those Barren Leaves*, and Lawrence only *Lady Chatterley*. Babbitt I don't know, nor any American writers. As you see, my ignorance is fairly vast, so you can choose what to send me. Don't send too many, though, because if I'm only here for a while, my intention is to study during the day and only read in the evening. And if I'm with you, I plan to spend all day out and about. To continue, I know nothing of Rousseau, I know Voltaire's novels and Diderot's *Jacques the Fatalist*. As you know, I know almost no German novelists or writers of the 19th and almost none from the 20th either. I'm now reading *The Case of Sergeant Grischa*, and I would willingly read *The Magic Mountain* and *Joseph and His Brothers*. Do you really want me to keep at it with my old friend Leibniz? We can talk about it further, but in any case it would be too bulky for now to drag along all the necessary volumes and materials. I will finish it one day, I believe. But for now I'm in more of a hurry to finish my physico-philosophical work and to complete my education in mathematics and physics. I also would like to read the letters and memoirs of famous men. I realized while reading *William II* that I have no aptitude for history, and that the only history books I can stand are these memoir or biographies.

Your Eugenio

♦ ♦ ♦

Trieste, 28 Dec. 1938

My Ursula,

I still have a lot to say about the things in your latest letters. You are absolutely right about Walt Disney's films. All he's done is take his cue from the story of Snow White in order to indulge his countless variations on the grotesque theme of the seven dwarfs, which is all he is capable of. Everything in the film apart from the seven dwarfs is flat, thin and banal. The character of Snow White is very weak and the scenes with Prince Charming (or whatever he's called) are truly pitiful. From moving, limpid and rhythmic, as you say, the story has turned into jokes and antics. But that's all he is capable of. Mickey Mouse is basically identical to the seven dwarfs. He's found his formula and he's sticking with it as long as it delivers. But how beautiful the story is, just as you said. And how beautiful it is to understand childhood, and experience your own so intensely. For me, my childhood is a nebulous, dull period with no colors that stand out. A mediocre little boy, a bit cocky, a bit angry, a bit of a liar. For you it was a world of strong feelings and true passions, of dances and rhythms, of falling asleep surrounded by ghosts, of enthusiasm for songs, fairy tales and pictures. Either I don't remember anything of my childhood, or I was nothing more than quiet, well-behaved, best in the class. But I hope our little moppet[1] has a childhood like yours.

And I also want to say something about what you were saying — whether a child needs impressions that are vivid and varied, or monotone gray (that is, the difference between your childhood and mine — but I think it depends more on nature than upbringing). In any case I wanted to say that this inability to concentrate, this letting yourself be pulled this way and that by your own thoughts is perhaps a female trait, but it is a trait that is essential to intelligence; and it's called imagination. The problem is finding that trick that enables you to channel it and make it productive (and by productive I also mean perhaps only that it gives you joy and a sense of fulfillment). It's almost a question of instinct and flair. You need to be a bit selfish, and have that "organic patience" Goethe talks about — and also, just a bit, you have to know how to say no — that is, how to manage your own capacity to enjoy, and to choose between enjoyments. It's what I would call epicurean asceticism. The danger is "living" always on the edge. You always have to be just a little bit outside yourself, a little bit the spectator, so you'll be able — not

---

[1]Their daughter Silvia [editor's note].

very much, I don't say abandon them entirely — but to choose between two daydreams.

Your Eugenio

♦♦♦

Ventotene, 21 Jan. 1939

My dearest Ursula,

I'm feeling better, but I'm afraid I'm still far from being really well because I still feel that my nerves are shaky and unable to handle any intellectual effort. Today I'm also a bit tired, because last night I stayed up very late reading the novel *The Stars Look Down,* which is really beautiful, perhaps the best contemporary novel I've read. You also write that you're often tired, and I assure you, the only medicine is to go to bed early. I read a little now (novels) and always think a little about the theory of imaginary numbers — but really without pushing myself, only when I feel like it, and only until I get tired. I wish I had a manual job, but here it's not easy to find one. Tomorrow I'm again waiting tables in the mess hall, but it's not a great job. And I have to say that even physically this inner nervous agitation makes me a bit weak. My usual nervous tics always come back out when I'm down, and I can't seem to get rid of them.

Many thanks for the excerpt from the encyclopedia article on Standt, which is very interesting. What I seem to get is that his method is very different from mine; but this is exactly why I would be interested to get to know him, so I could compare it with mine. Maybe you can find something in a specialized mathematics dictionary, or in a history of mathematics (for example that big one of Cantor's). And in general I would like to know if, even apart from Standt, there are ways of expressing imaginary numbers geometrically.

Your Eugenio

♦♦♦

Ventotene, 1 May 1939

My dearest,

I am fine, and getting on with working. The first chapter of

my semi-philosophical piece is almost done, and I feel quite good
about it. I've had to let the mathematics go a bit, but I'll get back to
it soon. Now and then I also still read Nietzsche, the only philosophy writer I'm able to read just now; and I think this is the basic
difference between a person affected by the philosophical illness
and someone who has recovered from it — whether or not they
can read Nietzsche. (In fact philosophers look down on him as a
non-philosopher). I don't know if you get what I'm saying — Nietzsche is much harder to read than Kant. Because the effort you
make to read him has to be renewed on every page, and there isn't
the sort of coherence that grabs you and pulls you out of your laziness. But one accusation and objection can be applied to him,
which I will express in his own words: "Der Liebhaber der Erken-
ntnis soll seine Ohren überhaupt dort haben, wo ohne Entrüstung
geredet wird. Niemand lügt so viel wie der Entrüstete."[2] Then I'll tell
you something Bradley said that I read in the philosophy book you
sent me: Metaphysics consists of looking for bad reasons to support
what we believe by instinct. And I tell you — I'm afraid I'm just too
lowbrow to understand Th. Mann. I will explain (I assure you this
is not a pose): your position here sounds superficial to my ears. You
still don't understand anything. What I mean is that everything he
writes, he writes with the idea that it should be rooted, you might
say, in something intimate, something deep, something intangible;
which out of good taste, an exquisite sense of proportion and a
certain modesty, he never expresses openly and aggressively, content instead to leave this something to those able to get it. Now, I
am still not able to; my ears are still too tough. I can understand
these things if someone tells me them in plain and simple black
and white, the way Proust does, for example. But to feel them as a
hidden world boiling under the flat, heavy prose of the stories of
Joseph, is for me too much work. But still, having understood this
is in itself a start at throwing off my uncouthness. And I came to
this while writing the philosophical illness, where it seemed ugly
even to me to say things in such a garishly open way. But I have to

---

[2]"The lover of knowledge should in any case put his ears in a place where there is no indignant talk. No one lies so much as someone who is indignant."

recognize that there is something unhealthy, "hesitating" I would say, about his style, which is so apparently honest and clean. I know from experience what a terrible illness it is to be committed to being "complete", to not leaving anything out. Maybe I can't put up with it because it's the same illness I have (the philosophical illness). And the way I know he has it is from one simple fact — that the novel was supposed to appear in two volumes (or three); four have already come out and it still isn't finished. This, my dear, is fear, fear of not having been honest or complete enough — it is a pang of conscience, a sense of guilt that won't leave you in peace. Tell me if you understand this. In the "philosophical illness" I should also write about you. I don't do so out of modesty, no, jealousy.

Eugenio

◆ ◆ ◆

Ventotene, 6 May1939

My dearest Pini,

Please, in your next letter don't forget Hölderlin's poetry. Where neither he nor Kleist, nor Nietzsche succeeded (all three of them went mad), George did. That's why I like him. Certainly you get the impression that this battle against the language completely exhausted him and that he didn't do anything else; and in his writings you sense the effort the victory cost him. But in Thomas Mann, I would say, there is too much resignation — the interminable alleyways he takes to reach his destination, seeing that the main road is blocked. It's almost an affectation. "Der Deutsche," Nietzsche writes, "ist beinahe des *Presto* in seiner Sprache unfähig."[3] This means that for someone who thinks at a "presto" tempo, the language in itself is a problem. But it also means that "style" — valuing language in itself, that is — is only to be found in those madmen who racked their brains trying to remake language the way they wanted it. In the others, including Goethe (and Nietzsche says this as well) you get the impression that the language dominated them. Now I can assure you that letting yourself be dominated by language, as did Goethe

---

[3]"The German is almost incapable of presto in his language."

and Mann, is exactly analogous to letting yourself be dominated by the philosophical illness — to say something you've thought of, you set out at a comfortable trot, and "prove it" from top to bottom over the course of four hundred pages without skipping anything, so as to be armored against any assault. This (you recognize every step of the journey) is fear. It is the need for armor, for a defense. In conclusion, I will let you love your language, on the condition that you love it like Hölderlin and Nietzsche and George — in order to do it violence; not like Goethe and Mann, to submit to it. Please keep writing to me on this subject, because I'm openly stealing from you a chapter for my book, entitled *The Deceit of Words*. And don't complain, because if you want to write these same things yourself it's fine, you still can — the two of us will always write so differently that we will always end up saying different things. In the meantime I will say that the Italian in your letter on Hölderlin was magnificent, lively, concise, perfect. And now the roll-call has rung.

Ciao, my sweethearts — all three. Eat a lot, all three of you.[4]

A hug from your

Eugenio

♦ ♦ ♦

Ventotene, 11 Dec. 1939

My Pini,

I've started reading *Marriages,* quite good right from the beginning, *The Good Earth* and Huxley's *Counterpoint,* which I would like to finish; what I'm saying, as you see, is that I feel able to read.

Eugenio

♦ ♦ ♦

Ventotene, 12 Dec.1939

Pinchen,

I'm reading *Marriages,* a mediocre novel with the usual types and the usual situations, but recounted, I must say, with a certain

---

[4]Ursula is waiting Renate [editor's note].

verve. But as always, reading a novel makes me think of you, and of us; I can't say exactly how. I would say that right now I don't need so much to talk to you as to be near you, to breathe the same air. And I get a feeling of nausea and suffocation every time we have to be apart. Between us there is nothing, or very little, of what there is in the husbands and wives in the novel — thinking of the other as an "other"; the reticence, saying some things and not saying others.

Eugenio

◆ ◆ ◆

Ventotene, 14 Dec.1939

My wife and friend,

I've read *The Good Earth,* a mediocre book in every way, and it makes me angry, this taking advantage of the sentimentality of most readers to make a book a big success. It's just as I imagined it from the title and from the people who like it — just the way I was hoping it wouldn't be. And it is not at all true that it displays a deep understanding of the Chinese soul — you find the same tone in every book that has peasants for protagonists, whether Chinese or Sicilian, or Scandinavian; apart from some local practices and customs — not talking much, that way of treating women, the slow, rapturous tone. These are very easy things to do and, especially mixed with a little rhetoric about the good and fertile land that humans cannot break free of, etc., they have a guaranteed effect on the majority of the public. Note that I am the last to deny that agricultural life has its merits, and a depth and variety that we city dwellers would do well to take in. But this unctuous and rhetorical way of glorifying it makes it unpleasant to me rather than attractive. When will somebody write a book on peasant life that doesn't carry on about the myth of the land, about the man who falls asleep amid the furrows breathing the air of the plowed clods, who picks up a handful of earth and shouts at his children: don't leave here, because this place is your life? Only then will we begin really to understand what agricultural life is, its beauties and its novelty. After that, reading *Counterpoint* is truly refreshing. It is not a book of paradoxes. It is a very serious book, very deeply experienced. You absolutely must read it. What is a paradox? It is that part of truth that is not commonly expressed. Stating it on its own makes it seem exaggerated and "paradoxical." But it is stated on its own like this precisely because it's the only part that's still worth saying, since the rest is known already by everybody. Every truly intelligent person invents very few things that are new and important as compared with those that already exist. If he talks only about the things he has invented and doesn't remind us that they have to be put in with the many other things that are already known, he is called paradoxical. But this is no reason not to be interested in what he says. Quite the contrary.

Always thinking of you and chatting with you, your friend,

Your Eugenio

♦♦♦

Ventotene, 18 Dec. 1939

My Pini,

I had a great day yesterday — I felt really good and I began to work a bit writing my philosophy piece. Today though, I'm a bit down; but it's not really important, because in general I'm doing better. I'm reading a book of Huxley's essays, and Lawrence's *Sons and Lovers*. When I feel a bit more in the mood I'll write more. But today I'm feeling lethargic.

Eugenio

♦♦♦

Ventotene, 25 Dec. 1939

Pini my darling,

I'm reading Lawrence's *Sons and Lovers*, which is a good book overall — but it always amazes me, in these autobiographical books, when authors speak so well of themselves. Aren't they embarrassed? Can't they view themselves with a bit of distance? The author's own defects are always so likable.

There are two authors who manage to find themselves disagreeable and see themselves ironically: Huxley and me. And with that I will take the liberty of reminding you that I am and will always be your devoted and affectionate and loving

Eugenio

♦ ♦ ♦

30 Dec. 1939

I've finished Lawrence's *Sons and Lovers,* a very interesting autobiography that explains a lot of things. It tells how he was so tied to his mother that he was not able really to love any other woman; and there's the very interesting story of his painful love for a girl, which he resisted inside himself. You can see that the book was written with no control, and is more interesting as a document than as art. But this is exactly what I like about it. There's a sort of untidiness about the scenes and descriptions that make you feel that he's setting them out just as they happened, without "constructing" them in the least. But reading this book casts a new light on his other book — and you realize that what he presents there as a spontaneous account, the immediacy of actual experience, was for him nothing more than liberation from a nightmare, his joy at the fall of certain inhibitions that had earlier tormented him.

Then I read *School for Wives,* which disappointed me. The treatment of the theme is perfunctory and heavy handed. I think you would be able to do it ten times better. There are extremely astute and profound observations that could be made (that you, from your own experience [and I'm being serious] would be able to make); and instead his observations are just coarse and banal. The only scene that comes to life is the one with the mother and daughter.

Bye then; I know I'm a bit like that husband. But with this difference — you can always tell me about it and, even though maybe not right away, in the long run I'll end up catching on.

Always love

Your Eugenio

♦ ♦ ♦

Ventotene, 4 Jan. 1940

My dear friend,

So, the thought for the day is this — that novelists can be divided into two types: 1) Those who need to express things symbolically and set the scene in abstract, unreal worlds. They have one bright idea and then press ahead with that as key — among these I would put Kafka, Chesterton, Pirandello, Molnar (in the *Legend of Liliom*), and the American, Steinbeck, whose little book I read — *Of Mice and Men* — quite moving, but entirely built around a very simple device. Among the painters I would include the surrealists (in contrast to Van Gogh and Cézanne, who are another thing altogether). Among the musicians, Stravinsky. Their originality lies in saying ordinary things in strange ways. This is why they attract, but in the long run they don't last. 2) The others, who have the simple ability to express and photograph their world of ideas. And then the point is to see if their world of ideas is alive, interesting and new, or not. For example, with your permission, the world of Gerhardt Hauptmann is nauseating. I had to give up on the book, fed up with being told that a transatlantic liner is a colossus dominating the elements, and tired of his talk about the intimate chaos that oppresses modern man, caught in the vortex of mechanical civilization. The main character miraculously escapes a shipwreck, and the moment he is brought, still dripping, aboard the rescue ship he wonders, "To what end have our lives been spared?" This is someone who needs to be punched. It's that empty and rhetorical pseudo-profundity of the professional and the merchant, of Mr. average. Plus which, the book is forty years old. But as you said, even now his brothers are easily recognizable scions of fashion. The present analogue of Hauptmann I would say is Wassermann. In a certain way it's amusing to read hugely successful books, to have an idea of public tastes.

Your Eugenio

◆◆◆

Ventotene, 8 Jan. 1940

My dear Pini,

Your husband has read another book of Huxley's, *Chrome Yel-*

low, and now wants to attack Anatole France. Most recent thought: great rage against the German novelists, who are utterly devoid of irony. Even the stylized ones I was talking to you about in the last letter in general go about their business in a tone that is a bit strange, between the charlatan and the humorist (think of Picasso, Chesterton, the futurists, etc.); there is a certain posing as original types that they do that makes you think they don't take what they do completely seriously. A Kafka, no — he needs to present himself as a near saint, a martyr, the victim of his artistic demons; he never smiles; he is tragic, lugubrious, infatuated with his work. He takes it so seriously that one day he will die, crushed by it. To me this is horrible. Not because it might be a contradiction in one who is serious, but because we are not permitted to take his own pose seriously. Someone who is truly serious doesn't really need to shout about it and adopt these obsessive attitudes. Out of all the theories of art as contemplation and objectification, the only thing that stays with me is this: a certain calm and sobriety, and if we are saying symbolic and stylized things, a certain irony. But it's still better not to say things that are symbolic and stylized. Many more things can be said speaking in a direct way; and these symbolists — I always get the feeling that they somehow have to hide what little they have to say. Among them, I'm sorry to tell you, I include Th. Mann, who in order to talk about modern man, needs to symbolize him using figures from the Bible.

Your Eugenio

◆ ◆ ◆

Ventotene, 11 Jan. 1940

My friend,

I'm now trying to read Anatole France, without much success; he's a spirit we know by heart and who hasn't got much left to tell us. But probably what we know by heart is what he taught us. And with that I will move directly to the next philosophical thought: The scientists of antiquity, even the greatest of them — no one reads them anymore. And why is this? Because by now they have been incorporated into our consciousness. Now this is true, in the end, even for artists, or at least for people of taste and culture. Why do I no longer need to read Anatole France? Because I have already absorbed his revelations about taste and culture just breathing the air of my era — because his contribution is already completely dissolved into my culture. The result is this paradox — the more influence an author has in his own time and the more his teachings have been heeded, the less posterity will need to read him. We remember such authors with gratitude, the way we remember Galileo and Newton, whose original works, however, no one reads — not even scientists.

And so which of the classics should we read, in that case? Those that for some particular reason were not assimilated by history and taste, and which therefore still have something to say to us — that is, those that have been forgotten and are not called classics. Or those that have only formal value and are appreciated only for "how" they said things — but even this "how," the "style," easily becomes a common heritage.

This, I would say, offers artists a lesson in modesty. In the place of the ambition to create something immortal that will endure over the centuries, the ambition to say something new, something that will be so well assimilated in their own time that reading the original work will become superfluous, remembered only with a debt of gratitude.

Your Eugenio

♦ ♦ ♦

Ventotene, 18 Jan. 1940

Pini my dear,

I'm reading another book of Steinbeck's, *Tortilla Flat*, another stylized story, but one that has a certain restful and calming effect, with repeated adventures, all more or less the same, like in *Don Quixote*. And I thought some more about books that come to be read by posterity and those that are absorbed into the tastes and culture so that they don't need to be read. Which are the books that are perennially re-read? Those in which the essential thing is "form" — certain poets, for example (Dante, Shakespeare, Goethe), who have given perfectly sculpted expression to certain attitudes and states of mind. You always come back to them when you want the thrill of that rich content enclosed in those few perfect verses. This is why great art is very often in the form of proverbs (and a "quotation" is but a form of proverb). Or you re-read the authors who, despite everything, failed to be assimilated by our tastes. Why do we re-read Plato? Basically, because he is distant and different from us. If he were a nearby relative we wouldn't need to read him. (You answer: then I must be very close to Plato, because I feel no need to read him). At this answer I am seized by an access of rage. I fling everything aside, tear up the letter, decide never to speak to you again of these serious and refined things, which you are unable to understand. I get upset, I torment myself, and I finish by declaring myself your most devoted and affectionate husband.

Your Eugenio

IV: Adult Eugenio

Eugenio Colorni, Writer

Two Mistakes

She commanded the hearts of the cavalry lieutenant, the tax attorney, and the trial judge. Yet she was not beautiful, and she was in her late thirties.

When I first saw her come into the dining room with that light, confident step, it was like I had known her forever. I think I would have been able to guess word for word the exchange that immediately took place between her and the gentlemen at the table at the other end of the room.

Born and living in Vienna, divorced a couple of times, accustomed to making a living by sketching and modeling fashions, she was the classic type of independent middle-European woman. So I immediately told myself that I wasn't interested.

So why did I end up becoming friends with her? That was my first false step. And what I think is that I needed to show her and myself that her whole way of being, so exotic and extravagant to the hotel guests, simply put me at ease — nothing about it fazed me in the least. All routine for a seasoned traveler who acts like he already knows everything in a new city where other tourists walk around astonished and bewildered, heads straight for the most exclusive and refined places and talks to the porters in the local dialect. I wanted her to know that she had nothing to teach me. But the result was unexpected. We both felt joy (I did too, why not confess it?) at finding each other again, remembering experiences in common and places we had seen — speaking the same language. She immediately fell into a confidential and intimate tone with me. The subtext was always "we understand each other," and she did not flirt with me. She paid me the respect of a more straightforward and honest approach.

We ended up sitting at the same table. She told me all about her life in Vienna and about her husbands, with lavish technical details. She had studied with great passion the sexual lives of animals and could vividly describe spicy episodes involving turkeys and swans, with great and somewhat pathetic self-admiration. She told how in a certain period she had chosen to be a maid in a hotel rather than earn her living in any other way. I have no scruples, she said, I go with whom I please. But when I want to, not for reasons of convenience.

"Central European women like me," she continued, "are soft and agreeable by nature. Even in a casual encounter we know how to set a mood of affection and intimacy that pleasantly deludes both parties. In Italy it's the men who are like that. It's sweet to hear words of love, even if you know deep down that they only come from passing sensual desire."

Why did I answer her in that same tone? I don't know. I was laughing at myself as I did it.

"I can't agree with you," I confided gravely, "this comedy of love irritates and bores me. I can desire a woman without feeling I have to look her in the face or say the slightest tender word to her. When I like a body I want a body, not a soul." And we shook hands companionably.

She looked at me a bit thoughtfully, and then: "It's true, what you say. This way you have of looking at things is healthy and refreshing. I'm grateful that you got me thinking about it."

I didn't need to ask twice to get her to come to me. One day when I wasn't expecting her she turned up, joyful and serene. And it was a relaxed moment, free of troubles or burdens. We sat for a long time talking over our relationship. "You have good instincts," she told me, "but you still have a lot to learn." We agreed that what we had between us was only an erotic affair, and we agreed that it should stay that way. The word, "erotic," I don't know why, bothered me a lot.

That was when I made my second mistake. I felt I wanted to talk to her about myself. It was a weakness, I admit it, a lack of manliness. It was a silly appetite for showing off, and that exact same need for amorous illusion that I had scorned not long before. It was that sweet and languid desire a man has, after he has had a woman, to get something back for the effort he has put into conquering her by letting go, relaxing, ceasing to care about her — so he can be completely himself. Revenge, almost, for past courtships.

It was all this, perhaps, but more than anything it was a desire to escape any misconception she might have, to let her know once and for all that I belonged to her world only as a joke, that I actually hated and despised it. It was with some resentment that I said to her one day:

"You haven't got the slightest idea what intelligence really is." She stared at me in amazement. "No one has ever said that to me." Then she absolutely wanted me to explain. "Maybe because I don't have a high school diploma? Because I don't understand math?" It had never occurred to her to see herself as anything other than extremely intelligent.

And I didn't know how to explain. What is intelligence? It's seeing certain small differences, noticing that things are more complicated than they seem, I don't know. . . . "You see," she interrupted, exultant. "You can look at it any way you like, but between you and me there's not much difference." And she was back in a good mood. "But actually," she continued, "I want to talk about something serious. For the last few days I've had bad thoughts going through my head. I keep thinking that little by little I'm getting myself into a dead-end. What am I going to do in a few years? The fact is, when it comes down to it, a woman's place is next to a man. There's Tonino, you know — he adores me. And the lieutenant I also really like. But what do I do with this love? Can I seriously be thinking about marrying them?"

I felt sincerely sympathetic. She had finally realized, poor thing, what was plain to everyone. I noticed a couple of gray hairs and thought of the horrible loneliness waiting for her. "Do you think you could still fall in love?" I asked her. "Oh yes, that for sure! I think I'll always be able to as long as I'm alive. If I had a husband and eight kids I would abandon them in a second if I happened to fall in love."

But I hadn't meant to ask her if she was capable of walking out on a man. I wanted to know the opposite, whether she thought it was possible for her to stay with one. I tried unsuccessfully to get the point across: "Haven't you ever, in the past, had one true great love?"

"Yes, for my second husband."

"And?"

"Well, when you wake up one morning and find your great love coughing in a way that annoys and irritates you, and for the first time you can't stand that he goes into the bathroom bowlegged with flip-flops on his feet; well, from that morning your great love is dead."

I felt really bad. So true! And so difficult to admit!

"This is what is so amazing about you," I replied. "This rushing immediately to the final outcome; this lack of caution, you might call it, this failure to take better care of your own love. This just setting it adrift at the mercy of the first gust that comes along, with no protection at all. Things like this happen to everyone. But not everyone just breaks off everything because of it. These are problems that someone who really loves has to get to grips with. You have to be able to choose between love and idiosyncrasy."

"I know the theory. Bear it and be silent. Suffer in silence. Put up with it, sacrifice. . . . But why? If there were children, that would be one thing. But when somebody is just such a. . . ."

She hadn't understood a thing.

"That's not what I mean, my dear child. It's not about bearing and sacrificing. It's about undoing these knots and giving them life by expanding your feelings. A great discovery that allows you to love is this — that the other person exists. They exist in their way of being, their past, their habits, their defects and their dullness. Really loving this person means wanting them to be just the way they are, expecting nothing from them, no change. And if you hit a bump that blocks or deflects the current that binds you, hate yourself and love them, not vice versa."

I stopped because I realized she was staring at me. It was a serious, impenetrable look and I wouldn't have been able to say what it held.

"Bravo," she said, "really great. And I say this without the slightest irony. I can see you really love your wife. In a way I envy her, and I envy you. But the fact is, my situation is different. My husband didn't earn enough. It was on me, with my work, to support the family."

"What's that got to do with anything?" I shouted in annoyance. "What do I and my wife and your husband's job have to do with it? Who mentioned anything personal? I'm not trying to confide in you about myself or instruct you about how you should have behaved. I was just trying to explain a state of mind, to get you to understand another way a person can be. Leave the comparisons out of it. Don't make all this into a confession."

"Oh, but listen to you; now you've lost me. You're not going to tell me now that you learned these things out of books. If you talk about them it means that in some way you've experienced them yourself. Now you get offended because I dared to mention your family. Well okay, excuse me, I won't do it again. So then, what do I have to say to you? What I have to say is that this, what we're doing, is not what I want. We agreed (no?) that between us there was an erotic relationship and that's all. It was so beautiful, so good for both of us. I told you right then on the first day: 'Enjoy it and shut up.' But you had to talk, you ruined everything. You started mixing in intelligence and love and morality. You wanted to dot the i's and put me in my place. You trampled everything like an elephant — oh, you did a really good job of it. And it's too bad, because we were really good together. And now I have to suffer for no reason. If my confession boosts your pride, take it, go ahead, I give it to you. Examine it with your intelligence. And another satisfaction I want to give you is that for the first time in my life I am ashamed of what I have done."

She left and never again wanted anything to do with me.

A LOVE

There had been something between them in the past — some little flirtation, a small fling that she had wanted more than he did, abruptly cut off when he had responded to certain advances, almost against his will, with words that were a bit too crude.

But in both of them there had remained a sense almost of dissatisfaction with the less than normal way it had ended, and seeing each other again after several years had been like coming across something stored in some forgotten corner of a closet.

Paola had made the appointment without even bothering to justify it, as if it were the most natural thing in the world. She hadn't even said to herself, "After all, what's the harm?" which precedes any action where there is harm. Entrenched behind her love for Emilio, it seemed to her indeed beautiful and pleasant to find herself with an old friend — not considering that Roberto's visit might bring him under suspicion. But on the scheduled afternoon, saying goodbye to her mother, who headed out to do errands knowing nothing of the impending visit, she caught herself imagining a scene of Roberto making advances and herself refusing him.

Roberto arrived punctually. On the way over and as he came in he thought of nothing — he had guessed the relationship with Emilio even though the latter had never wanted to confess it to him, and this official ignorance, and consequently the possibility of an involvement with Paola without offending his friend, gave him a certain sensual thrill. He had a vague feeling that he could take advantage of Emilio's silence to punish him for it and for his lack of trust in not telling Roberto anything, and even though he didn't actually intend to do anything, he enjoyed the idea that he had permission. He had always liked the girl, even though she was now the target of that sense of faint contempt one sometimes has for friends' girlfriends.

Faced with a friend who was in love his attitude was one of benevolent pity, almost of incomprehension — the superiority comes with the confidence of being able to move without hindrance, of not owing anything to anybody. And in the case of a woman someone else loved, and whom he didn't love himself, he had the same unconscious opinion that in fact anyone would: "not worth the effort." He told himself he had accepted Paola's invitation out of duty, because "a man can't refuse," and tried to convince himself that he was annoyed at having to waste his time with a girl that, he added with deliberate cynicism, he would never get "everything" from. He dawdled on the way, thinking of other things, hoping he might run into someone who would take up his time and make him late, but he didn't meet anybody and turned up on time.

Things went the way both of them might have imagined and almost predicted, and there was a sense of weary necessity about what happened, an inevitability that at times took on fatalistic tones, at others the easy and carefree feel of familiarity. Paola had a gift for ignoring the stakes of their earlier encounters, and the visit began with an almost deliberate cheerfulness, popping and fizzing with reminiscences of the past, with gentle allusions and good-natured banter.

Roberto put up with the drift of the conversation and responded almost automatically, without effort, drawing on his experience as a man of the world. But his mind was elsewhere. He glanced at the drapes, the paintings, the photographs; and if he looked at Paola he felt by turns aroused and gripped by a feeling of disdainful indifference. When they started dancing (for some sentimental reason she had put on a record that Emilio liked) he tried to kiss her. It was a predictable move and she executed the parry she had prepared. She shook her head and broke off the dance: "My dear Roberto, this is going nowhere."

They sat on the couch. Roberto was past the point where he could retreat — his move had committed him to go through with what he had started. But a feeling of boredom washed over him, and he would almost have preferred to be kicked out of the house rather than be compelled to maintain the position he had taken. He began to speak in a low, weary voice, lost eyes staring into the void. Yes, he had loved her so much and for so long — ever since the time of their youthful flirtation. The feeling had come rushing back when they had again met, and he had tried to avoid her to keep it from growing in his heart. It wasn't possible that she didn't love him because there is no love that is unrequited.

He spoke as if to someone else and no one else — to all the women he had kissed without knowing why, almost to justify himself. The ordinary words were spoken at first almost out of necessity but he ended up believing them. Love, yes, it was deep love, this moving tenderness, this languor he was now feeling — this desire to relax, to rest his head, not to think any more, not to control himself, to be caressed. The distracted kiss and the moment of lucidity that followed it had made it clear to him that there was only one way he could go. And in that case, since he had to go that way, wasn't it better to believe in it? Why fake what you could be honest about? And so when he heard the generic words come out of his mouth, as if from some other person, he gradually came to agree with them and make them his. He ended up taking this other person's place and owning them himself, in good conscience — and they were tender words, that came from a love that was not at all sensual, words almost of gratitude for the peace and tranquility they brought him.

He held her around the waist and kissed her hands. She let him do it with heartfelt sympathy — out of compassion, she said to herself. She was actually a bit sorry now that she loved Emilio. And when she spoke of her attachment to Roberto, it was with the satisfied dignity of fulfilling a duty, and at the same time with the tender satisfaction of interposing one of those impediments that makes a sentiment more delicate and foreign. "If I love someone else," she said, "it can't be helped," as if it had nothing to do with her. But that love, undenied, gave this one a pleasurable flavor of uniqueness and mystery.

Index of Names

INDEX OF SUBJECTS